For the Love of Israel and the Jewish People

Essays and Studies on Israel, Jews and Judaism

FOR THE LOVE OF ISRAEL
AND THE
JEWISH PEOPLE

ESSAYS AND STUDIES ON ISRAEL, JEWS AND JUDAISM

NATHAN LOPES CARDOZO

The David Cardozo Academy
Machon Aaron and Betsy Spijer

URIM PUBLICATIONS
Jerusalem • New York

For the Love of Israel and the Jewish People: Essays and Studies on
Israel, Jews and Judaism
By Nathan Lopes Cardozo
Copyright © 2008 Nathan Lopes Cardozo

Printed at Hemed Press, Israel. First Edition.
Layout design by Satya Levine

ISBN: 978-965-524-010-8

Urim Publications
P.O. Box 52287, Jerusalem 91521 Israel

Lambda Publishers Inc.
3709 13th Avenue Brooklyn, New York 11218 U.S.A.
Tel: 718-972-5449 Fax: 718-972-6307, mh@ejudaica.com

www.UrimPublications.com

In the years before the Balfour Declaration, a member of the House of Lords asked Chaim Weizmann, "Why do you Jews insist on Palestine when there are so many undeveloped countries you could settle in more conveniently?"

Weizmann said: "That is like me asking you why you drove twenty miles to visit your mother last Sunday when there are so many old ladies living in your street."

৵ ৵

"Some people like the Jews and some do not. But no thoughtful man can deny the fact that they are beyond question the most formidable and the most remarkable race which has ever appeared in the world."

–Winston Churchill

DEDICATED TO OUR HOLY SOLDIERS

RON ARAD

ZACHARYA SHLOMO BAUMEL

ZVI FELDMAN

EHUD GOLDWASSER

GUY HEVER

YEKUTIEL YEHUDA NACHMAN KATZ

ELDAD REGEV

GILAD SHALIT

MAY THEY SOON COME HOME.*

* This page was sponsored by: Michael Braunold, Moshe Ditcher, Michael Freund, Steve Farber, Werner and Jeannete Fink, John Fisher, Jerry and Alice Gess, Roger Gladstone, David Goodman, Montgomery Green, Marilyn Hilkowitz, Alex Igel, Ilana Julius, Wayne and Adeena Karsseboom, Rabbi Jay and Ruby Karzen, Neil Kaye, David Kestenbaum, Yehudith Levy, Sol and Barbara Liebgot, Benja Philipson, Richard Polak, Norm and Tzipora Pomeranz, Richard Rinberg, Yehuda Saar, David and Shoshana Schwartz, Glen Shear, Raoul Stein, Elliot Tannenbaum, Steve Vago, David Wenner, Shmuly Yanklowitz, Harry and Chava Yellin

In honour of our beloved children
and grand children

.

Bettina, David
Daniel, Jonathan,
Raquel, & Jacob

Ariella, Charles
Melissa, Althea, Sabrina,
Alessia,
Joseph & Zack

Marc, Natasha
David, Anouska
& Daniel

and in loving memory of our parents *z"l*

Mourad & Bahie
Blanga

Joseph & Rachel
Politis

who instilled in us the value of family,
the thirst for knowledge
and the love for Eretz Israel

 Nelly & David Blanga

IN MEMORY OF

SHIMON AVRAHAM BEN SHABTAI, *z"l*

PINHAS YOSSEF BEN AVRAHAM, *z"l*

YEHUDA DAVID BEN PINHAS YOSSEF, *z"l*

In memory of
Abraham and Esther Hersh, *z"l*
by their children
Ronny and Toby Hersh

છે   છે

In memory of
Mrs. Bertha Lopes Cardozo, *a"h,*
who with her warm personality
meant so much to the Kehillah of the Netherlands
and particularly to her sons and their families.

A great example of a Jewish daughter.

May her memory be a blessing.

**Rosa van Driel
The Netherlands**

With much thanks to Hashem, we feel privileged to contribute to the publication of this book. In this merit, may our children, Atara, Akiva, and Hayim, grow to have a tremendous love for the Land of Israel and all of Klal Yisrael.

David and Ilene Brookler

જ ૯

In honor of

Danielle Klein

and her children

In memory of her husband and their father, my dear friend

Ha-Tzadik

Michael Moshe Ha-Cohen Klein, *z"l*

Nathan Lopes Cardozo

CONTENTS

PART I: ESSAYS

LOVE FOR THE LAND

THE JEWS

ISRAELI SOCIETY

ISRAEL AND ITS NEIGHBORS

ANTI-SEMITISM

PART II: STUDIES

PART III: TWO LECTURES

INTRODUCTION

THE LAND OF ISRAEL and the Jewish people are bound together in mysterious ways that are difficult to grasp. The relationship between them goes beyond the conventional. Here is a nation with "too much history and too little geography," as Sir Isaiah Berlin once said. By conventional wisdom its history, which contains an enormous amount of pain and disaster, should have led to its destruction, but to the surprise of the world's greatest philosophers and historians, it led to the rediscovery of its geography. Yet that geography was never absent. When the Jews were exiled from their land, the Land of Israel was lifted from its native soil and transformed into a portable homeland that could be taken to all corners of the earth. Every Jewish home became Israel on foreign soil. The Jewish nation, which loved its homeland deeply, was never without it because that land lived inside the people and not the other way around, as in the case of the other nations of the world. The Land of Israel travels to the four corners of the earth. It has no boundaries and accompanies its people wherever they go. It was able to settle in Rome, Greece, Babylon, Spain, Poland, Russia, and other places. Yet it never dwelled in any of them; it merely stayed there, waiting to return to its native soil.

Moreover, Israel's topography, its location on the world map and its climate all allude to the nature of its people, the Jewish nation. They all reflect radical instability and uncertainty. Nothing can be taken for granted. By its very nature, Israel is a vulnerable place. Since it is located at the juncture of three continents, it has always been envied by many nations who have tried throughout history – and are still trying – to possess its territory, knowing its strategic importance and its central role in mankind's spiritual history. Yet it always was, and still is, incapable of becoming a major power itself.

Israel's climate is also unstable. Its most important resource, water, has always been unpredictable. Since the land is completely dependent on rain, its crops and fruits can never be guaranteed. In the past the land was often struck by severe famines that forced its inhabitants to leave, and this issue looms over the country to this very day. Unlike its neighbors, such as Egypt, whose water source is the Nile River, Israel has always had to look toward heaven for its sustenance. There is more than a little symbolism to this. Egypt has to look *down* for water, whereas Israel has to look *up*. This literally reminds us of the Torah's warning that "It drinks rain from heaven" and that "the eyes of the Lord your God are continually on it from the beginning of the year to its end" (Devarim 11:12). Nor is it a fertile plain but a land of hills and valleys in which, after much labor, one can produce sustenance for only part of the nation.

The same is true for Israel's security. The land is extremely small and cannot sustain a large population. Since its borders are difficult to defend, nearly all of its cities are vulnerable to attack by its many enemies, who live only miles away. Since biblical times it has had to defend itself against hostile nations or tribes in the south, such as the Philistines in the past and Hamas today. Also, as in the past, neighboring empires call for its destruction.

The nation of Israel is tiny, "not to be counted among the nations," as the gentile prophet Bilaam said (Bamidbar 23:9). There was never a time when it could rely on numbers. Today, its population is tiny. One is reminded of Milton Himmelfarb's observation: "The sum total of the Jewish people today is smaller than a statistical error in the Chinese census."

Just as the land is tiny, the Jewish nation, too, is small in number. Its small size makes survival a challenge. Thrown into many exiles, it was always on the brink of dying, fighting to keep its head above water, surviving on the edge, but never able to find much security. Even now, since the establishment of the State of Israel, it has not succeeded in obtaining the kind of security for which it always longed. Its topography became its history.

However, its influence on the world has been enormous. Just as the Land of Israel is small but finds itself at the heart of many continents, so too this small nation occupies a central and crucial role in harvesting the greatest human accomplishments ever achieved. Besides its enormous contribution to the religious world, it has given a boost unparalleled in human history to science, psychology and many other human endeavors. But above all, it caused an upheaval in humankind's moral fiber. The Jewish people gave mankind the idea of equality before the law, the sanctity of life and the dignity of all human beings. It introduced the notions of personal responsibility, conscience, and redemption. As long as the world lasts, all who want to make progress in righteousness will come to Israel for inspiration. No other nation has had such an impact on the way people think. "One of Jewish culture's gifts to Christianity is that it has taught Christians to think like Jews, and any modern man who has not learned to think as though he was a Jew can hardly be said to have learned to think at all."[1] "The Jewish vision became the prototype for many similar grand designs for humanity, both divine and man-made. Therefore, the Jews stand precisely at the center of the perennial attempt to give human life the dignity of purpose."[2] As is the land, so are its people.

"We will have babies and they will have conferences. Let's see who wins!" remarked a Haredi (ultra-Orthodox) Jew living in Israel when he heard about yet another conference about the problems and the future of the Jewish people. In many ways this observation sets the tone of much that occupies our people today. Will we survive? Will we have the resources to keep our young people proud of their Jewishness? What will become of the State of Israel? Is it doomed to vanish from the face of the earth? And so on.

Indeed, conference after conference is held on these and related matters. Most of the global Jewish leadership is anxious about our future. Assimilation, security issues and anti-Semitism depress us. Statistics predict a major decline of Jews throughout the world. Israel finds itself in a severe and dangerous identity crisis as many of today's Israeli youth do not know who they are and why they need to fight for the State of Israel's survival. They have lost the connection with the land and the people of Israel. Pessimism abounds.

---

[1] William Rees Mogg, *The Reigning Error* (London: 1974), 11.
[2] Paul Johnson, *A History of the Jews* (London: 1987), 2.

Yet there seems to be no pessimism in the Haredi world. As the above exclamation indicates, that world seems to be booming. According to several academic studies, by the second half of this century, both in the United States and in the United Kingdom the majority of the Jewish population will be ultra-Orthodox. The predictions concerning Israel are not much different. By the year 2020 the Haredi population of Israel will have doubled to one million, constituting seventeen percent of Israel's population, and one-third of all Jewish pupils will be studying in Haredi schools.[3] These are serious predictions. While the overall Jewish population throughout the world is clearly declining, the Haredim are the ones who are reversing this situation. This means that by the end of this century, the majority of Jews around the world will probably be religious. The rest will have faded away through assimilation.

However, the Haredi world is badly handicapped. Its continual increase in numbers, instead of being a blessing to the Jewish state, could become a major problem. The day may come when, due to its fast growth, the State of Israel will slowly but surely fall into the hands of the Haredim. To its utter surprise, the Haredi leadership will find itself with a state it neither knows how to govern nor has it ever agreed with. Unlike in the United States and European countries, the young Haredim in Israel are, with some exceptions, not receiving the kind of secular education that will prepare them to take on major roles in the building of the state. Not only will this be a serious problem as far as statesmanship is concerned, but also a large part of its society will be unable to provide for itself and become an impossible and dangerous burden on the state's finances. This will wreak havoc throughout the country and could lead to the undoing of the state no less than assimilation and extreme secularity.

The responsibility for this tragedy rests to a great extent with the Haredi leadership, its rabbis and heads of yeshivot. They will have to come to terms with the fact that they are part of a modern Jewish State and that if they want to continue to live in this land, they will have to make radical changes in their educational system.

Unlike many Haredi fears, this will not require any compromise as far as halachic requirements are concerned. In fact it will become possible for

---

[3] *The Jerusalem Post,* August 2, 2007.

many of its followers to become more deeply religious as they will be able to earn a decent livelihood, avoid non-halachic or objectionable means of earning a living and influence the State of Israel to become more Jewish merely by their example. There will be a need for more Orthodox physicians, psychologists and even scientists and, above all, religious leaders who know how to run a state and who understand the importance of international relationships. Many halachic and scientific problems will have to be solved, and it will be impossible to leave them in the hands of the secularists.

It is here that the modern orthodox world has a major role to play. It should initiate a dialogue with the Haredi leadership. Although it has much to offer, the Haredi world will only listen to its voice if the modern orthodox leadership pays much more attention to its followers' dedication to Jewish tradition and religiosity. It will have to emphasize religious inspiration and devotion. It must invoke in its followers a keen interest in holiness and purity. It must send a message that Judaism is not just a religion consisting of rituals such as Shabbat and kashrut. It will have to show its constituency that Jewish life is an experience of spiritual transformation in which even the so-called trivial is holy. It must realize that a major part of its community sees its Judaism as a Saturday morning religion and that this must change.

Yet even more important, to a great extent it is the secular Israeli world that is responsible for the unfortunate condition of the Haredim. The erosion of Jewish identity in general Israeli society but above all in the dominant secular school system is having disastrous results. In its frantic zeal to promote all sorts of secular universalisms, post-modernism, materialism and hedonism, the secular leadership is running the State of Israel into a catastrophic state that could be irreversible. By refusing to give Jewish heritage priority status in the secular school system, it has created a most dangerous situation for the State of Israel that is even more severe than those caused by the Haredi leadership. In its attempt to delegitimize Zionism, secularism blocks any chance for the Jewish state's survival. No nation can live on borrowed identity. One should never forget that the Haredi world never sold out on Israel's uniqueness nor did it fall victim to hedonism. It continues to promote Jewish meaning, and if one day its leadership wakes up and changes its attitude towards the Jewish state, it will have enormous resources at its disposal that could become a great blessing to the State of Israel.

Unfortunately, this cannot be said in the case of the secular community. Many of its young people are currently undergoing a severe identity crisis and will most likely leave the country with feelings of deep animosity.

The Haredi leadership is observing these developments carefully. Frightened of secularism and unable to cope with it due to its own limitations, the Haredi world has adopted a policy of ultimate disengagement. They will do anything to keep their followers away from modern life and education. They create spiritual ghettos out of the belief that this is the only way to guarantee a religiously observant life. The likelihood that this approach may backfire in the future is very great, and when it happens, the repercussions will be enormous. Yet until that moment, the Haredim will continue to build their walls. Had secular Israeli society maintained a connection with its Jewishness and not fallen prey to alien influences, the Haredi world would have had more reasons to emerge from its self-imposed confinement. Therefore, as things stand, the secular community is indirectly responsible for the Haredi disengagement.

Obviously, this does not justify Haredi policies. The Haredi world could have created a superb educational system that would not only cope with all the secular challenges but also be a challenge to the secular community. That it did not succeed in doing so is not only because it never set this as its goal, but also because most of the time it is completely unaware of the spiritual and the intellectual problems that the secular community faces. It is not enough to reject post-modernism as so much nonsense or ban scientific books whenever they seem to oppose Jewish tradition. The secular intellectual world is a serious place and needs serious answers whenever it challenges religious beliefs or looks for religious answers to its own quandaries.

The Haredi leadership needs to rethink its policies drastically. After all, it has a lot to offer. At the same time, secular Israel will have to wake up as well (with a start!) and realize that it is selling out on its most important asset: Judaism.

Nevertheless, things are changing. Some segments of the Haredi community are looking for ways to become more engaged with the modern world and the State of Israel so that they can earn a decent income by learning a profession. At the same time, as some secular communities become aware of their own undoing, they are looking for ways to engage in some kind of religious Jewish life and study. One can only hope that such initiatives will be encouraged rather than condemned. It appears that there is some light at the end of the tunnel. May that light soon become bright and warm.

HOW TO READ THIS BOOK

THIS BOOK CONSISTS OF THREE PARTS: Essays, Studies and Lectures. The Essays were written over a long period of time. They were sent to my colleagues, rabbis, students and friends as emails called "Thoughts to Ponder." Since they were written over several years and in the midst of the various Intifadas and horrifying terrorist attacks in the land of Israel, it is important not to read them at once or necessarily even in the sequence in which they appear in the book. Each essay stands on its own and must be read in light of its historical background. For this reason I have noted the dates when they were written. For obvious reasons some will overlap with others, due to the similar time span. Still, the careful reader will discover that each one contains its own uniqueness and flavor. I have left each essay in its original form and did not attempt to combine them. And if a reader should be called on to say a few words about Israel, he or she will have a large collection of possibilities from which to choose.

The Studies consist of in-depth analysis of topics that relate to Israel, the Jewish people and their relationship to the nature of Jewishness, anti-Semitism and the Israel-Arab Conflict. They should be studied in depth since they touch on the very foundation of what it means to be a Jew and what Israel should stand for. They also include suggestions of how to solve some major problems in the Jewish world. All of these studies were given as lectures at conferences and university conventions in Israel, the USA, Canada, England, the Netherlands and South Africa.

The Lectures consist of addresses that I gave in several Jewish communities and university campuses throughout the English speaking countries. They are of a more popular nature than the Studies.

ॐ   ॐ

At this moment (August, 2007), the security situation in Israel has slightly improved since the days that many of the Essays were written. There have been very few terrorist attacks in recent years, though many Kassam rockets land regularly in the south of the country claiming victims and creating much anxiety and damage. May the citizens of Sderot and its surroundings soon find tranquility in their homes and cities!

Some of the Essays and Studies deal with the Jewishness of the State of Israel and many Israelis' lack of Jewish identity. As mentioned before, this has also somewhat improved. More young secular people have realized that without some form of "religious" Jewishness, the State has no future and the Jewish people will not be able to survive. It may quite well be true that the alarm sounded by thinkers and educators like myself has somehow helped to bring this about. Still, much needs to be done. My warnings and suggestions in these Essays and Studies are still relevant and should be taken to heart, though some of my readers may maintain that my criticism is sometimes too harsh (I wish it were true!) or my optimism too unrealistic.

ॐ   ॐ

This book is dedicated to the MIAs and POWs of the State of Israel. The ongoing pain that they endure because they have not yet been brought back home is a dark chapter in the history of the State and the Jewish people and says much about our predicaments. We hope that these pages will give encouragement to their families. May God grant that this tragedy soon come to an end.

May Israel live and the Jewish people discover its own uniqueness!

Nathan Lopes Cardozo
Jerusalem
Menachem Av, 5767
August, 2007

ACKNOWLEDGMENTS

It is with great gratitude to the Lord of the Universe that I publish this work. Besides the fact that I feel His presence at every moment in my life, I am blessed to receive much encouragement from my dear wife Frijda Rachel and our children, children-in-law and grandchildren, who are a source of tremendous joy.

I wish to express my gratitude to my dear friend, Rabbi Francis Nataf, the educational Director of the David Cardozo Academy, my son-in-law, Rabbi Chanan Atlas, and our secretary, Mrs. Esther Peterman, thanks to whom I had the time to write this book. Thanks also to Gila Fine, Jeanne Arenstein, Amy Heavenrich, Jonathan and Dena Udren and the editors of Urim Publications for editing it.

This book was made possible by the financial support of the David Cardozo Academy, also called the Aaron and Betsy Spijer Institute, of which I am the dean and founder. With the help of Rabbi Francis Nataf it has become a well-known voice in the Jewish world. Its mission is to rediscover the original teachings of Avraham, the first Jew (Hebrew) in history, and to re-investigate the spiritual reasons why Avraham started what later became known as Judaism. Its unique approach offers an innovative look into classical Judaism. (See www.cardozoschool.org for more information.)

Special thanks to our dedicated staff and teachers: Professor Yehuda Gellman, Rabbi Zvi Grumet, Rabbi Dr. Alon Goshen-Gottstein, Professor Susan Handelman, Professor William Kolbrener, Professor Moshe Koppel, Rabbi Dr. Zvi Leshem, Professor Elliott Malamet, Rabbi Dr. Yehuda Schnall, Rabbi Dr. Eliezer Shore, Rabbi Nathan Slifkin, and Rabbi Professor Daniel Sperber.

Thanks also to the Board of the American Friends of the Cardozo School and its president, Rob Kurtz, the Board of the British Friends and its president, Charles Zeloof, and the Israeli board of Machon Ohr Aaron.

A special *chazak u-varuch* to Rabbi Dr. Marc D. Angel, Rabbi Moshe Benzaquen, Rabbi Joey Beyda, Rabbi Dr. Wim van Dijk, Rabbi Dr. Raph

Evers, Rabbi Meir Just, Professor Menachem Kellner, Rabbi Dr. Alan Kimche, Rabbi Moshe Shamah, Rabbi Shmuel Spiero, Rabbi Harold Sutton and Rabbi Stewart Weiss.

Special thanks to the following individuals and families (and not to forget their dear spouses!): Kam Babaoff, Richard Bentley, David Blanca, Marc Blanca, David Brookler, Bill Bron, Gerald Brounstein, Albert Cohen, Abe Dushey, Michael Feldmar, Werner Fink, Michael Freund, Elie Gindi, I.G., Raymond, Isaac and Sam Gindi, Joseph Gindi, Joe Harari, Efrem Harkham, Hart Hasten, Ronny Hersh, David Hidary, Michael Hidary, Dick Horowitz, Alain Iscovics, Frits Koetser, Marshal and Ellie Jaffe Kulman, Howard Jonas, Michael Kagan, Michael Kaiser, David Katzin, Ezra Kest, David Leventhal, Myriam Licht, Shimmy Lopian, Daniel Mahboubi, Brad Markoff, Howard Millendorf, Sean Namvar, Robert Neis, Aviva Pels, Norman Pomeranz, Stephen Rosen, Brian Ross, Steve Russo, Sunny Sassoon, David Sassoon, Shani Schwartz, Perry Shapira, Jerry Shatzkes, Stacy Sokol, Aric Streit, Isaac Sutton, Daniel and Caroline Tamman, Henriette van Driel, Elliot Tannebaum, Avi Tokayer, Salomon Vaz Dias, Steve Farber, Steve Feder, Peter Weintraub, Charles and David Zeloof.

My dear friends, Chief Rabbi Sir Jonathan Sacks and Rabbi Dr. Norman Lamm, are a constant source of encouragement.

My dear friends, Max and Jenny Weil and Rabbi Jay and Ruby Karzen, deserve special mention for all their help and encouragement.

I also wish to thank my friend Tzvi Mauer of Urim Publications, who has published many of my works. *Chazak u-varuch* to him and his staff!

This year I had the great misfortune of losing my dear mother, Bertha Lopes Cardozo, *z"l*. There are no words to express my thanks to her for what she has done for me and my family. No doubt she and my unforgettable father, *z"l*, are rewarded for all they did during their lives for me and for so many others. One day I hope to write a special book in honor of her.

I would also like to mention my dear brother, Jacques Eduard Lopes Cardozo, his wife Eva, his children and my sister-in-law Annemarie and her family. May they all be well, together with my only aunt, Mariana Lopes Cardozo, who with God's help will reach the age of one hundred next year. May she be blessed!

As I write these words, my dear mother-in-law, Rosel Gnesin, needs special mercy. May *Ha-Kadosh Baruch Hu* look after her.

Thanks are also due to Mrs. Irma Lopes Cardozo of New York. Her unforgettable husband, Chazan Abraham Lopes Cardozo, *z"l*, continues to be an inspiration to me.

I want to mention another special friend of my family, Betsy Spijer, *z"l*, of The Hague, the Netherlands, who left us only a few months ago. She and her dear husband, Aaron Spijer, *z"l*, were instrumental in making the David Cardozo Academy possible. Over the years, they helped me to publish my books and gave me the opportunity to study and teach. I also want to thank their and my own dear friends, Dr Leo Delfgaauw, Dr. Hans Wijnveldt and Dr. Michael and Eldad Eitje for their constant support.

May God bless Israel, the Jewish people and all good men and women in this turbulent world and grant them peace, health and happiness. But above all, may He bring meaning and a sense of a spiritual mission to all of our lives.

Nathan Lopes Cardozo

AN OPEN LETTER TO PRESIDENT SHIMON PERES[1]

17 Menachem Av 5767 (August 1, 2007)

THERE ARE MOMENTS in a man's life when he needs to speak up, usually when something dramatic has happened that requires a response. With your recent appointment as the President of the State of Israel, I feel that I must speak my mind.

First, some background: I am the child of a totally assimilated family. I grew up with both a Christmas tree and a menorah, and I found my way to Judaism after a great deal of struggle. It was a major upheaval in my life. I had to somehow become reborn and my "delivery" was difficult and painful. However, once I discovered the grandeur of Judaism, I convinced my parents of its beauty and they decided to have a traditional religious wedding ceremony thirty years after their civil marriage. To be honest, all this happened so long ago that I had almost forgotten about it.

Indeed, I had almost forgotten until last week when you, Mr. Peres, were sworn in as our new President. When I heard you speak at the Knesset about our future, your dreams, and the Jewish people in general, I realized that I had an obligation to write this letter to you. The reason is clear. Throughout most of my youth I did not know where I belonged or who I was. Was I a Jew or a gentile? I had no identity and let me tell you: almost nothing is worse than that. In a world in which everyone is doing his utmost to transform you into everybody else, you have to fight the hardest battle any human being can fight to decide who you really are. I was fortunate enough to arrive at that decision myself and so I decided to be a full-fledged Jew. As Matthew Arnold once wrote, "He who finds himself loses his misery."

---

[1] A shorter version of this letter was published in *The Jerusalem Post* on August 8, 2007.

And that brings me to you, Mr. President. We in Israel have lost our identity. Many of us no longer know who we are. We all recognize that we are in dire need of a new vision for Israel's future and our own. We need a powerful voice for change, and our eyes now turn to you. Newspapers have already been imploring you to uproot corruption, promote civility, fight domestic violence, mend Arab-Jewish relations, foster economic relations with Israel's neighbors and, of course, advance peace in the Middle East. Yet however important these goals may be, they are missing the point. These serious problems are the symptoms of the real crisis that has befallen us, which is the need to deal with our own identity. Let us not fool ourselves: a large percentage of our young people have no idea who they are. They are asked to serve in the Israel Defence Force, risking their lives for this country without knowing why. Many of our top leaders in the Knesset either have next to no knowledge of their Jewishness or look down on it due to an erroneous upbringing. More and more of our fellow Jews throughout the country lack Jewish self-understanding and wonder why they should live in this beautiful country called Israel. It is only a matter of time before we will find ourselves confronted with a majority of fine young people who struggle with an identity crisis of such proportions that many will leave this country out of sheer bewilderment. And let us be honest: this is extremely dangerous. It threatens the very existence of our people and our state. Human beings can starve from lack of identity as much as they can starve from lack of food.

What is Jewish identity? Even before the establishment of the State of Israel, many people tried to disconnect their identities from authentic Judaism. Yiddish-speaking societies such as the Jüdische Wissenschaft and Literarische Gesellschaften were created, as well as the Bund and various Jewish cultural events and movements. In this way, people hoped to stay Jewish while living mainly gentile lives. In our own time, we have told our Israeli youth that to be a soldier in the army is the pinnacle of Jewishness and that Zionism is the new religion. It was anticipated that all those movements and ideologies would successfully replace the old Judaism. But it was not to be. In retrospect, we must realize that all of these attempts have actually confused our people. These ideologies could not impart the sort of elevating spirit that would make Jews proud of their Jewishness, nor did they provide the same kind of meaningful destiny that our ancestors enjoyed for thousands of years.

These movements did not give us a mission that we would be prepared to die for. It is true that our wonderful soldiers are ready to sacrifice their lives for our country, but how long can this last unless we give them more than just a country? People are willing to die only for that by which they have lived. Ultimately, human beings will live meaningful lives only when they know that there is something eternal worth dying for.

The moment that we Jews began to define ourselves horizontally, we found ourselves prey to a range of syndromes from insecurity to aggression, from self-hatred to narrow ethnic pride. Like our forefather Yaakov after his wrestling with the angel, we began to limp.

This is the problem at the center of modern Jewish and Israeli life. As long as we do not give our people a sense of ultimate Jewish meaning, we will not be able to change their attitude towards life. No nation can live on borrowed identity. We cannot promote civility, fight domestic violence and uproot corruption if we do not first become aware of who we are. As long as we continue to be messengers who have forgotten their message, we will not be able to cause any real change in ourselves or in the world.

To be a Jew is to be a moral heir of those who stood at Sinai, to pledge ourselves to live by the truth of the great foundations of Judaism and to be part of a kingdom of priests, to be part of a nation that is dedicated to the wellbeing of all humankind through the teachings of the Torah. To be a Jew is to celebrate Shabbat, the greatest institution of liberty the world has ever seen, to observe our dietary laws because the act of eating is one of dignity and holiness, and to be imbued with the spirit of our prophets.

We must admit that all we have gleaned during the past years is that, in the long run, Jewish identity can only be understood in religious terms, albeit in terms foreign to other religions. We cannot predicate our survival on remaining a culture, a constellation of fading memories or some kind of nostalgia, or even on the Israeli army or Zionism. We must accept this. I cannot escape the feeling that we have somehow lost the script of the great Jewish story and we must now rediscover it.

It is here that your role as President of the State of Israel becomes crucial. You may either be highly successful or you may fail. The choice is yours. At this hour there is one characteristic which must stand out:

unbridled courage. You must lead the people back to their Jewish roots, and you must do this by personal example and with a clear vision. You are in the fortunate position of no longer needing to prove yourself. You are now old enough and wise enough to realize that a great man can ignore the applause of the multitude once he knows himself. There is a moment when human beings must realize that instead of being dedicated to fame, they are dedicated to a truth that surpasses their own interests.

Therefore, take a keen interest in Judaism. Start learning its great wisdom and forget what you may have learned in your youth that apparently turned you away from your roots. Try to rediscover it for your own sake. Let it do something to your being. Assemble Jewish religious thinkers at the President's Residence and listen to their words. Go to the synagogue on Shabbat and festivals and listen to the great Jewish prayers. Make Kiddush on Shabbat at home and sing the songs of our holy days. No, I am not asking you to become Orthodox, but to live a life that abounds with a great love for Judaism for everybody to see.

Do not be afraid of what people will say when you embark upon this change of direction. Nobody knows better than you that one can only answer for one's courage when one is in danger. Use radio and television to inspire people to follow your example. Tell them what you have discovered and organize open tents of learning in which both secular and religious Jews can study Jewish texts about civility and tolerance. I suggest calling these tents "Ohalei Avraham," the tents of Abraham, the very first Jew, who had the courage to change his ways when he was as old as you are now. As his message became eternal, so might yours.

Return to your people what they have lost. This nation is thirsty for identity and spirituality and it is your task to show them the road back. You have done great things for the State of Israel. Although, like all of us, you have made mistakes, you can now remedy many of them.

By doing so, you will have achieved more during your years as President of the State of Israel than you did in decades as a member of the Israeli parliament. If you live up to this challenge, you will leave a legacy beside which all your other achievements will pale in comparison. Only when the citizens of Israel return to themselves will they return to civility and domestic peace. Only when we all know who we really are will we be able to negotiate peace from a position of strength rather than weakness. (Would it not be wiser to look after our security before trying to make peace?)

Mr. President, we need a voice of greatness, and I believe you can deliver.

Nathan Lopes Cardozo

ISRAEL AND THE ARAB WORLD

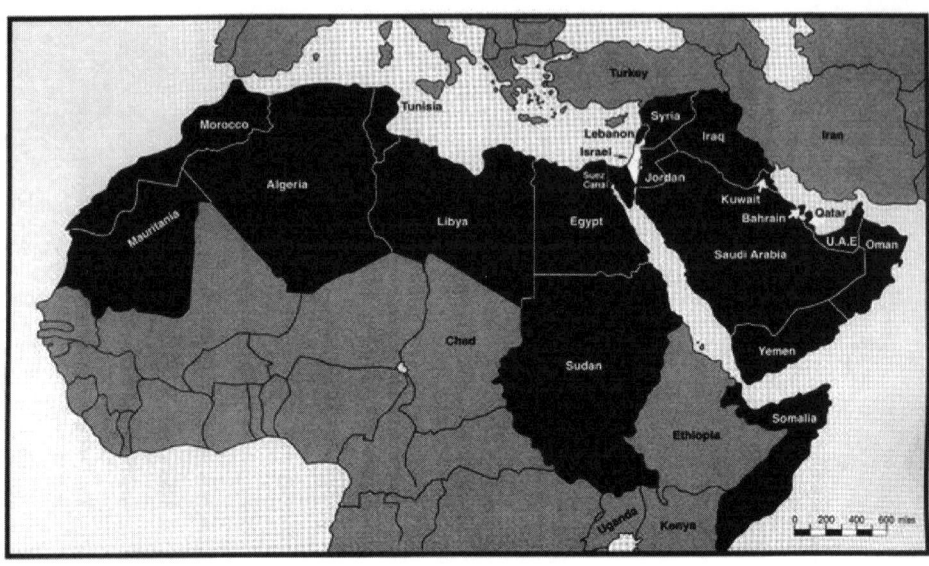

From *A Place among the Nations* by Binyamin Netanyahu.
New York: Bantam Books, 1993. Used by permission.

PART I

ESSAYS

LOVE FOR THE LAND

TO MERIT ISRAEL IS TO MARRY THE LAND

November 16, 2004

MARRIAGE AND THE MERIT OF LIVING in the Land of Israel have much in common. After Sarah dies, Avraham buys a parcel in the land of Canaan, which includes the cave of Machpela, in order to bury her. Speaking to the owner, Efron, Avraham says: "I will give you the price of the field. *Kach mimeni* – take it from me – and I will bury my dead there" (Bereshit 23:13). Efron takes the money, and Avraham becomes the official owner of this field and, hence, the legal landlord of a portion of the land of Israel.

The Talmud (BT *Kiddushin* 2a) connects this incident with the institution of marriage. In Devarim we read (22:13): "When a man takes a woman as his wife…." Because the same word, "take" (*kach* in Hebrew), is used as in the case where Avraham buys the Cave of Machpela, the Sages conclude that in the same way one buys the land of Israel, so one should marry one's wife – with money or an object of value such as a ring. This is an application of an interpretative rule called a *gezerah shavah*, which states that when two words are identical, even when they are stated in completely different contexts, both passages are subject to the same laws.

This Talmudic ruling has obviously drawn a lot of critique. How can one compare these two cases? Is marrying one's wife the same as buying a piece of land? This seems to be offensive and, in fact, in complete opposition to what a Jewish marriage is all about. Nowhere does Jewish law allow a man to deal with his wife as if she were his possession. In fact, if he does, the woman may demand an immediate divorce. Since Jewish law itself objects to any such comparison, why make it at all?

Many excellent explanations have been offered. Without denying their importance and truth, we would like to suggest a completely different approach. It may well be that the sages wanted to emphasize the holiness of the land of Israel by comparing it to a marriage. One does not buy a piece of the Land of Israel like one buys a piece of land anywhere else in the world. In Israel's case, one *marries* the land! The land becomes a loving partner, and one's love for this land is of a completely different nature from buying a piece of land or living anywhere else! Jews treat the land of Israel as a living personality with whom one has a deep emotional affinity. They do not relate to it as a possession to use but rather, as a living personality with a soul. It is not the love for a country of which the average native speaks. Like marriage, it is a covenant, and a covenant is built on the basis of duties rather than of rights. It is a pledge, and one does not betray a pledge. Just as during the marriage ceremony the groom gives the bride an object of value as a symbolic expression of his willingness to make sacrifices for her sake, so one "pays" for the land by making a financial offering. Just as in matrimony, where one marries for high and noble goals, so one betroths the land in order to achieve holiness, to transform oneself into a more dignified person and make the world into a better place. The many laws related to the land show that one needs to care for the land almost as carefully as one attends to the needs of one's wife. The Jewish relationship with the land is a love story, which is why Jews were unable to divorce themselves from this land even when they found themselves in exile for thousands of years. One does not abandon one's wife! For other nations this may be difficult to fathom, but for the Jew it is the very air he breathes.

It was Rabbi Moshe Avigdor Amiel (1883–1946), the chief rabbi of Tel Aviv, who gave this thought still another important dimension in his work, *Derashot el ammi*. Just as the giving of a valued object at the time of the marriage ceremony to one's wife is only the first payment, so is the buying of the land only a first installment. No one should ever believe that Israel is an intrinsic inheritance because the Jewish people once bought it piecemeal. One needs to merit it every moment. Just as no marriage will endure unless one continues to toil for its success all the time, so the land of Israel demands one's constant spiritual labor to merit living in it. Anything less will lead to divorce.

2

TO MARRY, TO BUY AND THE FUTURE OF ISRAEL

August 9, 2005

IN AN EXTRAORDINARY STATEMENT IN THE TALMUD, we get a glimpse into the minds of the sages of Israel just after they witnessed the destruction of the Temple, the murder of millions of Jews, and the complete breakdown of Jewish life in the ancient land of Israel.

"By right we should issue a decree that Jews should not marry and have children so that the seed of Avraham will come to an end of its own accord" (BT *Bava Batra* 60b).

No statement could better express total despair than these words. Once they realized that the small remnant of the people of Israel had been exiled and forced to live among violent anti-Semitic societies, they concluded that there was no longer any hope for a better future. So why continue to suffer when they could simply fade into oblivion?

Nevertheless, the Talmud reports that the simple Jews of that time chose not to give in to despair. Instead, they opposed their leaders' arguments and decided to rebuild Jewish life wherever possible. This showed courage of an unprecedented dimension. With no country, army or economy and surrounded by millions of enemies whose hatred towards Jews was well-known, these Jews found the strength to marry and raise families. Despite the total collapse of Jewish life, they opted for the seemingly impossible: to continue to build the people of Israel as they had been taught to do by the very leaders who now despaired.

In a similar vein, the book of Yirmiyahu (chapter 32) tells the story of the Babylonian siege of Jerusalem. In its third year, the Babylonian army caused an unprecedented famine, and deadly plagues killed hundreds of thousands of Jews. When Yirmiyahu predicted that the city would soon fall and that the king himself would be captured, King Zedekiah had him thrown in prison.

While Yirmiyahu was in the dungeon, God appeared to him and told him to buy a piece of land near Jerusalem from his cousin, a man named Hanamel. Only a moment later Hanamel indeed appeared and suggested that Jeremiah buy this piece of land. Consequently the prophet signed a contract with his cousin and had the document placed in an earthenware jar and buried in order to preserve it. Then he announced: "Thus says the Lord of Hosts, the God of Israel: Houses, fields and vineyards shall again be bought in this land" (Yirmiyahu 32:15).

It is utterly astonishing that under the terrible circumstances in which the Jews lived at that moment, one simple Jew had the nerve to walk up to the very prophet who persistently predicted that utter disaster was imminent and dared to offer to sell him a piece of land! No doubt this piece of land was full of corpses and located in a war zone that prevented the new buyer from visiting his property. Who would think of trying to sell, let alone buy, in such a market?

Indeed, it is not Yirmiyahu who serves as the story's hero, but rather his low-profile cousin Hanamel. After all, God told Jeremiah to buy the land, so how could he refuse? On the other hand, Hanamel had heard no word from God telling him to sell. So where did he get the courage even to suggest such a transaction?

Nothing would stop Hanamel from going on with his life. His faith allowed him to buy and sell with the absolute knowledge that one day everything would fall in place and a beautiful Jewish life would start again in our ancestral homeland. Today things may be dreadful, but one day there will be joy. This is the unprecedented faith of Hanamel, which even Yirmiyahu had to acknowledge.

3

THE FAITH OF THE PAINED

July 8, 2004

ONE OF THE MOST ASTONISHING FACTS about the current situation in the land of Israel is the unprecedented outpouring of faith. While confronted by ongoing terrorist attacks in which hundreds of people have been murdered and thousands injured, we are encountering a new phenomenon in modern Jewish history: in the face of unparalleled pain and disaster, the enormous capacity of trust in God and in Judaism by those who should have been the first to lose it.

Listening to the voices of those who have lost their parents, children or spouses, we realize the infinite power of their faith. Not once have we heard about a case where people walked out on their Judaism because of their immense pain. The religious community, which is currently paying an extremely heavy price, rather than weakening in its commitment to Jewish tradition, shows clear signs of an unprecedented strengthening of its observance and commitment to Halacha and Jewish faith. On more than one occasion young children, while burying a parent – and sometimes both parents at once – have called on their family and friends to increase their religious devotion, study of Torah and love for their people and country. And even in less religious or completely nonobservant circles, there is no abandonment of Jewish values, no flight from the land, but even a certain increase in religious practice.

It would be both vulgar and cheap to invoke Freud's argument of wishful thinking to explain this phenomenon. To argue that people in pain look for a God or a religious way of life in order to cope with their pain will not do. There are just as many arguments for people to abandon religion after suffering atrocities. The best proof of that is the Holocaust. Many survivors or relatives of those who perished abandoned their belief in God or their Jewish observance during or after the Holocaust. And while we would not dare to compare both cases – we surely admit that the Holocaust was a much greater national disaster than anything we are experiencing now – we cannot deny that on a personal level the pain of those who have lost their family in terrorist attacks has been no less.

Faith within the land of Israel is made up of different components than faith outside the land. In the early days of the State of Israel, American diplomats used to complain that whenever they discussed war-related strategies with Israeli ministers, they would become irritated because the latter would, as a matter of course, anticipate the occurrence of a few miracles without which any chance of winning a war would be unfeasible and the whole strategy a farce.

Israel is the land on which God keeps His eye from the beginning of the year till the end. It is the land to which one makes aliyah, to which one *ascends,* and not to which one descends. It is the land whose stones heard the voices of the great prophets, where the dust on which one walks still holds the footprints of holy biblical Jews and where the air carries the millions of prayers that were sent from all the corners of the world. It is a land that not only touches heaven but that represents heavenly conditions in earthly manifestations. It is the country where faith was born and whence it was carried throughout the world. It seems that faith has permeated the very essence of the land and its inhabitants like air in the heavens.

The secular population is also caught by its powerful manifestation. Even when they do not realize it and perhaps even deny it, they carry the seeds of faith in their subconscious and continue to believe in the unbelievable. They also realize that Israel's predicament at this moment is not just another accidental event in man's history, but rather one with enormous religious meaning. Just like the religious population, they do not know what it entails in terms of a higher meaning, but they also hear a perpetual murmur from waves that reach our shores from a world beyond.

It is like a kind of awe, transcendence and intimation of the divine that enter our space but have not yet landed on the surface of our world. As such, it is not possible to declare war on faith. It is too deep and too authentic. Secular explanations do not have the ability to grasp the profundity of the hour. Even in this struggle, Jews realize that there is a holy dimension to all that happens. Also the realization that the land of Israel still experiences many great miracles, even in the midst of all the atrocities (together with awareness of the utter absurdity of a situation packed in doses of normality so that life is able to continue), allows Jews to remain unmoved to the calls of extreme secularity.

Without diminishing the unspeakable pain of the hour, we should listen carefully to those who have been more affected by this pain than anyone else: those who have lost relatives and will never be able to return to a fully normal life. They, rather than we, the less affected, are the beacons of faith. This is most significant. We had better listen.

4

THE PAIN OF LACKING PAIN
COMMENTARY ON A EULOGY IN ISRAEL

October 18, 2004

THE STORY IS TOLD OF A GREAT RABBI who was known never to be involved in any secular endeavor. His whole life was dedicated to spiritual matters, to the study and teaching of Torah. Once, when his students saw him reading *The New York Times* before he left home for the morning prayers, they were shocked. How could it be that their holy teacher would lower himself to read such mundane material as *The New York Times*?

"My dearest children," said the rabbi, "I always read *The New York Times* before I go off to pray. Do you know why? Because when I read about the anguish of so many people in our world, Jews and non-Jews, I feel more in touch with them and then I know what to pray for."

As many tragedies befall our nation in the land of Israel, many of us, especially those who are not personally harmed, have difficulty "staying in touch" with these calamities. This also includes the author. The ongoing tragedies in which men, women and children are killed or severely injured by terrorists create a psychological condition within us which makes us slightly immune. While we are upset and deeply affected by these events, we go on eating and drinking, trying to live a normal life, as much as possible.

Yet as we do this, we feel guilty. Sometimes we wonder whether there is something wrong with us. How can I continue my daily life when I know how much pain there is on the other side of the street? Such a reaction is normal, and it is important to be aware of it. Still, we would argue that our failure to stay fully in touch is also a blessing, however painful.

One of the most paradoxical laws within Judaism is the need for mourners to refrain from mourning on Shabbat (even in the first week after burial, during which one is commanded to sit on the floor and refrain from any joy). Mourners are asked to celebrate Shabbat in an optimistic way, putting on their Shabbat clothes, eating a tasty meal, preferably accompanied by Shabbat songs.

We might ask: How is it possible to sing songs and act almost as if nothing happened when one has just lost a loved one?

Our sages give many reasons for this strange paradox. We would like to suggest yet another approach, one that will reveal the great insight of Jewish law into the human condition.

In order for human beings not to fall victim to total despair, it is important that they stay in touch with the joy of living. Even in the depths of tragedy there must be an opportunity to taste a better life. It is for this reason that mourners are asked to get up from their mourning on Shabbat and live a life of joy even when it is for only one day and even when it is a little artificial. It saves them from infinite despair, which otherwise would ruin their lives forever. It is for this reason that Jewish law asks them to become a little immune to their own loss and, as such, helps them to go on with their lives later on.

The same is true with a society or a nation. They must go on in spite of all the tragedies. One must prevent a national trauma at all costs. If not for the fact that we are able to distance ourselves from tragedy a little, our society would fall into total paralysis. If we do not heed this call, our nation will not have the strength to overcome and fight the enemy. Life must go on even when war surrounds us. We owe it to ourselves and our children.

Nevertheless, this does not solve our problem entirely. After all, there is still the possibility of indifference within our souls, of too much living normally. While all that we mentioned above may be true, we still must fight dimensions of apathy within ourselves. We need to be pained by an absence of pain.

There is one answer. It is the same one that the rabbi offered his students. We should choose a text which will take us straight into the shattering pain of others. We should read it before we go to pray or when we feel that our souls are turning cold. We should dwell on it to such an extent that it pierces our hearts. But once we have done so, we should put it aside and only permit it to slumber in the back of our minds. We must be able to return to our responsibilities of assisting our families and friends, to give them hope, meaning and joy. By doing so, we honor those who died for these ideals.

Not often are we provided with a text that can give us an opportunity to feel the pain and hear the hope. Last week, in the middle of the Intifada, a young man of twenty-one by the name of Tzvi Yehuda mourned, together with nine of his siblings, as he buried his father and mother, Rabbi Yoseph and Chana Dickstein, and his ten-year-old brother, Shuva-el, who had been murdered in a terror attack in Pesagot.

Tzvi Yehuda led the burial and the weeping crowd of thousands in a tearful recitation of *selichot* (prayers of supplication), beginning with the Thirteen Attributes of Divine Mercy. The speech was accompanied by almost constant weeping from his siblings and many other mourners. Read it and let it pierce your heart, but then put it aside and go back to your responsibilities and the joys of your home, however difficult that may be. When your soul is cold or you need to pray more deeply, read it again, but never too often.

In a broken but strong voice, Tzvi Yehuda said the following:

> Abba, Ima [Father, Mother], "who were beloved and pleasant in their lives and did not part even in their deaths,"[1] sweet Shuva-el, what can I say now? What words can describe the magnitude of this calamity? How can I speak in the past tense about all the people whom we loved the most? About Abba? About Ima? And Shuva-el? Suddenly, everything has been cut off in the middle. Abba, on Thursday night until two-thirty in the morning, we were working together on the sukkah, and we were in the middle of a passage in *Le-Netivot Yisrael* [a religious text]. Who will continue this?

> Know, Abba and Ima, that we, your children, received a strong education, an education with ideals, and even when you are not here physically, it continues to strengthen us according to your path.

---

[1] 2 Shmuel 1:23.

You decided to leave the neighborhood of Givat Sha'ul [in Jerusalem], the easy life, the workplaces that were close to home, even though there was nothing pressing. But still you decided, during these difficult times for the Jewish people in general and for Pesagot in particular, to move, and to try to strengthen and be strengthened, to acquire by deeds the beloved Land that you so loved, the love of which you imparted to us, with trips – many trips – around the country, and by teaching us.

"Beloved Land, do not cover their blood."[2]

All your efforts, all the foundations of our home, everything – drew its spirit and soul from this *bet midrash* [Rabbi Avraham ha-Kohen Kook's yeshiva], from the worldview that Rav Kook, of saintly memory, laid out for us, and his son, our teacher, Rabbi Tzvi Yehuda, may the memory of the righteous be for a blessing. All the time, Abba, you would tell us stories about them, and you gave me his name.

Therefore, it was obvious to all of us, the whole family, that this funeral must begin from the foundations of our home, from this *bet midrash*. I promise you, Abba and Ima, that we will continue in this spirit, in this ideology.

Abba, how happy you were that I am studying in Beit El. We studied together on Fridays. Ima relieved you from all the jobs, and you would come and we would learn for some two hours. As the time passed, we saw how our spiritual worlds began to take on parallel lines. You saw me walking in the same path that you took twenty-five years ago, when you started out as a student in Merkaz ha-Rav [Rabbi Kook's yeshiva]. How much joy and satisfaction you had from me. Abba, I so much wanted to be like you. To be "a son like his father."

---

[2] Based on Iyov 16:18.

Last night, we sat together, all the children, and we all recounted how in this last period of your lives, you both felt satisfaction. Tzofiyah said that you told her just a week ago, "It's like we're dreaming. We have reached our *menucha* and *nachalah* [resting place and inheritance]." You knew that you had found your place. You felt good in Pesagot. You succeeded in fulfilling all of your ideals in the best way.

Yes, you reached the *menucha* and *nachalah*. Abba and Ima and Shuva-el, you reached it in Pesagot.

But what will be with us? Who will be the Ima of Adiel? Who will be the Abba of Shirel? You so much wanted to see us getting married. Who will lead us to the wedding canopy?

Everything that you built in the house was built with the future in mind. You wanted there to be room for everyone – everything on a large scale…. Now you won't merit seeing your grandchildren….

Abba, Ima, Shuva-el: I, Tzvi Yehuda, your eldest son, whom you counted on so much, allowed me at every opportunity to be responsible, promise to be a good father, a concerned father.

In my name, and in the name of all the children, we promise to preserve the unity of our family, to stay together, even at the price of giving up personal dreams. This is what you wanted all these years, and this is what we will try to do.

We, the family, believe that this tremendous sacrifice that we made is not just a personal sacrifice. Our pain is not just a private pain. Abba and Ima were not killed in a gang war, or in a car accident, or because of any sins of theirs. Shuva-el, who had never tasted sin, certainly was not murdered for that. Abba and Ima and Shuva-el were murdered, in the light of day, in front of their children, by a cruel, debased murderer, because they were

Jews who lived freely in their state that they so loved, without fear.

Am Yisrael: this sacrifice is for all of us! Everyone must feel this pain. Everyone must understand, know, and feel that they have taken the best sons of our nation.

The Holy One, Blessed be He, is speaking to us via the [day-to-day] reality. He is shaking us and telling us: Wake up! Understand who we are and what we are doing here in Eretz Yisrael! Why are we here?

Unfortunately, we have been tested with many tragedies of late. To tell others that "the Land of Israel is acquired with tribulation," that that which is acquired with difficulty is an eternal acquisition, that Hashem only tests those who can withstand the ordeals – that's not so hard. But to tell it to ourselves – that's hard. And to really feel it – that's even harder. But no one asked us whether or not we want to be heroes. We didn't want that, and no one asked us, and we weren't ready, but we were forced. We were forced to be strong. We will try, with the help of all of you, to be strong. We will add faith, we will add courage, we will add strength. We don't know how we will keep going in this insane situation. We don't know what will be with us – both the little ones, and those of us children who are somewhat older but still feel little. But we know with certainty that we will go on. We will work hard, and we will strive, and we will overcome, and we will go on.

All that we have been saying about accepting the Divine judgment with love does not take away one whit of responsibility from those who were supposed to be in charge: The leaders of the state and its ministers, who are abusing the offices to which they were elected, and are not doing enough to prevent incidents like this, or to uplift the nation. That is their job. If they don't want to do it, then they should give it to someone else who can do it.

We, the family, decided yesterday to bury you in Pesagot, in the land that is precious to you, the place we decided on our own that it would be our place. Abba and Ima spent the last two years and all their resources to build this house. The fear never occurred to them that we would not be able to live everywhere in Israel. I myself heard people who tried to weaken them, but Abba and Ima were strong and did not break. Abba and Ima decided that this would be their place and that of the family. We the children are setting up our base in Pesagot.

Residents of Pesagot, know that our struggle is that of all of Am Yisrael. Am Yisrael throughout the generations is with us. Abba and Ima and Shuva-el are with us. We will continue together, without fear.

I want to thank you, residents of Pesagot, for all your help when we moved in, starting with the first night. You turned out to be angels, and then, from the minute we learned of this catastrophe, these pure angels – from Pesagot and elsewhere – enwrapped us, and helped us. There are no words for us to thank you.

Shuva-el, the little one, so cute…. I called you Bukish. I remember when you were born. It was Friday. You were born the fastest of all. A boy who was all joy to his parents, a good boy, a good influence on his brothers. Such a good friend to Benayah and Shlomo. So sweet, a tzaddik [righteous being]. You never had to be reminded to study, the one whom everyone loved, a smart boy who read books. They murdered you as you were reading, and your head fell on the book. A tzaddik, so pure – you never did wrong to anyone.

Abba and Ima and Shuva-el – they let me see you today. You looked so serene. I saw that it was well with you…. Please watch over us from where you are, over your sons and daughters: Tzvi

Yehuda, Tzofiyah, Ayelet, Didi, Renanah, Shuva-el, Shlomo. And watch over the little ones, Benayah, Shirel and Adiel, who will not get to know their own parents.

Watch over all of us, the orphans – it's hard to digest that we are called orphans – and over Grandmother Shula, and Grandfather Aharon and Grandmother Miriam and over all your brothers and sisters and the whole family. We know that you are with us. Help us to be strong.

Before I conclude I want to ask, in my name and in the name of all the children, forgiveness from you – for any offense that I did you, or chutzpah, or argument. I beg that you forgive us, holy Abba and Ima, and Shuva-el.

"And Hashem will wipe away the tears from every face, and swallow up death forever."

❧ 5 ❧

AN ANGEL CALLED CHAYA HODAYA
SCHIJVESCHUURDER[1]

August 9, 2001

My hands shake and my body trembles
As I hear of the tragedy that befell my dear friends:
Mordechai Rafael ben Joseph Schijveschuurder, of blessed memory,
His wife and three children
Who came up to the land
To join their people and to fulfill
The commandment to settle.
From the land of exile,
The country of Holland,
They ascended to heavenly Israel.

"He is to me like a bear lying in wait,
Like a lion in hiding.
He led me off my way and tore me to pieces.
He has made me desolate.
He bent his bow and set me
As a mark of his arrow.
He drove into my heart
The arrows of his quiver.
I have become the laughingstock of all peoples,
The burden of their songs all day long."[2]

---

[1] Written after the terrorist attack on the Sbarro restaurant in Jerusalem (August, 2001), in which several members of the Schijveschuurder family were murdered.
[2] Eicha 3:10–15.

I hear the sound of angels:
Not of those who live on high,
But of one who dwells on earth,
Chaya bat Rabbi Mordechai Rafael
Schijveschuurder, of blessed memory,
Eight years in body,
venerable in spirit.

And she spoke and said:
"Everything that happens here,
It is all a miracle.
Those who live and those who die.
Nothing happens for no reason and God knows what He is doing.
He wants to tell us that we have to behave better,
That soon the Mashiach will come and my parents will rise again,
And I will continue to smile."

And for just a moment the land of Israel
Was silent,
And millions of tears
Ascended to the Heavenly Throne
And asked for mercy.
It shall come to pass in the latter days....
For out of Zion shall go forth Torah
And the Word of the Lord from Jerusalem.[3]

Death is horrible, hard and black,
A source of anguish.
Our first reaction is consternation.
We are dumb and broken.
Slowly but surely
Our feeling of dismay makes place for a sentiment of mystery,
The *mysterium magnum*.

---

[3] Yeshaya 2:2, 3.

Suddenly life that we believed we knew
Seems to hide behind a veil of the Great Secret.
Our speech stops. Our understanding fails.
In death there is only silence and an acknowledgement of the Other.

Real life starts long before existence commences.
It comes from far.
It travels through experience:
Growth, suffering, insight and deed.
Life is always on the road, also after death.

In the Torah nobody dies.
One is "gathered to one's forefathers."
"When will your days be fulfilled that you will be with your fathers?"
Does the *neshama* become dust?
Will spirit become ashes?
It is only the *neshama* that creates immortal words,
Art, and thoughts.

Life is beautiful when it is carried by the body,
But still more beautiful is life in the word.
The word is greater than the world.
Due to the word of the Ribono shel Olam,
The world came into being and the universe was created.
The Torah is the creation of the word in kedusha,
And if a great human being dies,
Then his *neshama* becomes a word and that word lives in the book of the Creator.[4]

Mordechai Rafael Schijveschuurder, aged forty-four.
Tzira Schijveschuurder, aged forty-one.
Ra'aya Shulamith Schijveschuurder, aged fourteen.

---

[4] See also "Death as Homecoming" by Abraham Yehoshua Heschel. In *Jewish Reflections on Death,* edited by Jack Riemer. New York: Schocken Books, 1976.

Avraham Yitschak Yedidyah Schijveschuurder, aged four.
Chemda Bracha Schijveschuurder, aged two.

In fire and with "Shema" on your lips you left this world.
You are our eternal teachers!

6

A CALL TO FAST AND PRAY:
GUSH KATIF AND THE TSUNAMI

January 24, 2005

"When Moshe's hands became heavy, [Aharon and Chur] took a stone and placed it under him and he sat on it. And [Moshe held] his hands in steady prayer until sunset."

Shemot 17:12

When Amalek, Israel's biblical arch-enemy, attacked the Jewish people in the desert, Moshe was no longer physically able to fight together with his beloved people. Therefore he decided to climb the hill in order to be able to oversee the war and give his people religious and psychological support.

"It happened that whenever Moshe raised his hand, Israel would prevail, but whenever he lowered his hand, Amalek would prevail" (ibid, 17:11).

The Talmud (BT *Taanit* 11b), concerned for Moshe's well-being, asks the question why Moshe's right-hand men, Aharon and Chur, did not give Moshe a cushion on which to sit. Although both men helped him to keep his hands up so that he was able to pray with great fervor, it must still have been a difficult task for Moshe. So why not make his situation a little easier by providing him with a cushion?

The Talmud responds with great sensitivity:

"This is then what Moshe meant to convey: "As Israel is in distress, I will be in distress.""

As it says in an earlier statement:

> "Our Rabbis have taught: When Israel is in trouble and a Jew separates himself, two ministering angels who accompany every human being place their hands on his head and say: So-and-so, who separates himself from the community, shall not behold the consolation of the community. Another *baraita*[1] taught: When the community is in trouble let a man not say: I will go to my house and I will eat and drink and all will be well with me. Instead, a man should share in the distress of the community.

It is for this reason that Rabbi Yoseph Karo in his monumental codex, the Shulchan Aruch, lays down the law that in time of severe drought one should fast and after some time even lessen one's business dealings, building for pleasure and sexual intercourse (unless one has not yet fulfilled the obligation of procreation) (*Orach Chaim* 575:7).

It is clear from the Talmudic text that Moshe's refusal to sit on a cushion or the suggestion that the people withdraw from all sorts of pleasure during a time of drought is not part of an attempt, as in the case of prayer, to ask God for mercy. While no doubt such behavior will be pleasing in the eyes of the Lord of the Universe, the main purpose is altogether different: namely, the prevention of indifference.

The worst sin towards our fellowmen is not to hate them but to be indifferent to them. It is for this reason that the Talmud makes it clear that Moshe refused to sit comfortably on a cushion and that no man should ever say: "I will go to my house and I will eat and drink and all will be well with me" while others suffer. As William Redfield once said, "To try, maybe to die, but not to care is never to be born."

Many people do not realize that human beings are not aware of their own insensitivity. Conscious insensitivity is a contradiction in terms. While many are most sensitive for matters of small concern, sensitivity for great matters often escapes the human heart. Yet this is exactly what the Talmud is concerned about. Only through *acts* of compassion is one able to fight indifference. Merciful thoughts have little effect in time of distress. One must act the way one thinks or end up thinking the way one acts.

---

[1] *Baraita:* early rabbinic teaching not incorporated into the Mishnah.

As is well known, Palestinian terrorists continuously attack our fellow Jews in Gush Katif and its environs. Soldiers and fathers, some of very young families, and several children have lost their lives. As far as humanly can be seen, these attacks may well continue for a long time and possibly escalate, bringing many of our soldiers and fellow Jews in an even greater danger.

At the same time, the Asian tsunami tragedy is far from over. Millions of people are homeless and traumatized, hunger is rampant and thousands of children have become orphaned. Many have been kidnapped and sold into slavery.

All of us should be deeply concerned by the fact that we can easily fall victim to indifference. Thus, while most of us live far away from the places that were struck, Jewish law and morality ask us not to sit idly by. As no other country, Israel has shown great sensitivity by providing food, funds and rescue workers for the tsunami victims. However, religious Jews, who represent Jewish religious values, should respond with even greater sensitivity. This is even more so when the first shock has passed. Likewise, we should make ourselves more sensitive to the situation of our fellow Jews in Gush Katif and let them understand that we care and stand with them in their pain.

Therefore, I humbly call upon my colleagues, friends and students to observe a private half day fast next Thursday, the seventeenth of Shevat (January 27) and to intensify our prayers on behalf of our fellow Jews in the land of Israel and the tsunami victims in Asia.

Let us not say: I will go home, eat and drink and all will be well with me. Let us not suspend our sensitivity.

7

WHAT WILL YOU TELL YOUR CHILDREN?
AN OPEN LETTER TO MY FRIENDS AND
STUDENTS ABROAD

July 7, 2004

You shall not stand idle by the blood of your neighbor.

Vayikra 29:16

As THE JEWISH YEAR 5761 DRAWS TO A CLOSE, it is most appropriate to remind ourselves that it has been nearly twelve months since Israel found itself in a guerrilla war with deadly terrorists whose main goal is to kill as many Jews as possible. The Palestinian Authority and the Arab world have indoctrinated the world with their lies and manipulations, creating a global atmosphere of anti-Semitism which has turned governments and media against the State of Israel and its citizens.

Hundreds of innocent Jews were killed in bomb explosions and many were injured, never to return to a normal life again, while soldiers and policemen lost their lives trying to defend their fellow Jews. By now many Jewish children, in some parts of the country more than twenty percent of school pupils, have lost one or both parents. Intense suffering has become the ongoing experience of thousands, if not of tens of thousands of Israeli families who have lost family members and friends.

Meanwhile, an ongoing threat of war hangs over the entire population of Israel. Tens of thousands of Israeli parents have nightmares about their children who serve in the army, live in settlements and drive on dangerous roads.

The economy, which has been badly affected by all this, stands on the verge of collapse. Medical care has reached a low point so that many people are no longer sure that they will receive the minimum amount of medical help.

Psychologists emphasize the fact that this time, Israelis are not coping well with the situation. After so many wars since 1948, they have become tired and worn out. Seeing no end to this struggle and hearing high-ranking IDF officers speaking about the possibility of this guerrilla war continuing with increased violence for the next five years, hundreds of thousands of Israeli Jews feel utterly hopeless.

As if this were not enough, Israelis are now also confronted with a new phenomenon that they had never dreamt about and which they previously thought would be impossible. For the first time Israeli Jews feel utterly left alone because it has become clear as the light of the sun that the vast majority of fellow Jews abroad are showing deadly indifference to the situation. Utterances such as "We are with you in this war," "We stand behind you," "We cannot tell you how painful it is for us to be so far away" have become meaningless to most Israelis. However good the intentions of those who speak these words, to the average Israeli they appear empty. The reason for this is obvious. Very few Jews actually came last year to show solidarity with their Israeli brothers and sisters. Already for months Israeli hotels have been standing empty. Some have closed down, causing the dismissal of many workers. The tourist industry has been dealt a death blow to the point that Israelis working in this field have been forced, against their will, to move their families to other countries in order to support them.

While waiting for an unprecedented influx of hundreds of thousands of American Jews to this country (in which case hotels would not have been able to accommodate all the guests for lack of space), Israelis had to wake up from this dream that they believed to be one of unprecedented solidarity. A shattering silence has made them realize that in the moment of truth, they are alone. Instead of listening to their fellow Jews in Israel and coming in unparalleled numbers, American Jews preferred to listen to the State Department's warning not to travel to the Middle East.

(Lately, more and more Israelis complain about the fact that American Jews have seemingly become used to the Arab violence so that they no longer bother to phone their friends or family after a terrorist attack to ask how they are doing.)

Also, I have been utterly disappointed. Throughout my travels in America last year I asked and begged my dear students to come, if for only a few days. I explained that not only is it important for Israelis to see American Jews coming to their country, but it is of the greatest importance that American Jews prove to themselves that they really care for their fellow Jews. At the time I received many promises. People were going to organize flights, contact hotels, and get to Israel as soon as possible. Synagogue boards and outreach programs admitted that they really had to become active and make their members understand that this was their minimum obligation.

However, with few exceptions, it has become clear that until now, nearly nobody has come. When asking about this I was told that people "could not take off from work," that "the Israeli hotels were too expensive" or that they "would be bored in Israel" since it would not be possible to go out and have fun. Most disturbing was the fact that some of the same people went on vacation somewhere else to hotels that were more expensive, suddenly finding the time off from work which only a short time before they had considered impossible. Instead of being pleased to help Israeli hotels to stay open, the tourist industry to flourish, and sending a clear massage to the Arabs that American Jews could not be scared off, they actually gave in to Arab pressure and showed the world what Jewish solidarity was all about.

Even more disturbing is the unsolicited advice Israelis receive from their American Jewish friends: "If we were you, we would bomb the Palestinians or evacuate them by force, even risking a war, since this is no doubt the only solution." All this is said by people sitting in comfortable chairs while Israeli soldiers risk their lives to protect their fellow Jews and try to pave the way for a more peaceful existence for the children and grandchildren of those who remain in the United States.

One is reminded of Rabbi Shlomo Riskin's observation when he asked his American audience whether they consider Israel "Disneyland" or their motherland. If it is indeed nothing more than a land to have a good vacation in, then there is indeed no moral obligation to come here in solidarity. But if, as most American Jews clearly believe, Israel is their motherland, the question is obvious: "If your mother were unwell, would you not go to visit her?"

American Jews, including the religious community, will have to ask themselves some penetrating questions this Rosh ha-Shana. Above all they should be fully aware that one day their children will turn to them and ask: "Dad, Mom, what did you do for Israel when it was in this terrible situation some years ago? Did you at least go and visit your fellow Jews and ask them how they were doing? Did you call them regularly on the phone?" Woe to those who cannot give the right answer.

THE JEWS

THE PERMANENT PRECIOUSNESS OF
THE SECULAR JEW[1]

March 23, 2006

WE ARE LIVING IN AN AGE of blatant irreverence. Debunking has become the norm and wherever we turn we experience a need to reveal that even the greatest of our heroes had feet of clay. While people often mention human dignity, it has become a farce in real life. Instead of deliberately looking for opportunities to love our fellow men as our holy Torah requires, many have rewritten the Golden Rule to read: Distrust your fellow human beings as you distrust yourself. Human beings' disbelief in themselves has overflowed into their relationships with others. Fear of their own deeds and mediocrity has led them to believe that the spiritual giants have left us and that we are a generation of spiritual orphans.

This belief has slowly penetrated the subconscious of segments of the religious community as well, although in a more subtle form. Influenced by materialistic philosophies, many religious personalities who were once known for their reverence for their fellow human beings have become part of the problem without realizing it. Instead of sending a message of pure love and respect for their fellow Jews, whatever their background or beliefs, many people within the religious Jewish community have fallen victim to a kind of faint debunking that has led to a most worrisome situation in and outside the land of Israel.

When we observe even those who are fully committed to helping their fellow Jews find their way back to Judaism, we see an attitude that is foreign to religious life and thought. Without denying their love for their fellow

---

[1] This essay was inspired by some writings of Abraham Joshua Heschel.

Jews, we cannot escape the impression that a kind of talking down to secular Jews has become the norm.

Constant emphasis is placed on the need to cure the secular Jew's mistaken lifestyle. While such an attitude is no doubt born out of love for one's fellow Jew, it lays the foundation for endless trouble. It is built on arrogance. It sees the religious Jew as the ideal while turning the secular Jew into a second-class member of the Jewish people. It is the secular Jew who needs to repent for his mistaken ways. Such an attitude is built on the notion of contrast and lack of affinity. The secular Jew will always feel inferior. As such, the point of departure through which one would like to bring fellow Jews closer to Judaism is at the same time its undoing. The suggestion that one should throw oneself into a burning furnace rather then insult another person publicly (BT *Berakhot* 43b) may very well apply, since it is the community of secular Jews which is being treated with the notion of inferiority.

In order for Jews to bring their fellow Jews back to Judaism, there is a need to celebrate the mitzvot which secular Jews have been observing for all or part of their lives, not their failure to observe some others. Only through the notion of sharing in mitzvot will an authentic way be found to bring Jews back home.

The foundation should be humility, not arrogance. There is little doubt that secular Jews, consciously or unconsciously, perform a large number of commandments. While many of them may not be connected with ritual, there is still massive evidence that mitzvot that govern behavior between people enjoy a major commitment among secular Jews. Beneath the divisiveness of traditional commitment lie underpinnings of religion such as compassion, humility, awe and even faith. Different are the pledges, but equal are the devotions. It may quite well be that the minds of the religious and not religious Jew do not fully meet, but their spirits touch. Who will deny that secular Jews have no sense of mystery, forgiveness, beauty and gentleness? How many of them do not have inner faith that God cares or shows contempt for fraud or double standards? Each of them is the deepest of religious values.

Not only does this call for a celebration, but it may well become an inspiration for religious Jews. This is not just done by honoring secular Jews for keeping these mitzvot but in becoming inspired ourselves with *their* mitzvot and good deeds. There is a need to make so-called irreligious Jews aware that they are much more religious than they may realize. It is the realization that God's light often shines on their faces just as much, if not more, than on the face of religious Jews.

Just as irreligious personalities need to prove that they are worthy to be the friends of religious Jews, so religious Jews need to be worthy of the friendship of their secular fellow Jews. It would be a most welcome undertaking if religious Jews would call on their irreligious fellow Jews for guidance in mitzvot that demand greater commitment on their part.

There is a great need to call Jews back to their roots by showing them that they never left. Once religious Jews start to learn that irreligious Jews are their equals and not their inferiors, a comeback to Judaism on the right terms will come about.

One of the tragic failures of the ancient Jews was their indifference to the Ten Tribes of Israel, which were carried away by Assyria after the Northern Kingdom was destroyed. Overlooked and not taken seriously by their fellow Jews, they were consigned to oblivion and ultimately vanished.

This is a nightmare that at this moment in Jewish history should terrify each and every religious Jew: the unawareness of our being involved in a new failure, a tragic dereliction of duty.

AN OATH OF LOYALTY[1]

May 16, 2004

THE ACT OF CIRCUMCISION is like a marriage that Jewish parents in earlier centuries arranged long before their child was aware of the existence of his or her future partner. Just as they were convinced that this partner and no other was the ideal spouse for their child, so on a much more advanced level Jewish parents today bring their son into a covenant with the God of Israel as his most ideal Partner long before the child knows of Him. As such, circumcision is a moment in which the child becomes engaged to God and God to the child.

Circumcision is an eternal pledge that parents make to God whereby this child will not be an ordinary human being, but will live by His commandments and consequently guide humankind towards the final redemption, becoming a blessing to all nations (Bereshit 12:8).

Some of us will ask: what gives the parents the right to bring this child into this covenant without the child's consent? Why commit a child to a mission to which he may not agree? Yet on another level, should we not wonder whether it is even more unjust to bring a child into the world *without* a higher mission? While Socrates taught us that a life without thinking is not worth living, Judaism teaches us that life without a commitment is not worth being born into. The dignity of human beings stands in proportion to their obligations. And it is this dignity that we make our children share once we bring them into the covenant. To refuse them this merit is like denying them life altogether.

Circumcision is a word of honor, a moment that determines all other moments in the child's life. This imprint of God's seal should first of all be

---

[1] Inspired by Abraham Joshua Heschel.

on the body. After all, it is not the soul that needs to make a commitment. The soul *is* commitment. It is the body which, because of its inclination to look only after its own interests, has to make a vow that it will constantly stand in the service of God. Like a sheet that holds a treasure, the body is the vessel that contains the soul. Just as the contours of the sheet tell much about the contours of the treasury within, so the body should reveal the greatness of the soul. In case the body does not live up to this, the physical imprint of the circumcision is a constant reminder of what it means to live in the presence of God, a testimony of one's spiritual potential.

The revelation at Sinai is both an event that happened once and for all and an experience that happens all the time. What God does happens both in time and in eternity. So with circumcision. From man's perspective it happens only once but from God's perspective it happens continuously. The constant renewing imprint of God's seal on man's body is the eternal commitment of mortal man to God.

While monuments of stone may disappear, acts of spirit will never pass away. Circumcision is an act that transcends the present, history in reverse.

At Sinai the Jews committed themselves to the Torah with the words *naaseh ve-nishma,* "We will do and we will hear." Without yet knowing what they would be asked to do, they committed themselves to this open-ended, challenging task. On the eighth day of the newborn's life, at the time of circumcision, he is unknowingly brought into the covenant with God and stands in the same tradition of *naaseh ve-nishma.* The child's body starts on a road of commitment which is not yet known but no doubt is the most challenging mission in life: to become a blessing to all nations.

PROUD TO BE A JEW

July 7, 2007

IN THESE UNUSUAL DAYS, in which Jews are once more condemned for being Jews and some of our own brothers try to deny or even abhor their Jewishness, I believe, paradoxically, that the Jewish people will soon experience the most glorious opportunity of all time.

It is becoming increasingly clear to me that due to the present crisis, the Jewish people will ultimately be forced to recognize the profundity and spirituality of Judaism.

Circumstances are forcing the Jewish people to cleanse itself of many misconceptions, false philosophies and ideologies. Slowly but surely, more and more Jews will begin to see Judaism in a different light, and Jews will once more fall in love with their tradition, of which they have been robbed for such a long time.

Not only will Jews start to appreciate their own tradition, but Jewish religious values will move beyond the borders of the Jewish people, influencing a great part of humankind and transforming people's attitudes toward life in dramatic ways.

There is little doubt that ultimately this century will see the revival of Jewish tradition as never before. In our time, when many religions and secular philosophies have lost much of their influence due to their extremism and lack of moral fiber, Judaism will offer an answer to humankind's spiritual and material needs.

I predict that there will be a Jewish wave blowing through this world which will be unprecedented in its strength and sway.

There is nothing new in this assertion. Throughout the history of the Jewish people, gentiles of great influence have recognized all along what

Judaism has done for the good of humankind. It would be wise to quote some of them so as to create Jewish pride within ourselves and our children.

Here are some quotations that need no explanation. In order to appreciate them, it is important to read them carefully, since each one mentions another unique aspect of our Jewishness that it seems we ourselves have forgotten.

Heaven sometimes sends us great gentile souls in order to remind His people who they are. Let us listen carefully and act accordingly.

Leo Tolstoy (1828–1910), Russian novelist and social reformer:

> The Jew is that sacred being who has brought down from heaven the everlasting fire, and has illumined with it the entire world. He is the religious source, spring and fountain out of which all the rest of the peoples have drawn their beliefs and their religions.

> The Jew is the pioneer of liberty.... The Jew is the pioneer of civilization.... The Jew is the emblem of civil and religious toleration.... The Jew is the emblem of eternity."[1]

Lymann Abbott (1835–1921), American preacher and journalist:

> We Gentiles owe our life to Israel. It is Israel who has brought us the message that God is one and that God is a just and a righteous God and demands righteousness of His children, and demands nothing else. It is Israel that has brought us the message that God is our Father. It is Israel who, in bringing us the divine Law, has laid the foundation of liberty. It is Israel who had the first free institutions the world ever saw. It is Israel who has brought us our Bible, our prophets, our apostles. When sometimes our own unchristian prejudices flame out against the

---

[1] Quoted by Chief Rabbi J.H. Hertz, *A Book of Jewish Thoughts*. London: Oxford University Press, 1966.

Jewish people, let us remember that all that we have and all that we are, we owe under God, to what Judaism has given us.[2]

John Adams (1735–1826), second President of the United States:

I will insist that the Hebrews have done more to civilize men than any other nation. If I were an atheist, and believed in blind eternal fate, I should still believe that fate had ordained the Jews to be the most essential instrument for civilizing the nations. If I were an atheist of the other sect, who believe or pretend to believe that all is ordered by chance, I should believe that chance had ordered the Jews to preserve and propagate to all mankind the doctrine of a supreme, intelligent, wise, almighty sovereign of the universe, which I believe to be the great essential principle of all morality, and consequently of all civilization.[3]

Matthew Arnold (1822–1888), poet and critic:

The religion of the Bible is well said to be revealed because the great natural truth, that "righteousness tendeth to life," is seized and exhibited there with such incomparable force and efficacy. All, or very nearly all, the nations of mankind have recognized the important of conduct, and have attributed to it a natural obligation. They, however, looked at conduct not as something full of happiness and joy, but as something one could not manage to do without. But "Zion heard of it and rejoiced, and the daughters of Judah were glad because of Thy judgments, O Eternal." Happiness is our being's end and aim, and no one has ever come near Israel in feeling, and in making others feel, that to righteousness belongs happiness! As long as the world lasts, all who want to make progress in righteousness will come to

---

2 Ibid.
3 John Adams to F.A. Vanderkemp, February 16, 1809. In *The Works of John Adams*, edited by C.T. Adams, vol. 9, 609–610.

Israel for inspiration, as to the people who have had the sense for righteousness most glowing and strongest.[4]

Winston Churchill (1874–1965), statesman and leader:

Some people like the Jews, and some do not. But no thoughtful man can deny the fact that they are, beyond any question, the most formidable and the most remarkable race which has appeared in the world.[5]

Thomas Cahill (b. 1940), Irish author:

The Jews gave us the Outside and the Inside – our outlook and our inner life. We can hardly get up in the morning or cross the street without being Jewish. We dream Jewish dreams and hope Jewish hopes. Most of our best words, in fact – new, adventure, surprise, unique, individual, person, vocation, time, history, future, freedom, progress, spirit, faith, hope, justice – are the gifts of the Jews.[6]

William Rees-Mogg (b. 1928), former editor-in-chief of *The Times of London* and member of the House of Lords:

One of the gifts of the Jewish culture to Christianity is that it has taught Christians to think like Jews, and many a modern man who has not learned to think as though he were a Jew can hardly be said to have learned to think at all.[7]

Blaise Pascal (1623–1662), French mathematician and philosopher:

---

[4] Ibid., Hertz.
[5] Quoted by Geoffrey Wheatcroft in *The Controversy of Zion: Jewish Nationalism, the Jewish State, and the Unresolved Jewish Dilemma.* London: Sinclair-Stevenson, 1996, xi.
[6] Thomas Cahill, *The Gifts of the Jews.* New York: Doubleday, 1998, 240–241.
[7] William Rees-Mogg, *The Times,* quoted by Chief Rabbi Sir Jonathan Sacks in *Radical Then, Radical Now.* London: Harpercollins, 2000, 4.

It is certain that in certain parts of the world we can see a peculiar people, separated from the other peoples of the world and this is called the Jewish people…. This people is not only of remarkable antiquity but has also lasted for a singularly long time… For as the people of Greece and Italy, of Sparta, Athens and Rome and others who came so much later have perished so long ago, these still exist despite the efforts of so many powerful kings who have tried a hundred times to wipe them out, as their historians testify and as can easily be judged by the natural order of things over such a long period of years. They have always been preserved, however, and their preservation was foretold…. My encounter with this people amazes me.[8]

Paul Johnson (b. 1928), historian:

The Jewish vision became the prototype for many similar grand designs for humanity, both divine and man-made. The Jews, therefore, stand at the center of the perennial attempt to give human life the dignity of a purpose.[9]

Matthew Arnold:

As long as the world lasts, all who want to make progress in righteousness will come to Israel for inspiration as to the people who had the sense for righteousness most glowing and strongest.[10]

Olive Schreiner (1855–1920), South African novelist and social activist:

The study of history of Europe during the past centuries teaches us one uniform lesson: That the nations which received and any way dealt fairly and mercifully with the Jew have prospered; and

---

[8] Blaise Pascal, *Pensées*. Translated by A.J. Krailsheimer. Harmondsworth: Penguin, 1968. 171, 176–177.
[9] Paul Johnson, *A History of the Jews*. London: Weidenfeld & Nicolsohn, 1987, 2.
[10] Matthew Arnold, *Literature and Dogma*. London: Smithy, Elder: 1876, 58.

those that have tortured and oppressed them have written out their own curse.[11]

Perhaps the following quote, from Alfred Leslie Rowse (1903–1997), an international authority on Shakespeare and literary historian, is the most revealing:

> If there is any honor in all the world that I should like, it would be to be an honorary Jewish citizen.[12]

---

[11] Olive Schreiner, quoted by Chief Rabbi J.H. Hertz, 177, 180.
[12] A.L. Rowse. *Historians I Have Known.* London: Duckworth, 1995.

"NOT YET": JEWS BY CHOICE

May 16, 2004

READING THE STORY OF YITRO, Moshe's father in law and a convert to Judaism, is a serious challenge. For sensitive souls it is not merely a meaningful narrative but rather a painful confrontation with their own Jewishness.

After many years of separation, Moshe and Yitro meet again. Moshe has just taken the Jews out of Egypt and miraculously led them across the Red Sea. Yitro, together with his daughter, Moshe's wife Tzippora, and their children, were left behind when Moshe took on this great and almost impossible task. But now that the exodus has become a reality, it is possible for them to meet again. The text tells us that this meeting took place in the wilderness: "Yitro, the father-in-law of Moshe, came to Moshe with his sons and his wife to the wilderness where he was encamped..." (Shemot 18:5).

This piece of information seems to be superfluous since on an earlier occasion we were informed that Moshe and the people were in the wilderness. Rashi, recognizing the problem explains that this is a reference to the tremendous sacrifice Yitro made when he decided to become a Jew: "He lived in the world of glory. Still his heart moved him to leave it all behind and to go to the wilderness and hear the words of the Torah" (Rashi ad loc.).

Yitro possessed great wealth. He had occupied the prestigious position of the high priest in Midian (see Rashi on 18:1), which is analogous to the position of the Pope in Rome today. He was surrounded by servants, glory and abundance. The verse now informs us that he gave all this up to go to a "desert," a place that would no longer give him any of these glories. As a Jew he would become one of the many, no longer a man in his own right but just "the father-in-law of Moshe."

In fact, we are informed that Yitro became an outcast. When he rejected all the forms of religion and philosophies that were known in his days, he was abandoned and shunned by the society in which he lived. He had turned into a "lonely man of faith" and ended up in the wilderness. His love for Torah and the Jewish people made everything else seem of secondary importance. Only this and nothing else moved him: to be part of the Jewish people and participate in its mitzvot.

Yitro confronts us, for the first time after the exodus, with a new phenomenon: *to be a Jew by choice*. By doing so, he confronts all Jews with a major challenge: how to become a Jew by choice even when we have been born into the fold, how to feel the same burning need to live as a committed Jew as Yitro did. This is only possible when we are able to experience Yitro's way to Judaism in our own lives. No doubt it must have been a long and difficult road. It must have been a terrible challenge with many ups and downs. Once he adopted this path, Yitro must have invented an important device: a ladder of observance, step-by-step involvement with the world of mitzvot. He must have tried to engage the world of Halacha like a baby taking its first steps. He wished to feel its touch, to integrate it into his life and to feel absorbed by its spirit, like one who swims in water and feels it at every point of his body.

We, Jews born into the fold, must try to do the same, to build our own ladder of observance, to start again, to re-engage with a mitzvah as if we had never done it before and thus to become "Jews by choice." This does not mean that we should drop all the mitzvot which we have been involved in up till now and keep only a few, as no doubt Yitro must have done at the beginning of his road to becoming Jewish. Rather, we should begin a process by which we take hold of every mitzvah that we currently observe and transform it into something radically new, as if we had never observed it before.

It is told of the great Jewish philosopher and ba'al teshuva Franz Rosenzweig that in his earlier days, he was asked whether he put on tefillin. His answer was "Not yet." Although he may not have felt ready at the time to take on this great mitzvah, he made it clear that he looked forward to the day when wearing tefillin would become a real possibility. This does not mean that he should have been waiting till he was fully ready. After all, "it is in the deed that one hears," as he often said later. Only when one actually performs a mitzvah can one hear and feel its profundity, rather than the other way around. But what it does mean is that when one puts on tefillin, one has not yet performed the mitzvah as one should. Only when one comes to the mitzvah as a novice, like Yitro, can one experience its full power: not out of tradition or habit but out of a genuine desire to fulfill the word of God.

This is the road that Yitro took and for which he was prepared to give everything up. He therefore challenges each one of us. How much of Yitro lives within us? How much are we Jews by choice? If we would not have been born into the fold but into a world as far removed from anything Jewish as Yitro was, would we have moved to the desert and given up all our glory just to be Jewish? This is the ultimate question, and it requires our honest response.

❧ 12 ❧

ILAN RAMON *z"l*: A JEWISH ASTRONAUT

May 16, 2004

THE FIRST ASTRONAUT to ever be launched into space was Phileas Fogg. He was sent there by Jules Verne, the well-known author of *Twenty Thousand Leagues under the Sea* and *Journey to the Center of the Earth*. The launch took place in 1873 and became known worldwide through Verne's masterpiece, *Around the World in Eighty Days*.

At the time, few people believed that such a journey was possible. Even Verne was nervous as to whether his hero would make it within the time limit he had set for him. In the end, Fogg's money, courage and English equanimity, as well as the twenty-four-hour time difference between the eastern and western hemispheres, enabled him to arrive in time. However, the last detail would have made no difference, since Fogg forgot to add the extra day when he crossed the International Date Line for the second time. So he arrived on schedule although he cut it close.

Anyone who read this story at the beginning of the twentieth century and possessed some imagination wondered if one could travel around the world in perhaps forty or twenty days. Others dared to think of even five days, but they were considered wild dreamers who had lost all contact with reality.

Current space travel does not think in terms of days, hours, minutes, or even in seconds. Time as a measuring staff is far behind us. The late Israeli astronaut, Ilan Ramon, and his fellow astronauts traveled more than six million miles[1] during sixteen days, and he was only sixteen minutes away from his final destination when he and his fellow astronauts tragically perished.

---

[1] Speech by President George Bush, quoted in *The Jerusalem Post,* February 5, 2002.

Space travel has introduced us to completely different dimensions of our existence. It is not the result of a slow and steady development or some kind of breakthrough that had to come about. It is the start of something radically different that nobody dared to think of even a few years ago. We realize that we stand at the door of a new epoch before we have even rung its doorbell. "Proportionally," and in accordance with normal scientific development, it would have been impossible for hundreds of years for people to fly a distance of several million miles in sixteen days. In his remarkable book *Future Shock,* Alvin Toffler tells us that there is indeed a widespread agreement between historians, archeologists and others such as scientists, sociologists, economists and psychologists that all sorts of social and scientific processes are speeding up far beyond our understanding or wildest dreams.[2]

The Kabbala alludes to the fact that an immense increase in speed will take place in the days prior to the messianic age. Just like the Jewish home starts hurrying to ensure that it is ready for Shabbat, the world starts to hurry when the messianic age, the ultimate Shabbat, approaches: This is based on the verse: "I, God, will accelerate it in its time" (Isaiah 60:22) in which the word "it" is understood to mean the messianic age (Zohar 1:116b–117a). In times of great instability, the taste of the ultimate Shabbat becomes so overwhelmingly appealing that it starts to force its way forward. But speed also leads to accidents. While sometimes it may be necessary to do too much in too little time, this behavior incurs high risks because of the lack of proper preparation and contemplation. Just as if we were to decide to skate over thin ice at great speed and realize that our safety is in our speed, humankind runs to its ultimate destination with unparalleled speed, not always aware that it is taking considerable risks.

However, the greatest problem is that this kind of overwhelming speed is the result of using a highly sophisticated form of full automation which leaves human beings with very little to do. Most flight in space is pre-determined and beyond human intervention. While human beings are the original architects of the space shuttle and its journey, slowly but surely they become subordinate to their own inventions and lose their identity as human beings. They then become little more than instruments.

---

[2] Alvin Toffler, *Future Shock.* London: 1970.

When Yuri Gagarin, the first Russian cosmonaut, was asked what the most important date in his life had been, he promptly answered: "The twelfth of April, when I became a member of the Communist Party." The answer was automatic. Gagarin had become part of a system that stripped him of his humanity. When a famous Dutch author was introduced to a man who spoke twelve languages, he paused for a moment and asked: "But do you also have something to say in these languages?" This is right on track. After all, what is the use of knowing many languages when one has nothing to say? Merely knowing a language while being incapable of saying something original in it is also a form of automation.

Sending people into space in order to turn them into instruments is an embarrassment for all humankind. The paradox between the most sophisticated space shuttle and the simplicity of such a man is too much to bear. When somebody like Yuri Gagarin sees the climax of his life as the moment when he became one of millions of "yes-men," we experience a most dangerous process of automation. He may have traveled through space, but he never left his little home.

It was to the credit of the late Ilan Ramon that he lifted himself and all of us with him beyond the slightest possibility of becoming automatic. Not only did he stay human in space, but he surpassed his humanity. He taught the Jewish people that one should not become a number among the many. He refused to go along with the Israeli "yes-men," obsessed with the gentile world, who call for the secularization of Israel and strip it of its Jewishness.

While he was in space, Ilan emphasized the uniqueness of being Jewish. As a symbol of his pride in being Jewish, he brought a Sefer Torah that had been rescued from the Nazis during the Holocaust on board. With his kiddush cup near at hand, he revealed his deep emotions when he saw the Land of Israel from his spaceship. Since his view was broader than that of many of his assimilated fellow Jews, he left space for an even higher destination.

May his memory be blessed.

WHAT IS A *GAVRA RABBA* – A GREAT MAN?

February 19, 2007

THE TALMUD IN *MAKKOT* 22B discusses the identity of a *gavra rabba,* a great man or exceptionally great Talmudic sage. It quotes a remarkable observation by the well-known sage Rava, who says: "How foolish are some people who stand up out of respect for a Sefer Torah but do not stand up out of respect for a *gavra rabba,* an exceptionally great person, a great Torah sage."

When asked what is so exceptional about these men, Rava ignores their astonishing vast knowledge of Torah or even their outstanding ethical and religious qualities. Instead, he accentuates their power and courage to change the obvious and literal meaning of a commandment as mentioned in the Torah.

The example that Rava gives is telling:

While the Torah commands the Jewish court to administer forty lashes for certain offenses (Devarim 25:2–3), the Rabbis reduced the number to thirty-nine.[1] Rava says that the courage to change the literal meaning of the text is what makes them into exceptionally great people. They recognized their own authority as those who were invested with the power to interpret the biblical text in accordance with the spirit of the Oral Torah, which gave them the right and even obligation to change the literal meaning of certain biblical texts when it became clear that a deeper reading of the text and its spirit called for such a move. In our case they concluded that the number

---

[1] In earlier times, Jewish law would sometimes require corporal punishment under very specific circumstances, but only when the offender would be able to endure it without risk to his life or health. It therefore could happen that the court administered only several lashes since more of them would create a health problem. Torture, even of a criminal, is completely prohibited.

forty could not be taken literally and should therefore be reduced to thirty-nine. It is for this reason that Rava maintains that these sages should be accorded even more honor than the Torah scroll, which houses the actual biblical text. After all, the text is only the frozen aspect or outer garment of a living organism, the essential Torah. It is only in the Oral Torah as explained by the sages that the real meaning of the Torah becomes apparent.

Still, this cannot be the whole meaning of Rava's statement. If the power of the sages is revealed in their willingness to change the meaning of a text (such as in the case of the number thirty-nine instead of forty), one should ask why Rava does not quote the first case ever mentioned in the Torah concerning which the sages changed the specific biblical number to a lesser number and derive his proof from that.

After all, it is well known that they changed the number fifty into forty-nine on an earlier occasion. This is in the case of the counting of the Omer, where the Torah requires counting a full fifty days between the first day of Pesach and Shavuot, the day on which the giving of the Torah is celebrated. Shavuot would then fall on the fifty-first day.

Still, after studying the text carefully, the sages reduced the number of these days to forty-nine, stating that the fiftieth day itself should be Shavuot (Vayikra 23:16; *Torat Cohanim* ad loc.). Remarkably, in this case Rava does not state that their willingness and courage to reduce these days made them exceptional people. This is surprising, since it is the Talmud's custom always to bring proof for a specific teaching from the earliest biblical source possible, not a later one. However, in our case, it brings proof of the sages' courage from a verse mentioned later in the Torah (in Devarim)! This is perplexing. Why did they not use the verse in Vayikra?

It has been suggested that changing the meaning of the biblical text or the reduction of a number does not turn a sage into a *gavra rabba*. A sage becomes a *gavra rabba* when he reduces the pain of his fellow human being! When a sage finds, through biblical interpretation, ways to decrease the legal punishment of another human being, only then can we speak about a *gavra rabba,* an exceptional person.

In the above-mentioned case of the forty lashes that the Torah specifies as punishment for certain offenses, it is an act of mercy to find ways to reduce the offender's sentence and administer only thirty-nine. Such initiative and courage shows absolute moral greatness.

But in the case of reducing fifty to forty-nine so as to make Shavuot fall one day earlier, there is no reduction of human pain and as such, neither the Talmud nor Rava see such a sage as a *gavra rabba,* however brilliant he may be.[2]

Only when one makes a sincere effort to reduce the pain of one's fellow human being can one be called great.

---

[2] The above idea is based on an oral teaching that was quoted to me in the name of one of the chassidic leaders before the Holocaust whom I was not able to identify.

14

LEADERSHIP AND CAPTAINSHIP

March 12, 2005

Avraham passed away and died at a good age, elderly and
full of days, and was gathered to his people.

Bereshit 25:8

The day that Avraham our father departed from the world,
the great men of the nations stood in line and said: Woe to
the world that has lost its leader, and woe to the ship that
has lost its captain.

Bava Batra 91a

WHAT IS THE DIFFERENCE between the leader and the captain to which this
Midrash seems to allude? Are they not the same? If they are, why did the
Midrash speak of both? If one is the parable and the other the moral, the
Midrash should have first mentioned the captain (the parable) and
afterwards the leader (the moral). We must therefore conclude that the
Midrash tries to hint at a profound difference between both these tasks,
which throws light on Avraham's personality.

There are two major differences between a leader and a captain. A leader
always walks in front of his followers; he is the first, while a captain is the
last to leave the ship. Also, a leader has a personal interest in his destination,
while a captain does not.

A leader is not only a leader by virtue of his followers but also because
he is part of the group he leads. Their destination is also his. He needs to get
there as much as they do. Therefore, he does not behave out of character.

He himself benefits from leading the others. His self-actualization comes about through participating emotionally in the actual journey.

However, this is not true of the captain who has no personal interest in his destination. His task is to bring his passengers to their destination. Once they have arrived, it is likely that he will immediately turn around and travel in the opposite direction. He has no part in the group's desire to reach a specific objective. He travels with them only for their sake.[1]

Leadership and walking in front often entail a neglect of those who are left behind. The general cannot turn back to take care of the last soldier at the rear of the battalion. His mind is on his destination and his mission is accomplished when he reaches it. That some people pay the price for getting there is not his concern.

The captain's concern is completely different. He wants to take care of all his passengers, and if his ship should founder, he will ensure the safety of the very last passenger before leaving it himself.

We find a combination of these two qualities in Avraham's personality. As a spiritual leader who started a revolution that affected the entire world, he initiated a movement that to this day has had an unprecedented effect on humankind's attitude and behavior. His devotion to monotheism and ethics is legendary. He was an unparalleled leader who walked before everyone else. Yet he was also a captain who cared for those who were weaker and who argued with God in an attempt to spare the wicked people of Sodom and Gomorrah. While his eyes looked ahead, his heart was aware of what was happening behind him.

At the same time, he was a leader who shared in some of the goals of his generation and showed them the way in their own personal lives. Above all, he was the man who traveled with his passengers, often becoming involved in issues in which he was not instrumental and had no wish to be. On such occasions he was as selfless as a captain.

To be a Jewish leader is to be a captain as well.

---

[1] See also Rabbi Avraham Yitzchak Kook, *Midbar Shur*, Chayyei Sarah.

15

JEWISH NOBEL-NESS

December 15, 2005

In studying the Jewish people we are face to face with a miracle and I venture to say: he who will be attentive cannot be incredulous. Everything is miracle in this incomparable people. Everything is miracle: its history, its origin, its fall, its dispersion, its stubbornness. The contempt with which nations treat them who owe everything to them, who know the glamour of their past and the still greater brilliance of their future. Add to this the unprecedented fact that this people alone, among all the other nations, forms one family and that this family, though homeless and miserable, kept itself isolated from the rest of mankind…. This fact alone would be an undeniable miracle, even if a prophet [Bilaam] thirty-four centuries ago, at the frontier of Moab, had not said: "For from the top of the rocks I see him, and from the hills I behold him: lo, the people shall dwell alone, and shall not be reckoned among the nations" (Bamidbar 23:9). [1]

WE CANNOT HELP BUT THINK of the above when watching Nobel Prize laureate Professor Robert Aumann of Jerusalem receiving this most famous of all honors ever to be given to a human being last Saturday night in Stockholm. After celebrating Shabbat according to Jewish law, reciting the

---

[1] The Christian author S.R.L Gaussen in *Die Verkundnung des Evangeliums unter den Juden*, 376–377, quoted by Joseph Bloch, *Israel and the Nations,* Berlin–Vienna: Benjamin Harz, 1927, 376.

evening prayers and making havdalah as Jews have done for thousand of years, he proceeded to the hall where the King of Sweden waited to grant him this unprecedented award.

Here stood a Jew who took pride in showing his dedication to religious Judaism in front of all humanity, as only few Jews have ever been able to do. With his long white beard, his yarmulke clearly visible, surrounded by his wife, whose hair was covered in accordance with Jewish law, together with his children, their spouses and his grandchildren, all wearing kippot and modest dress, eating *glatt kosher* food while dining with another thirteen hundred guests of the world's most exclusive gentile nobility, he made it clear that he was willing to make no compromises and concessions to Jewish religious practice in order to receive this award. Only infinite Jewish pride was the mark of the day.

Throughout modern Jewish history, most Jews were ambivalent as to whether they wanted their children to live openly as Jews. While they did not want them to intermarry, they also did not want them to be conspicuous. They wanted them to be secular *conversos* – outwardly like everyone else, inwardly and privately Jews. This ambivalence haunted them and created enormous internal conflicts, often tearing them apart inside. Although they were Jews, they were dedicated to proving that Jews are no different from anyone else. Most of the Jewish community today inherited this conflict, whether they know it or not.

The venerable and deeply religious Professor Aumann showed all of us that there is another way which, instead of provoking conflict, creates unconditional pride. Like Avraham Avinu, he proved to the world that Jews have the courage to be different. Instead of becoming a Spinoza, Freud, Einstein, Rabin or Peres, this Nobel laureate refuted the belief that Jews can only buy their ticket into the most advanced world community through cultural and religious assimilation. Just as Judaism is the story of a sequence of utterly revolutionary discoveries, so the professor fulfilled the commandment given to Avraham, "Through you all the families of the world shall be blessed," by not only making one of the most remarkable scientific discoveries in history but above all by daring to be different. The refusal to accept the world as it is and the obligation to transform it is the underlying motive behind all of Judaism.

By demonstrating the religious commitment of his entire family to the world community, he sent a message to all humanity that it is possible – and in fact a great blessing – to give one's children the greatest of all gifts, that of tradition and mission and to enjoy it with all one's heart. While Socrates said that a life without thinking is not worth living, Judaism teaches us that life without commitment is not worth being born into. To refuse our children that merit is like denying them life altogether.

In the spirit of Shakespeare's Hamlet, the professor showed that although the Jew's kingdom might be bound by a nutshell, they should count themselves as kings of infinite space. One is reminded of the great non-Jewish literary historian, A.L. Rowse, who ended his memoirs with this surprising sentence: "If there is any honor in the world that I should like, it would be to be an honorary Jewish citizen."[2]

Ambivalence cannot sustain an identity. It has created havoc throughout the Jewish world, including in Israel. Attitudes that may have made sense to our grandparents have proven to be dysfunctional and unrelated to the world in which we live. Jews must face this and resolve the crisis before this destructive mentality overtakes us.

Professor Aumann has shown us the way. May he be blessed.

---

[2] A.L. Rowse, *Historians I Have Known*. London: Duckworth, 1995.

16

ISRAEL'S PREDICAMENT AND THE NEED
TO BE A STRANGER

January 15, 2006

As THE INHABITANTS OF THE STATE OF ISRAEL find themselves undergoing a critical moment yet again, one wonders why the Jews throughout the thousands of years of their history were never able to develop into a stable, secure nation as other nations did. The constant attacks upon the Jewish nation's very existence, its small numbers, the lack of its homeland for nearly two thousand years and its difficulties in living with itself are unprecedented in world history. Even today, with the re-establishment of their commonwealth in the form of the State of Israel, its power and its unprecedented accomplishments, the Jews remain a nation in constant flux, never sure where the next day will take them, confronted with crisis after crisis and incapable of predicting its future in any conventional sense.

This stands out as a total paradox, considering the nation's remarkable capacity to be constantly at the brink of extinction and yet not only survive but rejuvenate itself. Historians and anthropologists have difficulty understanding how this nation not only survives but outlives its enemies, draws the world's attention with its achievements and contributes to humanity in a manner that is totally out of any rational proportion to its numbers.

The quicksand on which all of Jewish history is built makes us wonder whether this is not essential to the very existence of the Jewish people.

One commandment which, unlike any other commandment in the Torah is almost endlessly repeated, is the one that requires the Jews to be concerned about the welfare of the stranger in their midst. According to one opinion in the Talmud (*Bava Metzia* 59b), this commandment is repeated forty-nine times in the Torah. Since no other commandment is repeated anywhere near that many times, we must conclude that we are nearing the core of the mystery of the Jews and Judaism.

It is highly significant that Jews are asked to look after the stranger on the basis of their own experience in the land of Egypt. "You know how it feels to be a stranger, since you were strangers in the land of Egypt." Here we are confronted with a crucial aspect of Jewish moral imperative. The demand of what appears to be the most important of all commandments can have sufficient authority only when it is based on an appeal to personal experience.

Indeed, it does not take much effort to realize that all of Jewish history is founded on the existence of "strangerhood." It is Avraham, the initiator of Judaism, who was called to become a stranger by leaving his home and country so as to find his Jewish identity. Early Jewish history is the story of a nomad people who, even after they reached their destination, was forced to leave it on many occasions and to live once more as strangers. They were forced to live for hundreds of years "in a land not their own" – Egypt – and under these circumstances, their identity gets "gestalt." It was only in sporadic moments that Jews actually lived in their own homeland. Even the Jewish *raison d'être,* the Torah, was not given "at home" but in a desert, in an existential experience of "foreignness." It is as if the Torah's commandments, without exception, find their justification, meaning and fulfillment only once one knows and experiences what it means to be a stranger. The more "recent" Jewish history of nearly the past two thousand years forced the Jews once more to live as strangers in other people's lands.

The stranger lacks security, a feeling of home and existential familiarity. Paradoxically, it is this lack that creates the climate through which people can become sensitive to the plight of their fellow human beings. It is the realization that there can only be moral hope as long as humanity is somehow unsettled. The quest for security will block humanity's search for meaning and purpose, while its lack of security will impel it to unfold its moral powers. Clearly, it is this fact that underlies the constant repetition of the commandment to look after the stranger "because you yourselves were strangers in the land of Egypt."

What this means is that to keep a nation sensitive and concerned about the condition of the "other," it must continue to live in some kind of "strangerhood" itself. It must never be fully secure and must constantly be aware of its own existential uncertainty. Therefore, Jews must be strangers. It is in that way that they can become a moral beam of light to the nations of the world – which, after all, is the reason for their Jewishness. The Torah is a protest against human overconfidence, since it is aware that the world will be a completely insecure place once people start to feel too much at home and consequently forget their fellow human beings.

Jews must live on the edge of eternal existence and insecurity even while living in their own homeland.

The great upheavals in recent Israeli-Jewish history that have denied the Jewish people stability and security may well be a divine message that it needs to return to much greater sensitivity towards the stranger and fellow human being. The nation must realize that God made it into a people of archetypal strangers in order to make it capable of living by the imperatives of the Torah. One not only needs to be sensitive to the non-Jewish stranger and one's fellow Jew but above all to realize that nearly all problems in society are the result of seeing the other as a stranger. Social injustice and crime are the result of seeing the other as an outsider. Most people do not understand what it means to be a stranger and how far it extends. "For a crowd is not a company and faces are but a gallery of pictures and talk a tinkling cymbal, where there is no love" (Francis Bacon). Most people are alone even as they are surrounded by others, and people suffer their loneliest moments while standing in a crowd.

This awareness should become a major basis for the future Jewish-Israeli society. To be an eternal nation while living with a lack of security is the great paradox that makes a real Jewish moral society possible. Nevertheless, once Jews create an inner awareness of their archetypal condition as strangers and create a society in which the stranger is fully cared for, they may proportionally remove the external circumstances which surround them so as to make the Jews aware of that very mission. The more the stranger is looked after, the less the need for the Jewish people to experience "strangerhood."

To put an end to the solitude of the other, one needs to be somehow a stranger oneself. Even God seems to be unable to exist in solitude and is therefore endlessly in search of humankind as His companion.

ISRAELI SOCIETY

ISRAEL'S UNIQUENESS AND ITS FUTURE

June 17, 2004

Rabbi Yochanan ben Zakkai once saw a woman stooping among the dung of an Arab's donkey to gather barley grains. She said to him: Do you remember, Rabbi, when you signed my ketubba?[1].... He told his students: I remember that I read that it promised millions of gold dinars from your father's house, apart from the wealth of your father-in-law. She began to cry. He continued: How praiseworthy are you, nation of Israel. When you perform God's will, no nation can rule over you, but when you fail to perform God's will, you are handed over to the lowest of nations, and not just to the lowest of nations, but to their beasts.[2]

ALTHOUGH THIS NARRATIVE appears superficial on the surface, it is profound. According to the Maharal of Prague (Rabbi Judah Loew, 1525–1609),[3] the story conveys one of the most fundamental concepts regarding the nature of the Jewish people. Careful analysis of this story shows a paradox. How does Israel's loss of self-rule reflect its spiritual uniqueness? Should Israel's loss of self-determination not show how ordinary it is? Why call even its downfall "praiseworthy," and how is such praiseworthiness reflected in the story of this woman?

---

[1] Document that sets forth the husband's financial obligations to his wife at the time of their marriage.

[2] *Ketubbot* 66b.

[3] Maharal, *Gevurat ha-Shem,* chapter 4.

The Maharal explains that unlike other nations, the very existence of the nation of Israel is supernatural. Its condition does not depend on the laws of historical necessity. Careful study of Jewish history proves this. By normal standards, the Jewish people should have become extinct long ago. The exiles in Egypt, Babylon, Greece and other empires should have cut off any possibility of survival. Therefore, the Jews' survival and peculiar history have constantly stunned and embarrassed historians and philosophers. In his *Pensées*, the famous French philosopher Blaise Pascal (1623–1662) applied the idea of probability to history and came to the striking conclusion that among all the myriad peoples that have lived on the earth, only one defies probability:

> It is certain that in certain parts of the world we can see a peculiar people, separated from the other peoples of the world, and this is called the Jewish people. This nation is not only of remarkable antiquity but has also lasted for a singularly long time. For whereas the nations of Greece and Italy, of Sparta, Athens and Rome, and others who came so much later perished so long ago, these still exist, despite the efforts of so many powerful kings who have tried a hundred times to wipe them out, as their historians testify, and as can easily be judged by the natural order of things over such a long spell of years. They have always been preserved, however, and their preservation was foretold. My encounter with this people amazes me.[4]

This fact is well-known and even explains much of anti-Semitism in our own days: Hatred for the Jewish nation is the direct consequence of its indestructibility. Those who do not follow the acceptable norms of our society are ostracized.

However, Maharal adds another dimension to this fact. One can see the uniqueness of the Jewish nation not only in its exalted moments, but also in its downfall. Even their subjugation is abnormal and does not follow the rules. Other nations go through high and low points in their history.

---

[4] Blaise Pascal, *Pensées*, trans. A.J. Krailsheimer. Harmondsworth: Penguin, 1968, 171, 176–177.

Assimilation and disintegration are set in motion according to natural historical patterns. Not so with the Jewish people, which can fall into turmoil within moments and with no precedent. At one moment it finds itself at its peak and suddenly, with very little warning, it falls to its lowest level. The Maharal explains that this is the meaning of the remarkable observation by Rabbi Yochanan ben Zakkai in the above-mentioned narrative. Just like a woman can have a *ketubbah* worth millions of dinars and lose it in a moment, thereby being forced to gather her food from animal dung, so Israel can fall within a moment and become completely dependent on the lowest elements in society. But even in that, Israel is praiseworthy because even its fall is unique. Once God withdraws His supervision in response to the Jewish people's failure to live up to its religious and moral obligations, the nation will be handed over not only to the lowest of peoples but even to its beasts.

The great Chassidic thinker, Rabbi Shmuel Bornstein, the rebbe of Sochaczew, points out[5] that this praiseworthiness is not only unique because the Jewish people has fallen so low, but also because one can simultaneously observe how low it has sunk. The Jewish people can watch it from close by. The fall is so sudden and radical that it violates all expectations and as such is visible for anybody to see.

When we observe the unsettling situation in the State of Israel, today we can only wonder how, in such a short period of time, the world has turned from admiration to total condemnation of Israel's policies. Careful study of this phenomenon shows a radical and sudden change which was unexpected and not at all self-evident. At the same time the Israeli leadership, which was once an example of determination, clear thinking and astonishing courage, has fallen to a low point where it appears not only to have lost its vision but also to have become the victim of many forces pulling it from all sides, resulting in total confusion. We dare to suggest that the leaders are themselves at a loss as to why they changed their minds regarding matters that were sacred to them only a short while ago. However much political analysts try to convince us that all of this can easily be explained by the normal state of political conditions, those who take a broader and deeper look at Israel's history cannot accept that. Too much is happening that

---

[5] *Shem mi-Shmuel,* Vayetze, 5678.

remains unexplained and that seems to indicate that another force may be at work.

Even more surprising are Israel's unprecedented successes even as all the political confusion and condemnation are taking place. While at war (and let us not underestimate the meaning of this statement), Israel continues to build its future as if it were not. Israeli doctors are at the forefront of medical research. Intel, Microsoft and IBM have a strong base here, and much of their development is being done by Israeli citizens. Together with two other countries, France and China, Israel has developed a satellite program that sent three satellites into space as of this writing. This is fairly surprising when we reflect that France has at least nearly sixty million inhabitants, China more than a billion and Israel just under six million. And all this without mentioning Israel's nuclear capacity, hi-tech economy, exports, and the fact that its citizens continue to live their lives and build institutions of higher learning, combined with many other successful endeavors, as if the nation enjoyed complete peace and tranquility.

All this comes as no surprise to the religious mind. The condemnation of Israel by the nations of the world and the confusion of its leadership, together with its unprecedented successes, are just more examples of its uniqueness. Paradoxically, the more the nations condemn Israel because it does not meet the conditions of normalcy, the more they prove Israel's distinctiveness.

Nevertheless, one wonders whether Israel's leadership is aware of this anomaly and whether it tries to come to terms with it. There is much evidence that it does not and that it finds itself in denial to a much greater extent than Israel's founders. While the latter were secular, they still understood the Jewish people's unique place in the world and its peculiar nature. Today's leadership, which comprises mostly native-born Israelis who had little exposure to anything Jewish, combined with very little knowledge of Jewish history, are no longer able or willing to admit this. Its determination to run the country as if it were a nation like any other shows a glaring inability to grasp Jewish history and its unique message. The more attempts that are made to deny Israel's uniqueness and classify it as merely another member of the community of nations, the more Israel will not be able to hold out as a nation altogether. Therefore, its leadership will only bring Israel to the brink of its capacity and, God forbid, to national disaster.

It is difficult to deny that Israel's sudden fall from greatness does not bring to mind the Maharal's observation that even its fall will be unprecedented. And while there is much reason to believe that things may still turn out well, Israel's political and religious leadership must change its thinking radically, considering new and better ways to call on its citizens to see their *raison d'être* in Judaism and thus come to value its own essence. However, this will only be possible when Judaism's teachers find new ways to inspire the people of Israel with its great message, so that everyone will see the uniqueness of the people of Israel once again.

KREPLACH AND BISSLI: REVELATION OF A LANGUAGE

April 25, 2004

> Words, in their primary or immediate signification, stand for nothing but the ideas in the mind of him who uses them.
>
> John Locke, "An Essay Concerning Human Understanding" (1690, 3.2.2)

LANGUAGE IS THE MOST REVELATIONAL ASPECT of the inner thoughts and attitudes of human beings. Freud made us aware of this when he discussed the "slip of the tongue" phenomenon. It is in language that human beings reveal their inner lives. Their subconscious overflows and, before they are aware of it, they have already exposed their inner selves.

Languages are constantly in flux. Whole societies could be identified by studying their changing attitudes toward their words and expressions, including words that have fallen into disuse and those that have replaced them.

Hebrew is a most powerful example of this phenomenon. A comparison of how the biblical and Talmudic mind used Hebrew and how the language has deteriorated in our day is most telling.

It has often been noticed that Hebrew does not possess a word that is equivalent to the expression "to have." In his monumental book, *To Have or To Be,* Erich Fromm commented on this:

> To those who believe that "to have" is a most natural category of human existence, it may come as a surprise to learn that many languages have no word for "to have." In Hebrew, for instance, "I have" must be expressed by the indirect form *yesh li* (it is to

me). In fact, languages that express possession in this way, rather than by "I have," predominate. It is interesting to note that in the development of languages the construction, "it is to me," is followed later on by the construction, "I have," but as Emile Benveniste has pointed out, the evolution does not occur in the reverse direction. (Erich Fromm, *To Have or To Be.* London: Abacus, 1979, 32)

This does not mean that there is no such concept as possession in Hebrew. Rather, the difference between the secular attitude towards property and the religious one is that the secular attitude emphasizes the development of private property in which property in itself becomes dominant (without a specific function), while the biblical attitude only knows of *functional* property – in other words, property that is owned not for the sake of possession but for use.

While a word that really represents "to have" still does not exist in modern Hebrew, the general use of the language is becoming more and more inclined toward possession.

Regrettably, we have experienced a vulgarization of the Hebrew language over the past several decades. This is not only noticeable in Israeli society in general but also among Israeli leaders and debates in the Knesset, Israel's parliament. While at the inception of the state one would be able to enjoy a Knesset debate because of the use of superior Hebrew, today we are confronted with a situation where we feel more and more uncomfortable listening to some of the members of this institution using Hebrew slang. Even rabbinical figures who used to speak a dignified language have lowered themselves in this respect.

This fact has entered into the collective consciousness of Israeli society. While in earlier days the content of Israeli advertisements reflected a Jewish outlook on life, today this is often not the case. Years ago, when trying to convince people to buy sweets and other delicacies, names such as "kreplach," "bagelach" and "rogelach" were used. All emphasize the relationship we have with other people. These names all end with the Hebrew word "lach," "to you." This is not accidental. While those who created these names may not have been aware of their choice of words, their subconscious revealed inherently Jewish values.

Looking into modern Hebrew advertisements we see a rather disturbing change: No longer is it "lach" which invites people to buy various tasty foods, but "li" (me): Bissli, Prili, Egozi, Ta'ami. A recent advertisement that we noticed says, "*Tihiyeh egoist ad ha-sof*" (Be an egoist to the end).

We would do well to notice this. Like the Freudian slip of the tongue, such expressions reveal more than we might like to admit.

Ultimately, it shows how Israeli society is falling prey to some Western concepts, which badly misunderstands values such as love. For many, love for others or even for spouse and child is nothing more than the use of other human beings for one's own pleasure. The expression "falling in love" is a case in point. Anybody who has any understanding of love knows that while one may be able to fall into a pit, one cannot fall in love, but only walk, stand or grow in love. It is even more important to remember that love does not exist if it is not motivated by a deep commitment to give. According to some authorities, the root of the Hebrew word for love, *ahava*, is *hav*, which means "to give." Those who do not know the art of giving do not possess the capacity to love.

Frank Leahy once observed that "Egotism is the anesthetic that dulls the pain of foolishness" (*Look* Magazine, January, 10, 1955). If Israeli society and the world at large were to start listening once more to the language of the Torah, it would prevent a great deal of unnecessary pain.

THE FAILURE OF THE RELIGIOUS PARTIES:
RABBIS WITH A KNIFE BETWEEN THEIR TEETH

May 16, 2004

NOW THAT THE CHESS PIECES in Israeli politics have been drastically moved and for the first time a mainly secular government is leading the country, it is high time that the religious parties, religious institutions and their leadership asked themselves some hard and uncomfortable questions.

How is it possible that after more than fifty years in power, the religious parties not only failed to inspire the majority of Israelis to feel a closer affiliation to Judaism and to foster a greater appreciation for the Jewish way of living, but also, as the last elections clearly showed, they have actually caused hundreds of thousands of Israelis to choose a more secular lifestyle and, in many cases, to identify with political parties that have explicitly committed themselves to attempt to do away with even the most minimal form of Jewishness in our country?

While it has been the custom of the religious establishment to point a finger at the media, the secular hardliners and the intelligentsia and accuse them of a deliberate attempt to misinform the general public about the religious world and its ideology, this approach no longer holds water. Although it is true that a great deal of misinformation about the religious community has been pumped into Israeli society, it is time both for the religious parties and the religious leaders to admit that for years, they have played their cards the wrong way.

Just as the Israeli government constantly fails to understand the mind of the non-Jewish world, so the religious parties have continually misread the minds and hearts of secular Israelis. Just like the Israeli leadership does not seem to grasp the basics of proper public relations policy, so the religious parties have in no way understood how to explain themselves and their values to a secular Israeli society. Just as this failure of the Israeli government has caused irreparable damage to Israel's image, so have the religious parties caused permanent injury to the image of Judaism.

There was and there is no reason for all this. Israel is unique in its sound moral obligation to defend its borders. No army has ever shown so much respect for the lives of its enemies as the Israeli army. No nation has ever been more concerned with the welfare of those who are intent on destroying its very existence. No army has ever dared to put its own soldiers in such dangerous positions so as not to injure the innocent among its enemies. No country has ever been prepared to give up whole parts of its territory, thereby endangering its own security, as Israel was prepared to do in its negotiations with the Palestinians.

No nation has so miserably failed to use these and other facts to explain itself to a world that, in turn should have generated an overwhelming admiration for this small country caught between hostile nations in the Middle East. In the same vein, the religious parties should have made use of the most advanced, uplifting teachings of Judaism, thereby creating unprecedented admiration for Judaism among the Israeli people. If anything should have impressed secular Israelis, it should have been Jewish values, genuine religious observance, integrity, impeccable example and high ethical performance in private and communal life.

But little of this has been the guiding principle of the religious parties. While we do not doubt the integrity and good intentions of some of the leaders, the political parties themselves have failed miserably. Instead of creating an atmosphere in the Knesset and among the Israeli population that proved that money, prestige and political infighting have no place in the making of the religious world view, most Israelis have been convinced that the Jewish religion is identified with party politics, questionable financial dealings, and self-interest. Indeed, since some of the religious party leaders would like us to believe that such incidents never actually occurred, we wonder even more how it was ever possible that such a devastating image of the religious parties ever came into being.

There is also no evidence that after this devastating blow in the Israeli elections, the religious parties did any real soul searching or even came close to admitting that something went terribly wrong. The religious party leaders need to realize that the outcome of the elections may be a forecast of what will occur in several years: that their fight for Judaism will be over and that their parties will no longer constitute any danger to the other opposing ideologies. While at this moment, the religious parties still hold power that cannot be ignored, there is enough evidence in political history that powerful parties, against all conventional wisdom, can easily become completely irrelevant only a short while later. Let us not make the mistake of thinking that such a situation cannot take place in Israel because of the high percentage of religious Israelis. There is little doubt that in the latest elections, more and more religious and traditional people, who were extremely disillusioned with the religious parties, voted for their secular rivals. However much the rabbinical leadership may try to stop this trend, it will not succeed.

What rabbinical leaders and thinkers need to do is to cook up a storm which will turn the whole of Israeli society pale – a storm that will prove that they have freed themselves from the sandbank in which they are stuck. In a completely unprecedented shift, they should lead the ship of the Torah with full sails right into the heart of Israeli society, causing such a shock to the Knesset that it will take days, weeks, or months before it is able to recover.

With their knives between their teeth, just like the prophets of biblical days, those religious leaders who are known for their impeccable and uncompromising conduct should create an ethical-religious uproar that will scare the moral wits out of the secular and religious Knesset members and weigh heavily on their souls.

Real religious leaders should not be "honored," "valued" or "well respected," as they are now, but as men of truth they should be *feared*. Israelis should be quaking in their shoes at the thought of meeting with them, but simultaneously be incapable of staying away from their towering, fascinating personalities.

Only then will Israeli society extricate itself from its ongoing predicaments.

THE DANGER OF HOLINESS AND THE
FUTURE OF ISRAEL

May 12, 2004

NO WORD IN THE TORAH is as central to Judaism as the word *kedusha* – holiness – and no word in Jewish tradition is as open to misunderstanding.

When the Torah discusses sexuality, food consumption and general human behavior, it calls on the people of Israel never to forget that everything needs to be sanctified and consecrated. The ultimate goal is to turn the whole nation into a holy people: "You shall be holy because I, the Lord your God, am holy" (Vayikra 19:2). This call is repeated many times. "Hallow yourselves, therefore, and be holy, for I am the Lord your God" (ibid., 20:7–8). "You will be holy unto Me" (ibid., 20:26).

For hundreds of years, there has been a difficult debate among Jewish philosophers concerning whether the Jewish people is inherently or only conditionally holy, but the above verses make one point abundantly clear. There is no opportunity or justification for any Jew to hide behind holiness that is not the product of an intensive effort to live an exalted moral life. Any view that frees Jews of their responsibility to observe the laws of the Torah because they are automatically considered to be holy is heretical and deserving of condemnation. Jews have no claim to anything that they have not earned through hard spiritual work and commitment. This is true regarding the possession of the land of Israel or any other matter. There are no automatic rights or claims based on inherent holiness. The people of Israel must *actually* be holy in deed and thought.

The sages were well aware of the danger of using the concept of inherent holiness as a way to justify the unjustifiable. We see this in their choice of the *haftarot* that are read on the Shabbat of parashiyot "Acharei

Mot" and "Kedoshim," those portions of the Torah that deal with the need for holiness. Altogether there are three haftarot for these two parashiyot.

The one that is read on a given Shabbat depends on whether the parashiyot are read together or separately and on whether the congregation follows Sephardi or Ashkenazi custom.

The haftara that is read when the parashiyot are combined discusses the equality of all human beings and Israel's mistaken view that it is something special because of its history and inherent holiness. "Are you not as the Ethiopians to Me, O Israelites? True, I brought Israel up out of the land of Egypt, but also the Philistines from Caphtor and the Arameans from Kir…" (Amos 9:7). In other words, the fact that God brought the Jews out of Egypt is not something unique that sets Jews apart from other nations. The haftarah continues with a harsh statement that removes any possible conclusion that Israel can rely on any inherent holiness when it sins. "I will give the order and shake the house of Israel through all the nations as one shakes sand in a sieve and not a pebble falls to the ground. All the sinners of My people – those who say, 'Never shall evil overtake us to come near to us' – shall perish by the sword."

Amos continues, "The eyes of the Lord God are upon the sinful kingdom, and I will wipe it off the face of the earth, yet I will not utterly destroy the house of Jacob, says the Lord" (9:8). While this is a promise that a remnant of Israel will survive, there is no promise that it will be in any way protected beyond basic survival or able to assert a claim to the land or to anything else when it does not observe the demands of the Torah.

The other two haftarot carry a similar message: When the people of Israel behave badly, "when Jerusalem sheds blood in its midst," when the people "disdain father and mother" and "oppress the stranger," "violate the menstruating woman," "take usury and interest," then "I will scatter you among the nations and disperse you throughout the lands. I will consume the uncleanness out of you. You shall be dishonored in the sight of the nations and you shall know that I am the Lord" (Yechezkel 22:15–16).

These haftarot are clearly a protest against all those who claim that the nation of Israel is inherently holy and *consequently* able to lower its standards of behavior or permit itself to deviate from morality. What makes the people of Israel separate and unique is nothing other than the result of its undivided commitment to live a life of holy deeds.

When we contemplate the re-establishment of the State of Israel after nearly two thousand years of exile, we Jews should never believe that the land is guaranteed to remain ours forever. It could easily be taken away as it has been in the past, and no army, law or international body will be of any help.

IT IS TIME TO GO TO THE SYNAGOGUE:
THE FAITH OF A HERETIC[1]

June 17, 2000

IN MY YOUNGER DAYS, when I was still far removed from religious observance, I knew a man who was a convinced and committed *apikorus* (heretic). I used to meet him every Shabbat morning in synagogue where he was a frequent worshipper and I was a visitor. He often would walk into the sanctuary, tell people that they were wasting their time coming to the morning service "since there is no God," and then he would proceed to his seat. Thereupon, he would cover himself with his tallit, open his prayer book and join the service with great fervor.

Intrigued by his behavior, I once asked him to explain himself. What is a committed atheist doing in a synagogue, praying as if his life depends on it? After a short pause he said, "The reason why I come to synagogue and join the prayers is the same reason I make kiddush at home on Friday night and eat kosher. I am a Jew, and I want to identify as a Jew. And it is these customs that make us into Jews. The synagogue is where we meet as Jews and these prayers give us our *neshama* [Jewish soul]. Without them, we are lost. Therefore I will come to this synagogue till my last day on earth, and I will eat kosher and make kiddush on Friday night. True, there is no God, but I am a Jew!"

In these days that are so trying for the people of Israel, I suddenly realize the great wisdom of this Jewish *apikorus*. Those who read Israeli newspapers, listen to the radio and watch debates on television cannot escape the fact

---

[1] While we believe that much has improved since this essay was written in the year 2000, many symptoms of what it describes still exist today.

that many leading and highly intelligent Israelis no longer attend synagogue. They seem to have lost their *neshama* and have almost completely separated themselves from the community of Israel. Unlike my friend, the heretic, they are no longer Jewish apikorsim but merely secularists. And that is the difference between heaven and earth.

Denying the Jewishness of the state of Israel or distorting it so that it loses all meaning is disastrous. To question the moral justification of the State of Israel is catastrophic. Telling fellow Jews that it would have been better to have founded our new homeland in Uganda is destructive. Changing our national anthem, "Hatikva," so as to remove its Zionist flavor or replacing the Israeli flag with a non-Jewish symbol is fatal. Trying to replace four thousand years of Jewish tradition with fifty years of Israeli culture is a tragedy. These are all signs that the carriers of those and similar proposals have lost their neshama.

For several years, many (though not all) university professors in Israel have taught hundreds of thousands of Israeli students a kind of nihilism, rejecting Jewish values and declaring them to be antiquated relics of our primitive ancestors. Famous Israeli authors have declared war upon Jewish tradition. Zionist leaders, once the heroes of secular Israelis, are now ridiculed and portrayed as unworthy people by those who previously admired them. Left-wing Israeli historians have made it their mission to prove that Jews never lived in this country, that the Temple never stood in Jerusalem and that there is no authentic Jewish claim to the land. Pop music has taken the place of Zionist and Jewish melodies, and drug and alcohol abuse are increasingly coming into style at Israeli parties and pubs. Modernism and its values have finally entered into the lives of many Israelis.

There is no greater danger to a nation than to demoralize it by making its inhabitants believe that their ancient culture is no longer of value, their traditions are meaningless, their ideology has become bankrupt and their claim to their land is unethical. This is homicidal and borders on treason.

While most young Israelis still admit that they are Jewish, it is becoming abundantly clear that more and more of them no longer see this as a privilege. Those who observe society in the land of Israel cannot escape the feeling that some kind of epidemic is spreading over the country that contaminates its inhabitants with an anti-Jewish spirit. It looks as though a kind of "Judaism-free society" is taking over, slowly strangling and killing the Jewish neshama.

It seems that the Jewish neshama is about to be buried, Heaven forbid. Yet although the secular Israelis will undoubtedly perform the burial ceremony with the respect that one accords to a world of the past and to one's ancestors, they will ultimately realize that they buried much more. They buried the very foundation of the Jewish state, their very identity and their future. Their cries for help afterward will be to no avail, and their attempt to resurrect the Jewish neshama will come too late.

True, the land of Israel is blessed with many proud Jews who take their Judaism very seriously and who embrace the country with their hearts and souls. Yet they are mainly in the religious or traditional communities. Regrettably, we are watching an entire generation of fine, young, secular Israelis fall victim to the desire to outdo the gentiles. While their parents still possess some kind of Jewish education, these children are not as fortunate.

Concerning them, the handwriting is on the wall. Since they have been deprived of a proper, inspirational Jewish education and a warm Jewish environment, they will no longer relate to the uniqueness of the Jewish soul. Left without an ideology or love for the land, eventually they will turn into people who despise themselves for what they are. This mentality, rather than the murderous intentions of the enemy, could lead to the downfall of the State of Israel, God forbid.

Therefore, it is time for Israelis to return to the synagogue and some level of Jewish living. That they are secular, apikorsim or atheists does not worry us as much as the fact that they are losing their neshamot. They should listen to my friend, the *apikorus*. It is time that they rediscover their souls and once more realize what it means to be part of that unexplainable "stuff" called Jewishness. Only in the synagogue and in a genuine Jewish environment is the Jewish neshama fashioned, kept warm and spiced with its special flavor.

Just like my atheist friend did, Israeli Knesset members, professors, historians, authors and many others should go to the synagogue and discover their Jewish souls. It will be an eye-opener for them. It will restore such warmth to their spirits that they will be proud to be Jewish, even though some of them may continue to be apikorsim or secularists. Above all, the people of Israel will see their leaders in synagogue and feel assured that these leaders are not merely Israelis but also Jews and therefore part of the *mishpacha.* Such a move will be a great relief and a great simcha to millions of Jews around the world.

Even our enemies will hear and understand that the Jewish spirit is not to be ridiculed.

FINDING ONE'S NESHAMA:
FRANZ ROSENZWEIG AND THE BERLINER *STIEBL*

June 17, 2004

IN THE PREVIOUS ESSAY we suggested that Israeli leaders, academicians and the Israeli public should find their way back to the synagogue and rediscover their neshamot. But this is easier said than done. Many have entered and left the synagogue without feeling any spiritual significance. In fact, many entered and became discouraged.

Going to synagogue is an art. One has to arrive there with a sincere urge to discover one's Jewishness, to reconnect with the Jewish people and with one's inner being. To enter the synagogue is to hope for a metamorphosis in one's soul and a transformation of one's personality.

When Franz Rosenzweig (Germany, 1886–1929), one of the most important Jewish philosophers in modern times, decided to leave Judaism and be baptized, he enacted this resolution by attending the High Holiday services in a *stiebl,* a small Orthodox synagogue in Berlin. This was a kind of final farewell to his former religion, with which he had never had a relationship. Arguing his case, he wrote: "We [Jews] are Christians in everything. We live in a Christian state, attend Christian schools, read Christian books; in short, our whole culture rests entirely on Christian foundations. Therefore, if a man has nothing to hold him back, he needs only a slight push… to make him accept Christianity."[1]

Yet to his utter surprise, he was deeply inspired by the services. As a result, he underwent a profound religious metamorphosis and left the small

---

[1] Quoted by Samuel Hugo Bergman, *Faith and Reason: Modern Jewish Thought.* Schocken Books: 1961, 57.

synagogue with such a love for Judaism that not only did he retract his decision to become a Christian, but he also decided to become a religious Jew. Consequently, he made a very intensive study of Judaism, wrote some remarkable works about his new-found religion and turned into one of the most important Jewish thinkers of modern times.[2]

What happened to Rosenzweig in those few hours in that small synagogue? What turned his life around and transformed him into a deeply religious Jew? How is such a metamorphosis possible, especially to a man of great intellectual perception? After all, Rosenzweig had spend years contemplating the possibility of becoming a Christian and had discussed it with many of his friends, who encouraged him to do so. Still, within only several hours he decided to put aside his earlier decision and become a committed Jew!

The solution to this problem may be found in a highly significant midrash which tells of a Jewish apostate by the name of Joseph Mechitha, who helped the Romans destroy the Temple.

> When the enemy [the Romans] desired to enter the Temple Mount, they said, "Let one of them [the Jews] enter first." They said to Joseph Mechitha, "Enter and whatever you bring out is yours." So he went in and brought out a golden lamp. They said to him, "It is not fitting for a common person to use this, so go in, and whatever you bring out is yours." This time he refused. Said Rabbi Pinchas: "They offered him three years' taxes, yet he still refused and said, 'Is it not enough that I have angered my God once that I should anger Him again?'" What did they do to him? They put him into a carpenter's clamp and sawed and dismembered him. He cried: Woe to me that I angered my Creator!" (*Midrash Rabba*, Bereshit 45:22)[3]

Rabbi Joseph Shlomo Kahaneman, the well-known Ponevezher Rav, once commented that this midrash conveys the mighty impact that the

---

[2] Rosenzweig's most important work is *The Star of Redemption*. For a thorough critique, see Eliezer Berkovitz, *Major Themes in Modern Philosophies of Judaism*. Ktav: 1974, chapter 2.

[3] *Midrash Rabba,* Bereshit 45:22.

Temple once had on human beings. The moment that Joseph Mechitha entered the Temple, he underwent a spiritual metamorphosis. He suddenly realized that he was a Jew and that he had been deeply touched by the unique atmosphere and the symbols he found there. Even though he removed a golden lamp, afterwards he realized that he could not enter the Temple a second time. His new-found neshamah would not allow it. Even when the Romans offered him enormous amounts of money and threatened to torture him to death – a threat that they subsequently carried out – he could not bring himself to defile the House of God again.

In his weekly parasha commentary, Rabbi Yissachar Frand[4] suggests that this midrash somehow explains Franz Rosenweig's sudden transformation when he entered the small synagogue in Berlin. Once he saw Jews deep in prayer, their tallitot over their heads, his neshamah awoke and his Jewishness was restored.

However, this needs further explanation. How do a synagogue and Jewish prayers suddenly awaken a Jewish soul that had been totally removed from anything Jewish? What was in the Temple that made Joseph Mechitha realize its overwhelming spiritual power to the extent that he could not enter a second time? As suggested above, it relates first of all to the kind of attitude that one has before one enters the Temple or a synagogue. After all, many people entered and were disappointed or even discouraged. Others even defiled the sanctuary without remorse, as Titus entered the Temple and had intercourse with two harlots in the Holy of Holies (*Gittin* 56b). Yet even when one enters with the right approach, what turns this experience into a religious metamorphosis?

Here we enter into the world of Jewish symbolism. According to kabbalistic thought, the physical symbols in the Temple, such as the altar and the menorah, are tangible reflections of the En Sof, the infinite Divine stuff that descends into this world like a kind of fog. These symbols are not fully comprehensible since their essence belongs to the metaphysical world. However, they are identified by the subconscious, which has its root in the Divine, since human beings were formed in the Divine image. Consequently, they invoke in human beings an overwhelming recognition of the higher world, which gives him the powerful feeling that he is looking into his own

---

[4] Parashat Toledot: Wer is Weise? (German), June 13, 2004.

soul. This is the deeper awareness of the neshama. The Temple was the representation of heaven on earth and its symbols caused the soul to hear a perpetual murmur coming from the waves of a fantastic seashell far beyond human reach. Such a divine manifestation ultimately leads to the metamorphosis which Joseph Mechitha experienced when he entered the Temple.

In a similar way, Franz Rosenzweig discovered his own neshama while attending the service in the *stiebl* in Berlin. Once he saw the symbolic objects that are so abundant inside a synagogue – representing the Temple – and simultaneously heard and read the prayers of the High Holidays, he entered into the heavenly realm that had been present within his own soul all the time. It revolutionized his inner being and brought heaven to earth. This experience did not stem from his observation of what took place in this small synagogue but rather from a desire to enter and become part of a significant religious experience.

This is what we suggest all secular Israelis try to do: to enter a small synagogue filled with dedicated and passionate worshippers and, as they do so, to remove all external and artificial components from their souls. They should allow themselves to merge with the surroundings in which they find themselves and let go. While indeed this requires great courage, the sudden feeling of belonging that will result in an encounter with what we call the world of the neshama will carry unexpected bliss. It will be a homecoming that can save the Jewish world from a great deal of self-imposed harm.

THE SITUATION IN ISRAEL: A PERSONAL LETTER

March 12, 2002

As I SIT HERE IN MY HOME in Jerusalem writing to all of you, I can hear heavy bombing that makes my home shake as if heavy mortars were falling in my back yard. I see missiles flying over, hitting the headquarters of our enemies. The radio informs us of an ongoing terrorist attack that this time does not seem to end. Six Jews were killed within the first minutes of the attack.

Last Saturday night I passed the Moment café in Rechavia, where a short while later a terrorist blew himself up, killing dozens of young people. The week before, many children lost their lives in Meah Shearim and one grandmother buried her daughter, son-in-law, and several grandchildren. The death toll between one Shabbat and the next is overwhelming. And so it goes on, week after week.

As the situation in Israel deteriorates every day and sometimes every hour, many thoughts come to mind, too many to express. Our thoughts are with the many who are still in hospital and those who have lost family members. We think of our family, friends and children who walk the streets, live in the so-called "territories" and ride buses, and we wonder if we will ever see them again.

Above all, we think of our soldiers and policemen and women. When we listen to their stories carefully, a feeling of unprecedented awe fills our hearts. The army's moral conduct when it enters the cities and refugee camps of the enemy, their near-abnormal concern with the welfare of the enemy population while carrying out house-to-house searches in order to discover terrorists, taking risks that no army in the world would ever contemplate, takes us totally by surprise. The Israel Police works day and night under impossible conditions. They are prepared to die in order to save their fellow Jews, as parents try to protect their children. They do not appear to be concerned about their own lives.

Here is a nation that offered its enemy weapons to defend itself, paid for them, and was willing to give in to nearly all of its enemy's demands, including the handing over of ninety-five percent of the territory of the West Bank, as long as peace for both parties would prevail.

Here is a nation that was willing to become so vulnerable that military experts of foreign countries called their actions outright suicide.

Here is a nation that, after its enemy bluntly rejected all of its concessions and chose instead to start a guerrilla war, is still prepared to continue to negotiate a peaceful solution.

Here is a nation whose government and army have to endure such biting critique by its own members for their slightest mistakes that it nearly collapses under its own obsession with justice.

Finally, here is a nation which, after all is said and done, is still called the aggressor par excellence by most of the world. To underscore this point, Israel's detractors do not restrain themselves from manipulating facts, creating stories of Israeli atrocities, misrepresenting human mistakes made by Israeli soldiers and deliberately forgetting that only a few of them, overwhelmed by stress that few people ever experience, behaved in unacceptable ways.

While other nations still destroy tens of thousands of their fellow human beings and such information receives no proper attention in the media, the accidental death of one Palestinian child hit the front pages of nearly all major papers and is shown again and again on CNN and the BBC.

While we observe the Israel Defense Force, one of the most powerful armies in the world, we realize that at this moment it is not even able to deal with small groups of terrorists that by any military terms should be no match for them at all. Its defeat by some outdated weapons used by Arab schoolchildren, its inability to prevent the destruction of one of the world's mightiest tanks, defies all imagination.

When we turn to Israel's government, we see a group of highly capable people who have become paralyzed and are incompetent to give any direction to its policies, while other members seem to have difficulty deciding which side of the conflict they are on.

Add to this the fact that the Middle East and its surroundings consists of more than three hundred million Muslims and that the Arab world is five hundred times larger than Israel, which makes this country look like a sliver of real estate, nearly undetectable on the world map. When we do this, we get some understanding of the incomprehensible.

This is not war or the history of conflict, nor is it unfair journalism. Rather, it is extreme absurdity for which human history has no real precedent.

This absurdity should wake us up. Anyone who has eyes to see and a mind to think should realize by now that we are not confronted with a serious conflict like other conflicts. This is a conflict *sui generis*. What we are experiencing is the encounter with another metaphysical order where different criteria and rules apply. It is as clear as it can be: no military solution of any order will succeed in bringing an end to this conflict, nor will any negotiations lead to true peace.

This does not mean that the army should not do whatever it can. Nevertheless, as Jews we should realize that the problem lies somewhere else. And the place where it lies is the place where it *should* lie. History is not so much the outcome of political deals, financial conditions and military power but, above all, of the spiritual and moral fiber of human beings. Whenever human beings do not see morality as their major reason for existence, history runs in directions that ultimately lead to disaster. This applies even more strongly to our own people, whose mission is to be a moral inspiration to all other nations.

The conflict that we are experiencing is an encounter with the Creator and Mover of the world who, it seems, is no longer prepared to accept the human onslaught against His creation, the undoing of His work, and the violations of His moral demands.

As Jews, we are obligated to look into ourselves and find ways to become better human beings and Jews. It seems that only in this way will we be able to see an end to this conflict.

It is our duty to make sure that our communities accept their moral responsibilities, making the care of their fellow human beings and the pursuit of justice their highest priority. We must understand that the continuous discussion of these ideals gets us nowhere. What is needed is action.

Here are some suggestions:

- Let us end the terrible traffic accidents in the land of Israel. It is absurd that there is an outcry about terrorist attacks when the same number of people (or even more) get killed on the roads in the Holy Land. It is absurd that there are tragedies that we can prevent, yet we refuse to take all the necessary steps to do so even as we protest the deaths of our fellow Jews at the hands of our enemies.

- Let us end the abuse of women and children in Israeli homes. Whoever would have thought that a Jewish country would experience such an evil?

- Let us end the violence in Israeli schools in which Jewish children hurt and get hurt.

- Let us abstain from saying anything bad about any Jew or group of Jews, or even about the Israeli government, unless it is constructive critique.

- Let us stop all forms of hurting our fellow Jews and other human beings when it is not necessary for self-defense.

- Let us refuse to listen to gossip or be involved in deception, lies or trickery.

- Let us cause the world to say "Blessed be the God of Israel."

- Let us be extremely careful about honoring our parents and spouses.

- Let us show great patience with people who bother us.

- Let us avoid losing our tempers and giving in to hateful feelings.

- Let us pray with great concentration for the welfare of our soldiers and police force and remember our many POWs and MIAs.

- Let us get up in the middle of the night and ask God for mercy on Am Yisrael and the world. (Midnight is a most precious time for prayer.)

- Let us enter our synagogues five minutes before the actual service starts. (Who could be even one minute late in these days?)

- Let us pray for the welfare of those Jews whom we do not like.

- Let us rise for elderly people and assist them.

- Let us smile at every person we meet.

- Let those who live outside Israel continuously phone their friends here and not transgress the law against standing idly by while the blood of one's fellow Jew is being spilled.

But let us also make it clear to the European nations that their continuous attacks on Israel's policies will not go unpunished. It takes little wisdom to realize that when humankind does not respond to this local Middle East conflict, put an end to Arab violence and stop giving credence to the arch-terrorist named Arafat, these hostilities will boil over into a world conflict that will find its way into the hearts of European cities in ways that will be many times worse than what happened in New York, Washington, DC and near Shanksville, Pennsylvania on September 11, 2001.

The clock is ticking. The alarm is ringing. Who does not hear the sound of the great Lion?

24

THE STATE OF JEWISH EDUCATION TODAY[1]

May 27, 2004

THE HOLY OF HOLIES in the Temple of Jerusalem was a place where only the High Priest was allowed to enter once a year, and only on Yom Kippur. Yet even the Holy of Holies needed occasional repair. To provide for such an eventuality there were openings in the upper chamber that led downward through the ceiling. Through these openings, which were close to the walls, the workmen were lowered in *tevot* (boxes) into this most holy place. These boxes had an opening on only one side, facing the wall, so that the workmen "could not feast their eyes on the Holy of Holies" (*Pesachim* 26a).

It is said that the upper chamber of the Holy of Holies was even less accessible than the Holy of Holies itself, for while the High Priest entered the Holy of Holies once a year, the upper chamber was entered once every fifty years to see whether it required any repairs.

Chassidic thought gave the above tradition an allegorical meaning. In Hebrew, the word *tevot* means not only "boxes," but also "words." Therefore, the words of Jewish tradition are seen as ways to enter the Holy of Holies of every Jewish person so as to repair and to revive his or her heart. But the words (*tevot*) of the Torah can only touch the outer walls in the human heart as well. Their deeper meanings are beyond human comprehension. What human beings can grasp are only the perpetual murmurs from a world beyond.

Jewish education is in need of radical repair. We are living in a time when the Jewish religious imagination seems to be exhausted. We no longer seem to know how to lower ourselves via the *tevot* into the Holy of Holies of the human heart.

---

[1] Inspired by Abraham Joshua Heschel.

We have fallen victim to a sociological and anthropological approach that has led to the vulgarization of Jewish education. We ask whether the Jews are a race, a people, a religion, a cultural entity, a historic group, or a linguistic unit. We do not ask: What are we morally? What are we spiritually? What do we owe the world and what is our mission? Although we may be busy repairing Judaism, we are descending from the wrong upper chamber into an artificial temple of secularity.

While Jewish education today deals with a great deal of information, it forgets that it is *transformation* that we are looking for. We are told that walking inside the Temple created new people. People were astonished by the many miracles that took place in the Temple. It was not Jewish continuity that the Temple guaranteed but rather a radical re-creation of the Jewish soul that made souls grow wings so that they could fly. It served as a protest against the stale and obsolete.

It caused human beings to be so taken in by the spiritual power of the Torah that they could see God everywhere, like the Chassidic rebbe who used to walk in the forest because he wanted to see how the tall, swaying trees were "davening *Shemoneh Esreh*."[2]

Jewish education must be like a work of art that is capable of introducing us to emotions that we have never felt before. It is boring unless we are surprised by it. Every thought is also a prison if it does not invoke an outburst of amazement within us.

---

[2] Reciting the Eighteen Benedictions while standing in great concentration, often accompanied by swaying of the upper body.

25

THE DAY AFTER DISENGAGEMENT, OR WHAT TO DO[1]

August 18, 2005

AS ISRAEL STANDS AT A CROSSROADS, with its existence challenged as never before, it is time to realize that the national trauma surrounding the disengagement is only a symptom of a much deeper and dangerous problem – the liquidation of the inner spirit of the Israeli Jew. While Israelis may be exposed to a great amount of information about their Jewishness and its traditions, they are exposed far too little to its spirit. There is a great deal of proficiency but too little reference, a great many skills but too few inner attitudes and appreciation. One cannot build a nation's eternal future solely on knowledge. It is urgently necessary to cultivate inner values and feelings, and to refrain from doing so is a serious abdication of responsibility. Israeli society, including much of its religious segment, has become hijacked by the mass culture that has captured the minds of old and young so powerfully. Hollywood, Madison Avenue and the desire for luxuries are a major threat to the independence, sensitivity and inner balance that are so vital to the spiritual freedom of today's Jews. The constant flattening of the inner spirit finds expression in spiritual boredom, which leads to the search for extreme materialism, cheap entertainment and a sincere lack of sensitivity towards one's fellow human beings.

There is a deep need for spiritual audacity, educational guts and defiance that will create a radically different atmosphere in Israeli society. It is suicidal to argue that unless the climate favors these principles, there is no chance of making major changes successfully. The environment has never been conducive to spiritual concepts. Judaism's major essence is warfare. It was Avraham, the first Jew, who declared war on spiritual indolence and

---

[1] This essay appeared in *The Jerusalem Post*.

desensitization. His daring personality turned the tables on the world, creating the greatest revolution ever to take place in the history of the human spirit. Although he knew that everything was against him, he was not discouraged. He knew that the inner human spirit could be rescued.

Why was Avraham so successful? How was he able to become the founding father not only of Judaism but of much of the moral value systems of other monotheistic religions and western civilization? Avraham realized that there was little value in teaching people about the oneness of God, the need to observe Shabbat or the importance of observing the dietary laws. Any insistence upon these important values would no doubt fall flat on the deaf ears of his generation. He realized that these concepts are conditioned by a set of assumptions and opinions that were totally alien and irrelevant to most of his contemporaries. Therefore, Avraham searched for a common dominator about which all people could agree, and concluded that this could only be found when he was able to reach the inner lives of his fellow men and women, the very core of their being – to cultivate their souls together with their minds. Avraham knew that deep down, human beings are searching for meaning and that moral beings look for empathy and reverence and, above all, need to do good for their fellow human beings. Only then can human beings discover their real selves. Only when they can find a sense of personal vocation and mission can they surpass themselves.

So Avraham started his Tent Revolution, which became the backbone of authentic Judaism. High on a hill, so that it would be seen by all, Avraham built a small, inviting structure that became the center of social intercourse and where people of opposing backgrounds could meet, speak and share. Here he started the greatest educational-interpersonal project in human history. It was through his astonishing dedication to treating his fellow human beings with goodness and showing love even to the coarsest idolaters that he reached the hearts of everyone he met and took the world by storm.

Israel needs to return to Avraham's Tent Revolution. It needs to build tents of Avraham throughout the country in which inspired teachers and laypeople, Orthodox, liberal and secular, teach, debate and exemplify the great Jewish ethical values as found in Judaism's classical sources. They must share their knowledge not as academicians or scholars trying to decipher ancient texts but rather as feeling human beings looking for ways to shape a society in which *menschlichkeit* is a guiding principle.

There are too many yeshivot and too few, if any, tents of Avraham. After elementary studies, most yeshiva students should be motivated to prepare themselves for the great task of bringing Jewish ethical values back into the center of Israeli life. In a time of great danger we can no longer afford to allow most of them to study Talmud for its own sake. Unless we make these tractates relevant to the needs of the Jewish people and share them with our fellow Jews, we badly underestimate the power of the Jewish tradition and rob our fellow Israelis of what our society needs the most: Jewish ethics. No doubt this requires a radical restructuring of the yeshiva curriculum. The need to read the great classical texts of Jewish philosophy will have to become the center of these studies. Whether these are found in the writings of Yehuda Halevi, Maimonides, the Maharal, Abraham Yehoshua Heschel, Franz Rosenzweig or Joseph Ber Soloveitchik is of secondary importance. What is important is that all of them focus on the powerhouse of Jewish ethical wisdom not as dry texts but rather as moving, passionate teachings. This applies even more strongly to many university teachers who sometimes, in their obsession with philology or comparative studies, lose sight of the great spiritual message of the texts that they discuss with their students.

Since the mass media is by now the most powerful way to create public opinion, Israeli society should include programs on radio and television which cause their audiences to want to emulate Israel's sages. Jewish tradition holds an infinite storehouse of inspirational stories that show the Sages' sensitivity towards their fellow human beings' feelings. Posters on bus stops and in shopping centers should ask Israelis whether they smiled at someone else this morning ("He who shows his neighbor the white of his teeth [who makes him cheerful] is better than he who gives him milk to drink" – *Ketubbot* 111b), helped an elderly person or child to cross the road, gave charity to the poor, a lift to a soldier, dropped in to see an old acquaintance, thanked their waiter or waitress. While some Israelis describe people with sensitive character traits as *freierim* (pushovers), they must learn that they are the backbone of our society. Better an Avraham complex than a narcissistic one.

Israel has an urgent need today for coherence and unity. This can only come about when Israeli society rediscovers its Jewish ethical and compassionate roots and recreates them with passion and commitment.

126

Only when we return to Avraham's tent will we overcome our problems in spite of all the obstacles. The great question in Israel is not whether there will be a Palestinian state but whether the State of Israel will be a Jewish one.

THE FUTURE OF THE STATE OF ISRAEL:
A REMINDER IN DIFFICULT TIMES

September 4, 2005

ON THE WORDS: "In the beginning God created heaven and earth" (Bereshit 1:1), Rashi quotes the famous but astonishing observation by Rabbi Yitzchak[1]:

> If the nations of the world accuse Israel of banditry by conquering the land of Israel... then the people of Israel will answer and say: "In the beginning God created heaven and earth. The entire universe belongs to Him. He created it and He gave it to whomever He deemed fit. It was His desire to give [the land of Israel] to the Canaanites first and it was His desire to take it from them and to grant it to us."

What is the meaning of this strange observation? How does referring to Creation help to justify Israel's claim to the land? Some commentators seem to believe that the objection of the nations of the world is not that the people of Israel should not be the owners of the land of Israel per se, but rather that it should be completely clear that it was God and none other who gave the Jews the land. Only then would it stand unchallenged, and even the nations would have to yield to the Divine will. But if the Jews were to

---

[1] It is not clear who Rabbi Yitzchak was. People are accustomed to believing that he was the father of Rashi. The Divrei David and the Taz share this view. However, this statement, which is quoted by Rashi, is also found in *Yalkut Shimoni*, Parashat Bo, Remez 177, quoting *Midrash Tanchuma*, where it is stated in the name of an anonymous scholar.

conquer the land by pure physical force rather than through God's clear intervention, then their occupation of the land would have no validity. It was exactly for that reason that the nations strongly opposed any Jewish claim to the land. To them, it was clear that God had not given it to the Jews since they conquered the land by conventional means – military might – when Yehoshua told them to do so.

It is here that the observation of Rabbi Yitzchak becomes illuminating. By referring to the creation of the universe he shows an entirely different way of looking at the Jewish right to the land. His point is that the account of Creation teaches us that all existence is miraculous. All Creation is ultimately inexplicable, and therefore everything that happens within creation is supernatural and the result of Divine intervention. Even the laws of nature are nothing but the frequency of miracles. Therefore, argues Rabbi Yitzchak, it is true that the conquest of the land by the Jews was a miracle. Just as God is the sole Creator of the universe, it is clear that God wanted the land to belong to the Jews!

However, this sidesteps the question: if everything is a miracle, what is special about the Jewish people's claim that God wanted it to have the land? Would not the same argument apply to the other nations when they lived there? Once they lived there, would it not mean that God wanted them to live there? Their possession of the land was as much a miracle as is Israel's.

The answer to the question is this: Within the "frequency of miracles," Israel stands out as a nation that exists through miracles that lack all frequency. They do not occur as part of the laws of nature, nor do they have universal applications. These "non-natural" miracles have an affinity with miracles such as the splitting of the Red Sea and the revealed miracles mentioned in other parts of Tanach and later Jewish history. Since they lack all frequency, they are just as non-natural as the original Creation.

In our own time, we would do well to take this observation very seriously: The people of Israel are only able to hold onto the land because of its miraculous nature. Otherwise they would not be able to inhabit this land for even one day. The mistake of the gentile nations is that they are not prepared to see the multitude of miracles that made it possible for the people of Israel to conquer the land. Instead, they are convinced that Jews won the land through conventional warfare in the past and again in 1948.

When we study Jewish history carefully from early Biblical times to our own era, we can only conclude that Jews were constantly accompanied by miracles, large and small. This was true when they entered the land in the days of Yehoshua and when they established the State of Israel in 1948 and held it till this very day.

Even after the downfall of the Jewish Commonwealth nearly two thousand years ago and while living in the Diaspora, Jews experienced ongoing supernatural protection even despite the many and terrible persecutions. The Jewish people survived six empires. They were exiled to all corners of the earth, restricted in their daily lives, incarcerated in ghettos with no defense or wealth, tortured and murdered. Nevertheless, Jews saw the demise of their enemies such as the Greeks, Romans and so many others. They outlived them all and returned to their homeland nearly two thousand years later, as lively as ever. All this is *sui generis,* unprecedented and, for many, too much to bear. It is a miracle that has no universal application.

In his book *The Meaning of History,* Nicholas Berdyaev (1874–1948), the famous Russian author and philosopher, asked his readers to take proper notice of this fact:

> And... according to the materialistic and positivistic criterion, this people ought to have perished long ago. Its survival is a mysterious and wonderful phenomenon demonstrating that the life of this people is governed by a special predetermination, transcending the process of adaptation expounded by the materialistic interpretation of history. The survival of the Jews, their resistance to destruction, their endurance under absolutely peculiar conditions and the fateful role played by them in history; all these point to the particular and mysterious foundations of their destiny.

When the State of Israel was established in 1948 it became even clearer that Israel survives through miracles. For more than fifty years, Israel has been surrounded by more than 350 million human beings living in many Arab countries larger than the United States. All of them, even those that have made peace with the Jewish State, consider Israel as a cancerous growth in their midst. Israel has fought war after war to defend itself against these nations. Logically speaking, Israel should not have survived, even with all its military might. That it has done so is completely beyond human comprehension and openly indicates the protection of a Higher Power. There is much truth in Ben Gurion's statement that those who do not believe in miracles are not realists. When we contemplate the fact that since the early days of the intifada, Palestinian terrorist organizations planned ongoing daily attacks on Israelis and that by normal standards tens of thousands of Israelis should have died every year, one gets a more realistic picture of the miraculous nature of the State of Israel. The fact that Israel continues to build and thrive in the midst of a guerrilla war against terrorists, while holding out against mighty Arab countries, fascinates and irritates the world. With a population of just over six million at this writing (with its sole partners powerful nations existing of more than a billion people), Israel has become a nuclear power. Meanwhile the fact that it is creating a strong economy and has become a prominent leader in the hi-tech industry, together with so many other accomplishments, has yet to be explained in terms of normality for a nation whose territory is so small that one can hardly find it on the map without a magnifying glass.

At this difficult time for the State of Israel and especially for the settlers of Gush Katif and northern Samaria, we should not forget that despite all the pain and trauma, the miracle of Israel continues. Although Israel was forced out of the Gaza strip, the fact that it still exists and continues to thrive is still a sign of its unprecedented miraculous nature.

Nevertheless, this should not encourage a fatalistic attitude. There is no way to predict the future. It would also not be right to rely on continued miracles. In any case, miracles should not be taken for granted. One needs to merit them and to recognize them as such. Israelis have become used to miracles, and that is exactly where the problem starts and why it is now being reminded that the land cannot be taken for granted – not only Gush Katif but also Jerusalem and Tel Aviv.

The question at this crucial moment in Jewish history is not whether the nations of the world understand the miraculous existence of the State of Israel, but whether the Jews themselves are prepared to see this reality. Miracles have only continued to be part of Israel's history as long as Jews both inside and outside the land have done everything to merit this Divine intervention by continuing to recognize the miracles. Secularizing the Jewish state, adopting anti-Jewish values, and destroying Jewish education and love for Jewish tradition will slowly but surely empty the land of its miracles. This is suicidal. But if Jews are proud of their tradition and are committed to Jewish values, history seems to teach us that miracles will continue. This is not wishful thinking but the realistic lesson learned from four thousand years of Jewish history.

GOD, GUSH KATIF AND NEW ORLEANS

September 15, 2005

WHEN WE CONTEMPLATE the terrible destruction of New Orleans and the tragedy of Gush Katif, we must be most careful not to turn God into a Being in whose name we can speak. Predicting that He will not allow the disengagement to happen or claiming that Hurricane Katrina is divine punishment are facile and superficial ways to explain His actions. It is like explaining three-dimensional reality using a flat surface.

It is well known that Jewish tradition forbids the pronunciation of the four-letter name of God. This name, rooted in the Hebrew word for "being," consists of the Hebrew letters *yud, heh, vav* and *heh*. According to the Jewish Sages, the Name reflects the different dimensions of being related to time: past, present and future, making God the One who lives in all three. The reason why we may not pronounce this Name is because the Name expresses the idea that God lives in these different dimensions simultaneously. Consequently, these dimensions are actually one and the same. God is beyond time – or, if we wish, in all time. Yet for humanity, which is bound by the limits of time, this is impossible to grasp. Human beings live in broken eternity. Therefore, we may not pronounce the four-letter Name since this would create the impression that when we call upon God by using the four-letter name, we actually grasp that God lives in the past, present and future simultaneously. This would not be true, and Jewish law forbids lying. God is incomprehensible and beyond all description, and his being cannot be expressed. It is for this reason that it is not permitted to pronounce this Name.[1]

---

[1] See *Chullin* 90b, *Yoma* 69b and Rabbi E.E. Dessler, *Mikhtav me-Eliyahu,* vol. 3, 314–316.

The great Kabbalist, Rabbi Moshe Cordovero, elaborates on this theme in his famous work, *Elima Rabati*:[2]

> When your mind conceives of God, do not permit yourself to imagine that there is really a God as depicted by you, for if you do this, you will have a finite corporeal conception, God forbid. Instead your mind should openly dwell on the affirmation of God's existence, and then it should recoil. To do more than that is to allow the imagination to reflect upon God as He is Himself and such a reflection is bound to result in imaginative limitations and corporeality. Therefore one should put reins on one's intellect and not allow it great freedom, but assert God's existence and deny the possibility of comprehending Him. The mind should run to and fro – running to affirm God's existence and recoiling from any limitations, since man's imagination pursues his intellect.

On a deeper level, this is the most important message of the biblical book of Job, which discusses human suffering as no other. While Job's friends argue that his terrible afflictions must be due to his sins, Job argues that this cannot be true because the punishment far exceeds the crime. Therefore, there must be more to his afflictions than sin. The rabbis, in full agreement, accused Job's friends of "wronging him with words." They argued that the idea that humanity can scrutinize God's ways is a kind of *avodah zarah,* trying to fit Him into a box in which He does not fit.

Still, it is not for human beings to argue that since Gods ways are unknown, they carry no message for humankind. While God no doubt has His own ultimate unknown reasons for allowing or even causing tragedies to take place, they may still carry important messages for us. Although the real reasons may be totally beyond our grasp, we are still obliged to contemplate what these messages may teach us from our own limited perspective. Just as God is in the past as well as in the present and future concurrently – and therefore incomprehensible – so it may well be that His reasons for evil are also rooted in a similar condition. However, from our subjective perspective,

---

2 *Elima Rabati* 1:10, 4b.

they may teach us an important lesson at the same time. Although we will never know the real reason, the subjective messages should not be lost on us.

Since it is impossible to know God's factual reasons, one cannot hold anyone else responsible for any natural disaster. There is no way of knowing whether the other is at fault. But what one *can* do is to suggest that there may be such a subjective correlation and ask the other to contemplate this accordingly. However, this can only be done in great humility and with the clear emphasis that this is nothing more than a suggestion with the obvious intention to help humankind. In matters of God, one must be open to all possibilities. One cannot risk missing out on a possible opportunity to hear His voice.

This applies to ourselves most of all. One must act as if one's own moral failures may have somehow played a role in causing the disaster. One must grasp with both hands any opportunity to learn and advance one's spiritual growth.

For the same reason, one cannot argue that prayers must work. One of the great teachings of Judaism is that God cannot be manipulated by human beings. While prayer may not save us, prayer makes us worth being saved if the divine plan calls for it. Arguing that prayer must work and that God must listen is making God into an idol in the service of humankind. To "force" God to respond positively to our prayers and expect Him to respond in the way that we would like Him to may be good enough reason for Him *not* to listen.

THE TRAGEDY OF AMONA

February 9, 2006

Liberty and democracy become unholy when their hands become dyed with innocent blood.

Mohandas K. Gandhi[1]

The Jew is that sacred being who has brought down from heaven the everlasting fire, and has illumined with it the entire world. He is the religious source, spring, and fountain out of which all the rest of the peoples have drawn their beliefs and religions. The Jew is the pioneer of liberty.... The Jew is the pioneer of civilization.... The Jew is the emblem of civil and religious toleration.

Leo Tolstoy[2]

TELEVISION HAS BECOME a major and unfortunate player in our obligation as Jews to create a *kiddush ha-shem* (sanctify God's name).

Our nation's privacy and inner struggles are challenged today as never before. What was once concealed from the eye of the world and dealt with as a local affair is now shown on the world stage and judged accordingly. While this is true for all the nations of the world, it has far greater consequences for the Jewish people and the State of Israel. This is because Israel's image is directly related to the *raison d'être* of Jews. How Israel and the

---

[1] *Non-Violence in Peace and War,* 1948, 1:357
[2] Quoted in J.H. Hertz, *A Book of Jewish Thoughts.* London: 1966, 135.

Jewish people are perceived touches at the core of Israel's mission towards the world.

The obligation to sanctify God's name is perhaps the most far-reaching commandment in the Torah. Its opposite, the desecration of God's name, is the only prohibition for which there is no repentance and forgiveness in this world. Once God's name is violated in public, a limit has been crossed for which there is no pardon.[3]

Judaism demands that the individual Jew and the Jewish people in general be a living advertisement for God and Jewish ethics. The commandment of *kiddush ha-shem* has many components. Perhaps the most crucial one has to do with the way that God is perceived by the world. While God Himself obviously cannot be desecrated, His Name can. The idea of "name" here is what we would call today reputation, standing and public image.

On several occasions Moshe admonished God not to destroy the Jewish people since it would give Him a bad name. Moshe uses this argument when he deals with the terrible consequences of the Golden Calf incident[4] and following the demoralizing report of the spies: "Moshe said to the Lord:... Will You now kill these people like one man? Then the nations... will say: It was because God could not bring these people to the land that He promised them that He slew them in the desert...." (Bamidbar 14:15–16).

God seems to be most sensitive to this argument, since when He hears it, He cancels His intended punishment. This is most difficult to understand from a theological point of view. Why should God be concerned about how the nations perceive Him? Since when are issues of truth dependent on public opinion? What has popularity to do with faith?

However, Judaism's response is quite clear: only through a human being's godly acts do we know about God's ethical distinctiveness. Humankind is created in His image and it is humanity and specifically the Jewish people who represent Him in this world by performing His commandments. Through the wisdom and the beneficial effects of these ethical demands, people recognize His greatness. How Jews behave is how God is perceived.

---

[3] Maimonides, *Mishneh Torah,* Hilkhot Teshuva, 1:9–12.
[4] Shemot, 32:12.

But it is also the Jewish people's highly unusual fate in history that reminds us of God. Just as God is unique, so are the Jewish people. Neither can be explained in conventional terms. God is the wholly Other and the Jewish people is "a nation that dwells alone and is not counted among the nations."[5] The eternity of God is reflected in the eternity of the Jewish people. Its strength to survive under all circumstances and against all odds makes them into a vehicle through which God reminds humankind of His very existence and involvement with the world. One is reminded of Nietzsche's observation when he wrote: "The Jews are the most remarkable nation of the world history.... They defined themselves counter to all those conditions under which a nation was able to live."[6]

By destroying the Jewish people, God would obliterate His own standing in the world. It is the Jews who, through their fate and commitment to the commandments, represent the divine in this world. Therefore, they need to serve as an inspiration to all the other nations of the world. Their role is to be an example, no more, no less. They are called on to be a kingdom of priests and a holy nation and it is their task to inspire and to make sure that the world follows in its path, imitates its deeds and walks in its ways. The Jewish nation is defined by its supreme ethical mission. It is for this reason that the commandment to create a *kiddush ha-shem* is vital to the very existence of the Jewish people. When Jews violate this commandment, they lose their very reason for existence.

It is in this context most important to remind ourselves of an unusual Talmudic ruling:[7] When there are legally or morally justified reasons to act in a certain way but the result will be the desecration of God's name, one is forbidden to do so. When God's reputation, and consequently the honor of the Torah, are at stake, the need to sanctify God's name must override any other consideration. Much of this depends on circumstances and how the public will perceive matters. This is the upshot of all Talmudic discussions about *kiddush ha-shem*. On numerous occasions, the Talmud obligates Jews to

---

5 Bamidbar, 23:9.

6 Nietzsche, *Twilight of the Idols and the Anti-Christ*, trans. R.J. Hollingdale. Harmondsworth: Penguin, 1968, 134.

7 *Gittin* 46a.

sanctify the name of God in the eyes of the world. When Rabbi Shimon ben Shetach bought a donkey from an Arab and his students brought it home, they found a pearl in its harness. When they suggested that Rabbi Shimon could legally and perhaps morally keep the pearl, he told them: "Do you think that Shimon ben Shetach is a barbarian? He would prefer the Arab to say 'Blessed be the God of the Jews' than possess all the riches in the world."[8] In fact, Halacha states that the desecration of God's name in relations with non-Jews is much more severe than with fellow Jews. Therefore, while Jewish field workers may eat part of the produce on which they are working, they are forbidden to do so when they work for a gentile since it could be construed as theft. There are hundreds of other examples.[9]

Only when it is a matter of life and death and there is no alternative may one do something that may be seen as contrary to the obligation of making a *kiddush ha-shem* in the eyes of the world.

During disengagement from Gush Katif, a non-Jewish journalist, Rob Hoogland of the well respected Dutch daily paper *De Telegraaf,* wrote about his total amazement on seeing how the Israeli army and the settlers behaved toward each other. Never, he wrote, did I see an army which, without any weapons, and with tears in their eyes and as softly as possible removed their opponents. "What an unbelievable army Israel has! Watching this taking place gave me goose-bumps. While Arabs shoot in the air when they are celebrating and no weapon is required, Israeli soldiers completed this most difficult task with no weapon in sight. What class! Well done, Israel. Shalom!"[10]

It is for this reason that the clash last week between the Israeli police and the settlers at Amona is so deeply tragic and unprecedented. There was no need for this conflict, which led to many injured on both sides and fueled even more mutual antagonistic feelings. Ultimately it also led to an unprecedented *hillul ha-Shem,* a desecration of God's name, in front of millions of viewers. There could have been no greater blunder.

---

[8] Jerusalem Talmud, *Bava Metzia* 2:5. See also *Devarim Rabbah* 3:3 and *Pnei Moshe* ad loc.

[9] See Semag, Mitzvot Aseh 74, Rabbenu Bachya, Vayikra 25:3. Also see Tzefanya 3:13 and the *Encyclopedia Talmudit,* volume 15: *Hillul ha-shem,* 351–360.

[10] *De Telegraaf,* August 20, 2005.

What both sides could and should have known was that the whole world would be watching this unfortunate event, and as in the case of Gush Katif, they should have shown what it means to be a Jew even when one Jew opposes another. Not only was an opportunity for *kiddush ha-shem* lost, but an elementary part of this special and undefined Jewish neshama and comradeship was badly injured. It is not just the future of the land that is at stake but the very essence and existence of the Jewish people. The government of Israel and the leadership of the settlements must do everything in their power to make sure that this will never happen again. May God have mercy.

RABBI YOCHANAN BEN ZAKKAI AND A.B. YEHOSHUA

June 4, 2006

IN ONE OF ITS MOST DRAMATIC TEXTS, the Talmud (*Gittin* 56b) discusses an episode in Jewish history that describes perhaps the most decisive moment which occurred before the Holocaust. It took place in the first century CE at the very hour that the Second Temple was about to be destroyed by the occupying Roman army. The Jews were killed by the tens of thousands. Food had run out. Despair was rampant everywhere. It seemed that there was no longer any future for the Jewish people since the Romans had decided on a "final solution."

There were only two choices: to surrender and survive, or to fight and surely die. Defeating the Romans was no longer an option – their numbers and determination to end all Jewish life outweighed the weak and exhausted condition of the Jewish people.

At that time, Rabbi Yochanan ben Zakkai was the unchallenged Jewish leader of his day. It was left to him to decide what to do. The sage was fully aware that if he decided to surrender he would save many lives, but at the same time he would cause the end of a people who were once called the Jewish nation. After all, the Romans would force the Jews to assimilate and adopt their way of living. The chosen nation, with its unique mission, would become extinct, and it would be made very clear that once the Jewish people no longer existed, the world at large would suffer as well. There would no longer be anyone to fight for moral values, human dignity and the knowledge of God. The world would become a place of immense moral pain, destruction and ongoing disaster.

At that moment, Rabbi Yochanan ben Zakkai made a decision which was as risky as it was courageous. Against all logic, it led to an unparalleled victory that miraculously saved the Jews and therefore the moral fiber of humankind. Rabbi Yochanan told his pupils to smuggle him inside a coffin beyond the walls of Jerusalem and to bring him to Vespasian, the general and future emperor. When Vespasian asked Rabbi Yochanan why he had come to see him, he offered the despot a full surrender on one condition: "Give me Yavne and its sages." Not realizing that the town of Yavne housed the core of the Jewish sages of its time, and therefore the source of Judaism's spiritual strength, Vespasian agreed.

This minor request not only saved Judaism from oblivion but also led ultimately to the fall of the Roman Empire. Because Judaism had been saved, many years later Christianity was able to bring some of the major Jewish and monotheistic values to the empire. This ultimately resulted in Rome's collapse. Had Judaism not survived, Christianity would not have emerged as a major force within Western civilization.

What made Rabbi Yochanan believe that the Jews and Judaism would survive once he guaranteed the continued existence of Yavne and its sages? It was because Rabbi Yochanan realized that the Jews possessed a religious tradition that could function beyond time and space if necessary. He realized that if the Jews were to be robbed of their homeland, they would still be able to live as Jews and keep Judaism alive, albeit on the periphery, as long as Jewish learning and Torah study continued to flourish. Such study would make survival possible even under the most difficult circumstances.

This is what the poet Heinrich Heine said so powerfully nearly nineteen hundred years later, when he claimed that the secret of Jewish survival may be found in the idea of their "portable Fatherland." When the physical homeland is lost, a spiritual one, the Torah, survives. Many years later, George Steiner made a similar observation when he called the Torah "our homeland, the Text."[1] Rabbi Yochanan was convinced that the interaction with this Divine text would make it possible for the Jewish people to continue where any other nation would succumb. If necessary, it would carry the Jewish people beyond the physical need for a homeland. Although the price would be enormous, it would work, as Jewish history has proven.

A. B. Yehoshua, one of the most influential Israeli authors of our century, would have been well advised to listen carefully to Rabbi Yochanan

---

[1] George Steiner, "Our Homeland, the Text." *Salmagundi* (Winter/Spring 1985): 4–25.

ben Zakkai's advice and strategy. Last month, in a highly controversial talk at a symposium of the American Jewish Committee in Washington, he made some important remarks about the contemporary Jewish scene but then lost credibility when he made some dubious statements about Jewish life in Israel and the Diaspora. He reminded his audience that "the Zionist solution, which was proven as the best solution to the Jewish problem, was tragically missed by the Jewish people."[2] Less than five percent of the Jewish people chose to make aliyah at the time of the Balfour Declaration in 1917, when the gates were still wide open and many more Jews would have been able to immigrate without opposition. "It certainly would have been possible to establish a Jewish state before the Holocaust... the State would not only have ended the Israeli Arab conflict at an earlier stage and with less bloodshed, it would also have provided refuge in the 1930 to hundreds of thousands of eastern European Jews who sensed the gathering storm."[3]

While this opinion may be challenged as wishful thinking, there is much truth in A. B. Yehoshua's belief that had the Jews taken the threat of radical anti-Semitism more seriously and if a more serious attempt had been made to establish the State of Israel at that time, many Jews would have been saved.

But A.B. Yehoshua did not leave it at that. He continued: "For me, Avraham Yehoshua, there is no alternative [to being Jewish]. I cannot keep my identity outside Israel. [Being] Israeli is my skin, not my jacket. You [Diaspora Jews], you are changing countries, like changing jackets. I have my skin, the territory [of Israel]."[4] He then claimed that one could not live a full Jewish life outside Israel and implied that the most secular Israeli in Israel was living a more Jewish life than his orthodox fellow Jews in Toronto or Brooklyn.

While we certainly agree that Israel is the only place in the world where one can live a full Jewish life, it is extremely naïve and ludicrous to claim that secular Israelis live more Jewish lives simply because they live in the State of Israel, surrounded by fellow Jews, governed by a Jewish government and protected (we sometimes wonder!) by a Jewish army. It is true that in Israel,

---

[2] See A.B. Yehoshua, "People without a Land," *Haaretz,* May 12, 2006.
[3] Ibid.
[4] *Jerusalem Post,* May 12, 2006, *Upfront* Magazine, 12.

Jewish culture is not a subculture and Judaism can flourish more fully here than anywhere else. But that does not mean that Israel is a Jewish country simply because (almost) only Jews happen to live there. A.B. Yehoshua mixes up two components that are not the same. Being Israeli is not the same as being Jewish. In order to be an Israeli one must live in the land, and when the land ceases to exist, there is no longer any meaning in being an Israeli. Yet – as Rabbi Yochanan ben Zakkai understood – if necessary one may remain a Jew, although surely not a complete one, without living in Israel. A.B. Yehoshua does not seem to understand that there would not have been a State of Israel had his own grandparents not continued to live a Jewish life in the Diaspora. Had they and their contemporaries lived an Israeli life, there would no longer have been any Jews and no State of Israel would have been established. Rabbi Yochanan taught us that Jews will survive without Israel as long as there is Torah, the portable Fatherland, but that Jews will not survive because of Israel, however powerful it may be, when Israel does not incorporate a large amount of resources from Jewish tradition. The belief that Jews will only survive because of the land of Israel is false and has no foundation in Jewish history or reality.

One need only ask one question to show the inadequacy of A.B. Yehoshua's argument. While we can be almost positive that the grandchildren of Orthodox Jews in the Diaspora will remain Jews, this cannot be said about the children of secular Israelis. A.B. Yehoshua is wrong because what he believes is his skin is in fact his jacket. While Orthodox Jews in the Diaspora may not live a complete Jewish life, Judaism is at the core of their lives. On the other hand, even if secular Israelis live among Jews and are governed by a Jewish government, their Jewishness is in their outer shell, not in their essence. It is their jacket, not their skin. Although they are living an Israeli life first of all that contains some strong Jewish elements, it is still their outer shell, in the public and national component of their lives, not in the core of their very essence.

Fortunately, many Israelis realize this and, although they are not Orthodox, they try to bring some inner Jewishness to their lives because they know that Rabbi Yochanan ben Zakkai was right and that A.B. Yehoshua is wrong.

A PHENOMENON CALLED ISRAEL:
REFLECTIONS ON A WAR

July 20, 2006

THROUGHOUT THE CENTURIES, historians, philosophers and anthropologists have struggled with the notion called Israel more than with nearly any other topic. While trying hard to place Israel within the confines of conventional history, they experienced constant academic and philosophical frustration. They discovered that any definitions they proposed soon broke down due to serious inconsistencies. Was Israel a nation, a religion or an altogether mysterious entity that would stay unexplainable forever? Sometimes Israel was seen as less than a nation and more as a religion, only to be challenged by others who believed the reverse to be true. Still others claimed that it could not fit into any of these categories.

It was clear that "Israel" did not fit into any specific definition or known scheme. It resisted all historical concepts and generalities. Its uniqueness thwarted the people's natural desire for an explanation, since explanation always implies arrangement in categories. Anything that flies in the face of such an attempt is alarming and terribly disturbing. This fact became even more obvious once Titus the Roman forced the Jews out of their country, specifically after the collapse of the Bar Kochba rebellion. It was at that moment that the Jew was hurled into the abyss of the nations of the world. Since that day the Jew was confronted with a new condition: constant insecurity. While humankind at large has always been confronted with moments of insecurity, destiny has denied the Jews even the smallest share of the dubious security that others possess. Whether the Jews were aware of it or not, they always lived on ground that could give way beneath their feet at any moment.

In 1948 Israel became a country once more. But many people forgot that while it became a country once again, it was not only a country. All the other dimensions such as nationhood, religion, mystery, the lack of definition and insecurity continued to exist. Today, the people of Israel does not find itself exclusively in the land of Israel, and instead of one Israel, the world now has two. But the second new Israel has up till now been seen as responding to the demands of history, geography, politics and journalism. One knows where it is. At least one thinks that one knows where it is. But it becomes clearer and clearer that this new and definable Israel is now seriously on the way to become as much a puzzle and mysterious entity as the old Israel always was. In fact, it already is.

Throughout its short history, the State of Israel has gone through the most mysterious events modern human beings have ever seen. After an exile of nearly two thousand years in which the old Israel was able to survive in contradiction to all historical criteria, it returned to its homeland. There it found itself surrounded by a massive Arab population that was and is incapable of making peace with the idea that this small, mysterious nation lives among them. After having endured a Holocaust in which it lost six million of its members, it was not permitted to live quietly on its tiny piece of land. Once more, Jews were denied the right to feel at home in their own country. From the outset Israel was forced to fight its enemies on all fronts. It was attacked and condemned for fighting for its very existence and for defending its population. Over the years it had to endure the international community's policy of double standards. Today, just as in the past, when it calls for peace, it is condemned for creating war. When it tries as no other nation to avoid harming the citizens of the countries that declared war on it, it is told that it is more brutal than nations that committed and still commit atrocities against millions of people. Simultaneously and against all logic, this nation builds its country as no other has done, while fighting war after war. What took other nations hundreds of years it accomplished in several. While bombs and Katyusha rockets bombard its cities and calls for its total destruction are heard in many parts of the world, its population increases, it gives birth to children, creates unprecedented technology and manages to create a stronger and more stable economy. Yet the more it succeeds, the more its enemies become frustrated and irritated – and the more dubious Israel's security becomes. And the more some nations would like to try to destroy it, the more the world is forced to deal with this small people and its survival capacity. By now its news occupies more space in any major newspaper than any other political issue or general topic, as if to say that its dubious security and its irritating population are at the center of world history.

Jews must ask themselves what this non-classification really signifies. Is it merely because of lack of vision and insight on the part of the nations? Is it that Jews could really fit into a system, but the nations have not yet allowed them to do so? Is it a negative phenomenon, a temporary one, until it rectifies itself in the future?

We have only one way to comprehend the positive meaning of this otherwise negative phenomenon – that of faith. From any other viewpoint, the Jews' inability to fit into any category would be intolerable and a meaningless absurdity. What we need to understand is that our inability to fit into any category is the foundation and meaning of our living avowal of Israel's uniqueness. Israel's very existence is the manifestation of a divine intervention in history of which Israel must give evidence. In it, history and revelation are one. Only in Israel do they coincide. While other nations exist as nations, the people of Israel exist as a reminder of God's involvement in world history. Only in Israel is humanity touched by the divine.

The realization of this fact has become modern Israel's great challenge. Its attempt time and again to overcome its geographic and political insecurity by employing world politics will not work. Driven by its desire to overcome its insecurity, it veers from geography to nationhood, appealing to its history and religious culture without finding a place that it can call its existential habitat.

When we read Israel's prophets, we see how they warned against such false notions of security. They predicted that Israel would perish when it insisted on existing only as a political structure. Yet it can persist, and this is the paradox of the reality of Israel when it insists on its vocation of uniqueness.

Israel was summoned to remind the world of God's existence, not just as a matter of religion but as a historical reality. There is no security for Israel unless it is secure in its own destiny. It must assume the burden of its own uniqueness, which is nothing other than to assume its role as God's witness. And it must draw strength from this phenomenon, especially in times such as ours when Israel's very existence is once more at stake. Once it recognizes its uniqueness, it will – paradoxically – enjoy security and undoubtedly be victorious.

THE FUTURE OF ISRAEL AND THE ZIONIST
ENTERPRISE: A DIFFERENT LOOK[1]

February 26, 2006

NOWHERE IS THE EXTREME SPIRITUAL CRISIS of the Jewish people more evident than in the State of Israel. A loss of purpose and direction has overtaken the vast majority of Israelis and most of the nation's leaders. Confusion and a feeling of hopelessness have become the order of the day for many people. Yet as we search for the cause of this bewilderment, it is crucial that we not become confused about the confusion. While many people may believe that this feeling of hopelessness is the result of Israel's sudden realization that there is a Hamas state in its back yard or that Iran is preparing to destroy it, we must realize that this is confusing the symptom with the cause. At the core of the crisis is a fundamental misreading of the nature and destiny of the Jewish people.

Israelis are slowly beginning to realize the attempt to transform the Jewish people into a normal nation now that it has its own homeland is nothing but a farce and is the cause of this traumatic perplexity. The attempt is exploding right in their faces. Not only has it become clear that the old secular Zionist dream that anti-Semitism would cease once the Jews had their own homeland was false, but also it is now obvious that the State of Israel's very existence has become the main reason for anti-Semitism. A normal Israeli state with a normal army, government and population has not transformed the Jewish people into a normal nation.

Right now, nothing is clearer that the old biblical truth that "Israel dwells alone and shall not be reckoned among the nations" (Bamidbar 23:9).

---

[1] Published in the *Jerusalem Post*, February 23, 2006.

Whether we like it or not, we are not a normal people and we can make no greater mistake than to try to "normalize" ourselves. The Jewish people's long history is by definition one of existential oddity.

> I remember how the materialist interpretation of history, when I attempted in my youth to verify it by applying it to the destinies of peoples, broke down in the case of the Jews, where destiny seemed inexplicable... Its survival is a mysterious and wonderful phenomenon demonstrating that the life of this people is governed by a special predetermination, transcending the processes of adaptation expounded by the materialistic interpretation of history. The survival of the Jews, their resistance to destruction, their endurance under absolutely peculiar conditions, are the fateful role played by them in history; *all these point to the particular and mysterious foundations of their destiny*. (Nicholas Berdyaev, *The Meaning of History*, author's emphasis)

Indeed, no other nation has overturned the destiny of all of humanity as much as the Jewish people. It gave humanity the Bible, together with the greatest prophets and people of spirit. Its spiritual ideas and moral laws still hold sway over all humankind, influencing entire civilizations. It gave birth to a man whom millions see as their messiah and laid the foundations of moderate Christianity, Islam and many secular moral teachings. It provided all of humankind with a messianic hope for the future and endowed human beings with dignity and responsibility. The Jews gave the gentile world the Outside and the Inside, their outlook and inner life. In his work, *The Gifts of the Jews,* author Thomas Cahill said, "We [gentiles] can hardly get up in the morning or cross the street without being Jewish. We dream Jewish dreams and hope Jewish hopes. Most of our best words, in fact – new, adventure, surprise; unique, individual, person, vocation; time, history, future; freedom, progress, spirit; faith, hope, justice – are the gifts of the Jews." All of this proves that Jews have a destiny and a mission that are radically different from those of any other nation. They are an eternal people with an eternal message and their history is one of extreme "abnormality."

This is the reason that the attempt by secular Zionism to "normalize" the Jewish people failed at the start. No nation can live with a borrowed national identity. In fact, it is the very attempt at normalization that ultimately threatens the state's very existence. The desire to escape Jewish destiny by way of secular Zionism has undermined the moral security of the people that dwells in Zion. Now that Zionism has spent its inherited resources, large segments of Israeli society are left with rootless secularism, no memories and therefore no expectations. Broad sections of Israeli society have been alienated from the historic continuity of the Jewish people and have become unsure of the moral validity of our claim to our ancestral homeland. And indeed, there is no *Israeli* claim to the land. There can only be a *Jewish* claim. Where there is no continuity, there can be no return. Only in the uninterrupted chain of Jewish generations may the certainty be found that this has been our land, all through our exile, and that it was taken from us by force. Our faith in our right to this land has been our eternal protest against anyone who held or wants to possess it. Yet this faith is inseparable from our Jewish destiny. Once we reject this fact, our claim to the land evaporates. Either we return to the Holy Land or there is no land to return to.

No doubt the time will come, sooner rather than later, that the government of Israel will realize that it has wrought havoc on its people by denying its people its Jewish roots. It will then beg for help from the very people whom they now reject: the young, religious and tradition-loving Zionists. The Israeli government could have made no greater mistake than to create such a serious rift between itself and those communities. It will realize that these young people, together with all those who have a deep Jewish connection to the land – although they may not be fully observant – are the ones who are prepared to die for it and therefore are the only ones who can restore it. They are the ones who have a deep love for Judaism and a keen understanding of Jewish destiny, and they are Israel's lifeline. The same broad segments of the Israeli population that have turned against them will one day realize that their physical and spiritual survival will depend on them.

Therefore, the leadership of the religious Zionist community bears a tremendous responsibility. It must prepare this community for the time when all of Israel will come to their doorstep, asking for help. It will therefore have to rethink religious Zionist ideology and make sure that the wellbeing of the people of Israel and their connection with Judaism remains their first priority. They will have to see the land as a means, not as an end in itself. They will have to remove that which is unnecessary and undesired and add what is important. They must make sure that the image of the religious or tradition-loving Zionist is one of great integrity and *kiddush ha-shem*. By that time, its members will have grown into a balanced, tolerant and pragmatic leadership that will bring pride to the Jewish people. It will connect them once more to their Jewish heritage and teach them that Jews will have a future in the State of Israel through their awareness of their *radical otherness*. Once that goal has been reached, it will become obvious that we will be able to resist any threat from without. Confusion will be replaced by certainty and bewilderment by calm.

ISRAEL AND ITS NEIGHBORS

ISRAEL IS GUSH KATIF:
THE PALESTINIAN CLAIM TO ISRAEL

May 12, 2004

IN TRACTATE *SANHEDRIN* 91A, we read a story that took place in the days of Alexander of Macedon, known as Alexander the Great (fourth century BCE.) Just after Moshe's death, when Yehoshua was leading the Jewish people into the Land of Israel, seven tribes hostile to the Jews occupied the land. Yehoshua offered them peace and security on condition that they commit themselves to the seven Noahide Laws, the basic moral code for all humanity. If they refused – which would constitute a statement that they would not adhere to civilized behavior – Yehoshua informed them that they could leave peacefully. Afterwards, he led the people into the land.

Since most of the tribes refused to accept either alternative, war broke out. The only tribe that actually left was that of the Canaanites. Tradition has it that they settled in Africa (Rambam, *Melachim* 6:5).

Centuries later, the Canaanites came to Alexander's international court with a claim that the land of Israel should be returned to them. When the court asked the reason, the Canaanites, who were also called the *bnei Africa* (the inhabitants of Africa), said that the Israelites had forced them out during Yehoshua's time and that this injustice should be rectified. When Alexander asked them for proof of their claim to the land, they responded that it was the very Torah of the Jews that supported it. Did it not say, "The land of Canaan with its coasts" (Bamidbar 34:2)? And, since Canaan was their ancestor, they had a legitimate claim to return to the land and take possession of it.

Consequently Alexander, who is known to have been somewhat sympathetic to the Jews, asked the sages to respond. An unlearned Jew,

Geviha ben Pesisa, who was known for his great love for his fellow Jews, asked to be allowed to defend the Jewish claim to the land against the Canaanites. "Let me go and plead against them before Alexander of Macedon," he pleaded. "If they defeat me, then [you can] say: 'You have defeated one of our uneducated people,' and if I defeat them, then say: 'The Torah of Moshe has defeated them.'" After the sages decided to give him their approval, Geviha ben Pesisa asked the Canaanites, "From where do you have your proof?" "From the Torah!" they responded. "I will also bring a proof from the Torah," he said. "It says that when Cham, one of Noach's children, had uncovered his father's nakedness, Noach said, "Cursed be Canaan. A servant of servants shall he be unto his brothers" (Bereshit 9:25). (Canaan was another name for the children of Cham.) Geviha ben Pesisa continued, arguing that since the curse made the Canaanites into slaves to the children of Shem (another son of Noach and the ancestor of the Semitic peoples and the Jews), the Jews would be the owners of the land in any case. According to Jewish law, "Whatever a slave acquires belongs to his master" since slaves are their master's property. "Moreover," he said, "you have not served us for years!"

"Alexander told them [the Canaanites]: 'Answer him.' 'Give us three days,' they said. They searched, but finding no answer, they left."

When we study this incident carefully, we find that several matters are difficult to understand. First of all, it is obvious that the Canaanites were guilty of reading the Torah selectively. Had they turned the page, they would have read that the land had been promised to Avraham already in earlier days and that the Torah reiterates that God gave it to the Jews. Even more mysterious is Geviha ben Pesisa's defense. Why did he use such a roundabout argument? Why did he not use the most obvious one – that the Torah makes it abundantly clear that the land was given to the Jews? He could have quoted dozens of verses to support his claim!

Rabbi Shmuel Eliezer Edeles (the Maharsha) argues in his commentary that the Canaanites' motivation was much more sophisticated than one might imagine. They had read the Torah very carefully and knew of the promise that God had made to the Israelites concerning the land. They reminded Alexander's court that they, the Canaanites, had been forced out of the country because of their immoral behavior. The Holy Land had no longer been able to contain them and had consequently spat them out. Yet, continued the Canaanites, the Israelites had become just as evil as they themselves had been! They had also become disobedient and had violated the moral code. Moreover, had not the Torah made it clear that the Jews would only merit the land when they were a holy nation, as the Torah demanded? In that case, the Jews no longer had a claim on the land and they, the Canaanites, who had lived there before the Jews, had every right to take it back!

Even an unlearned man like Geviha ben Pesisa understood the Canaanites' argument and had to admit that their point was somewhat valid. Therefore, there was no point in citing verses stating that God had promised the land to the Israelites earlier. The promise was no longer effective till the Jews repented. The only way that he could defend the Jewish claim was indeed a roundabout one, the one referring to Noach's curse of Cham. However, it does not take much to realize that this claim is weak and unconvincing.

We cannot but be reminded of this Talmudic narrative when we think of Israel's imminent disengagement from the Gaza Strip. Unless we are missing some major element necessary for understanding the logic of this measure, the plan to leave the Gaza Strip and Gush Katif makes no sense from any angle. Besides the fact that such a withdrawal can only be interpreted as rewarding terrorism, Israel gains no real benefit from it since there is no evidence that the Palestinians are capable of maintaining peace or that they even wish to. It only results in endangering a large contingent of Israel's population, which will now only be even more vulnerable to rockets and other terrorist actions. It is after all difficult to see why Afula and Ashkelon will be less endangered tomorrow than Sderot and Gush Katif today.

Common sense tells us that rather than saving the other settlements of the West Bank from ruin, disengagement will only whet the appetite of the Palestinian terrorists and the international community to force Israel into an ongoing surrender of more and more land until it will be impossible to defend its "Auschwitz borders," as Abba Eban called them.

Most disturbing is that there is no longer any serious opposition to the plan from anyone in Israel's top leadership, intelligentsia or, above all, the press. At this point there is no longer any strong, outspoken opposition in the Knesset. While many of the common people have protested in every way possible, no strong voices are challenging this plan. The press, which plays a major role in shaping people's understanding of what is really taking place, continues to fail in its moral obligation to inform the population of the facts. It is becoming more and more obvious that it deliberately sees its task as one of covering up the truth rather than revealing it.

A silence is covering the land as if its leaders, including the opposition, have been intoxicated by a kind of dream state like a person who has just awakened from surgery but, unable to resist the effects of the anesthesia, falls back into deep slumber.

Although nobody can fathom the workings of the mind of God, from a religious point of view we must ask whether this silence and ambivalence are not the result of divine interference. Could we be losing our grip on this land because we have lost our way as the people of God? One wonders whether the Lord of the Universe is preventing the Israeli leadership from waking up and seeing the facts as they are since they, together with much of the nation, have failed to understand the significance of the people of Israel in all its moral and religious dimensions. Therefore, it is playing into the hands of the Canaanites' old claim that we too have given up our right to this land.

Unless the governmental and religious leaders of Israel wake up and inject Israel with a strong moral code and a deep sense of Jewish religious content, Israel will fall more and more into the hands of those who, out of desperation and lack of vision, will keep on chopping away pieces of land until we are forced to recognize, to our utter bewilderment, that by having forfeited our Jewish connection to this land, we have forfeited the land itself. We will then be forced to wake up from our slumber and find that all of Israel has turned into one large Gush Katif.

What we will then discover is that it was not political errors that were ultimately responsible for our dangerous predicament. Rather, these errors were the direct result of our ongoing refusal to face our Jewishness. Only when the people of Israel realize that its moral-religious mission is crucial to its survival will it be able to understand its relationship to the land. It will then become clear that without a strong attachment to Jewish identity, a deep involvement with Jewish living and religious authenticity combined with the highest level of moral behavior, the Lord of the Universe may no longer be prepared to guarantee this land as an obvious inheritance of the people of Israel.

Since it is becoming ever clearer that the secular and religious establishments in Israel are incapable of turning the tide, common people of Israel must undertake the task of insisting on radical changes in order to force the governmental, educational and rabbinical leadership to take action, or otherwise replace them.

One of the characteristics of a dream is that nothing in it surprises us. It permits us to be quietly and safely insane without being aware of it. It allows human beings to live in a world of deafness, impervious to the cries of the real world.

Nevertheless, we should never forget that the efforts that we make to escape our destiny only lead us into it.

Let us also be aware that miracles do take place and that all may turn out for the best. Still, we must remember that human beings create miracles when they use the courage and intelligence that God gave them.

CAMP DAVID AND THE CITY OF DAVID

May 6, 2004

I stand at the Kotel, the Wailing Wall.
I see the Wall with her frozen tears
And her passing clouds with many sighs.
I read secret books and hundreds of thousands of names.
Names from Egypt, Babylon, Rome, Poland, Spain, Hungary, America and South Africa.
Names from Auschwitz, Buchenwald and Dachau.
I see the auto-da-fés, the Crusades, the pogroms and the Roman torture chambers.
Mothers crying about their children,
Women of all ages.

There is also the businessman standing in tears.
The movie star, the politician, the housewife, the yeshiva student and the strong soldier.
Yeshayahu stands next to me;
A little further on, Rabbi Akiva.
My teachers: Maimonides and Yehuda Halevi, Hillel and Shammai,
Behind me the Gaon of Vilna, occupied with his thoughts
And the Baal Shem Tov in deep meditation.

Men, women, children, Mitnaggedim, Chasidim, Ethiopians, Yemenites, Sephardim and Ashkenazim, Jews of all colors.

There is no time, no clock, no early or later.
I stand but cannot grasp.

I say my tefillah.
Then the truth descends on me: I know
I have never left this place.
I find myself here for four thousand years.

The return to Zion is unprecedented,
a happening *sui generis.*
The creation of the State of Israel is a surprise and a shock.
It confuses. It is a breach in a world where people do not want to be
surprised.
And therefore Israel irritates.

"The Egyptian, the Babylonian and the Persian conquered the world with
much noise, pomp and splendor and disappeared.
The Greek and the Roman followed with their drumbeat and war-carriages
and died out.
Others came and held their torch high and burned out.
The Jew saw them all, surpassed them all and stayed immortal."[1]

The Jews never left Israel. They were driven out against their will.
Titus and his army.
And the people of Israel protested.
They said, "No" to anybody who made a claim.
In their prayers, in their songs, in their homes, in the *bet ha-midrash,*
At the time of his chuppah and his burial and in his sermons.

Yerushalayim.
It is only the Jews who keep on praying for its rebuilding, for two thousand
years
and no other nation.
It is only the Jews who mourn for two thousand years for its destruction
and no other nation.
It is only the Jews who fast and sit on the floor for two thousand years on
the day the Temple in Jerusalem was destroyed

---

[1] Based on Mark Twain.

and no other nation.

It is only the Jews who for two thousand years break a glass under their marriage canopy out of sorrow for Jerusalem

and no other their nation.

It is only the Jews who for two thousand years build a house and leave one part of the wall unplastered because of the loss of their Temple

and no other nation.

It is only among the Jews that women do not wear all their jewelry at once out of reverence for the destruction of Jerusalem

and no other nation.

It is only the Jews who cover their dead with the dust of Israel when they bring their dear ones to their last resting place outside the land of Israel

and no other nation.

Is not every Jewish house in exile a piece of Israel on foreign ground?

This is the history, the reality and the future of Israel.

PRAYER FOR THE JEWISH SOLDIER

June 17, 2006

Lord of the Universe:
We, the soldiers of the people of Israel
Come to You in humility
And pray for your help.

Once more we are asked to defend our
People and
The Holy Land against our enemies.

We ask You to have mercy on us and
Help us watch over our people
With clean hands
And with a heart filled with mercy.

Let our people have the strength to
Stay in good spirits
And live in unity and
Walk in Your ways,
The ways of justice and truth.

Let us not make mistakes
And hurt those who are not guilty,
Who do not understand
And have no part in this conflict.

Please,

Let our bullets not hurt those children of our enemies
Whose parents place them deliberately in dangerous spots,
Fire on us
And then shield themselves
Behind their own offspring against
Our forces so as to fault us when their children
Are wounded or even killed.

Remove the evil spirit of these parents
And make them realize the wickedness of their actions.

Stop their teachers from manipulating their students
With hate for us in their schoolbooks
On the radio, television and
The Internet.

O God,
You know what one of our prime ministers once said:
"We may forgive our enemies one day
For hurting and killing our children
But
We cannot forgive them for having made our children
Into those who needed to kill."
We beg You, do not let our Jewish souls have to undergo

This ordeal that we cannot bear.
We are the children of Avraham, your servant, who
Prayed for the evil people of Sedom in the hope that
They would repent and live decent lives.

So, we beg you:
Make our enemies repent.
Make them understand that
We are good people
Who wish to live in peace with
All our neighbors.

O Lord,
Remove from their thoughts atrocities such as those
In which they dip their hands
In our blood.
As Jews, we
Cannot fathom
Doing this to even our worst enemies.

You commanded us to live in a country that
Is little more
Than a tiny island.
Our population is smaller than that of
Many single cities.

You asked us to live there so as to send
Your holy Word to all the corners of the world.
But
We are surrounded by many nations who
Contain more than a hundred million people.
They inhabit one of the largest regions of the world
But deny us the right to live in even the smallest corner of the world.
They do not want to listen
And only wish our death.

Give the Arab nations
Leaders
Who pursue justice and who really
Care for their people
And do not wish to bring their own brothers to despair
And unbearable pain
With the intention
Of accusing us
Of grave injustice.

Now,

After thousands of years of our dwelling
In this world and after many exiles, tortures, pogroms,
Expulsions and Holocausts
We finally found our way back to our
Small homeland
That You promised to our ancestors.

Yet once more our dreams of peace
Have gone up in smoke
While we try, at the risk of our own lives,
To find a way to
Allow our Palestinian neighbors to
Live their own lives.

While we were prepared to make sacrifices
For the welfare of these people
As no other people ever did
While we offered them land, peace, finances
And even firearms so as to defend themselves,
We once more pay the price for being a people
Who believe in the honesty of another nation and its leaders
And once more we feel misled.

Oh Lord, remove the evil intentions of the
Security Council, which distorts the truth.
Remove the deliberate lies
From the hearts of those who head the
Media.
Why do they want to portray us
As an evil people?
They do so
To deny Your existence and Your moral
Demands.
They hide behind their own wickedness
And cover up their own and their ancestors'
Immoral acts that they committed against us

166

And our ancestors for thousands
Of years.

O God, You know
That
No army in world history has used as much restraint
As ours.
No army is so careful not to hurt or kill
As ours.
But what shall we do when they are not even prepared
To give us the option
To prove this to the world?

Please, God,
Bring peace into the hearts and minds
Of our enemies.
Let them be uplifted with a spirit of righteousness.
Stop them from hating us because we are Your people.
Let us sanctify Your name as this is our
Mission and our dream.
Give us the possibility once more to teach
Your ways to the peoples
Of the world
And make them hear and
Understand.

We hate war as nobody else does.
We abhor the need to wear weapons.
We cannot stand the sound of our *own* artillery
And our tanks.

We are the people of the Book,
The Book that demands holiness,
Kindness
And integrity.
Our heroes are not the generals or the marshals

But our prophets and our sages,
Righteous people.
So deliver us from this anguish.
Bring peace to the nations.
Let us not be forced to use our strength against them
For they will have no escape.
But
Let the blessing that you gave to Avraham come true –
"Through you all the families of the earth will be blessed" –
For this is our hope.

EFRON AND ARAFAT: TWO OF A KIND

July 7, 2004

As HE TRIES TO BUY A PIECE OF LAND to bury Sarah, Avraham becomes involved in lengthy negotiations (Bereshit 23). After he has turned to the children of Chet, he asks them to speak to Efron the son of Tzohar, the owner of the Cave of Machpela. It is in this cave that he would like to bury his dear wife Sarah.

At first, Efron gives the impression that he wants to give the land to Avraham without any monetary compensation. But when Avraham refuses to accept this offer, Efron states that in that case, he would like to receive four hundred shekels,[1] an abnormally high sum of money, with the sarcastic comment that this price is of no significance "between me and you" (23:15). Avraham hands him the amount and buries Sarah.

The commentators carefully examined every part of these negotiations and suggested many explanations in order to understand what they were all about. Some suggest that Avraham refused to receive this piece of land as a gift because he realized that the children of Chet wanted him and his family to become part of their culture – in other words to assimilate and become one of them. By giving the land to him instead of selling it, they would draw him in as "one of the family" and all distinction between him and them would be blurred.

Avraham, on the other hand, wanted to make it abundantly clear that he needed to stay a "stranger" and secure a piece of land where only Hebrews would be buried. Any attempt to assimilate him into the culture of the children of Chet was unacceptable.

---

[1] The Bible scholar E.A. Speiser states that Avraham could have bought a whole village for this sum (*Anchor Bible*, 171).

Others maintain that Avraham wanted to impress on all those present that one day, in the messianic times, the dead will be resurrected, and that therefore a burial place should hold the bones of the deceased for eternity. Therefore, such a place could never be touched or ploughed.

Efron, who does not believe in any of this, suggests that he could easily give the land to him since after several years they would clear the land of any remains and the original owner would be able to use it again for agriculture. Therefore, he would not really lose the land by giving it to Avraham for several years. It was just a temporary arrangement. The commentators have offered many more solutions.

However, there may be another reason why Avraham was not satisfied with the circumstances under which he could become the owner of the land. Efron may have intended never to give or sell the cave to Avraham. Avraham realized that all Efron's diplomatic talk and his generous offer to give him the land for free was nothing but a clever way to refuse any such deal. Even when Efron actually asked for money, it was never truly his intention to sell Avraham the cave.

In order to understand this properly, we must enter Efron's frame of mind at the time of the negotiations and understand something about human psychology. We need to examine Efron's position before and after the negotiations.

In all probability, Efron was an unknown figure before this incident. He did not stand out, had no special status in the community of the children of Chet, and but for this particular incident, it is likely that no one would have heard of him. However, he suddenly becomes the center of attention. All eyes turn to him and in a matter of moments he realizes that he has become the most important man. He and nobody else has to deal with Avraham, a man whom the Hittites called "the mighty prince among us" (23:6), one of the most impressive people of his time.

At that moment, Efron tastes power. He realizes that the very idea of Avraham negotiating with him gives him, Efron, a great amount of prestige and standing in his community. (This is analogous to a case in which an average citizen of the United States is invited to the White House for a private audience with the President.)

If Efron reaches a settlement with Avraham, he can no longer enjoy this spotlight and will have to return once again to the status of the common man. The only way he is able to ensure that he stays at the center of attention is by dragging out the negotiations as long as he can. Therefore, Efron is not at all interested in solving the "problem." The reverse is true: he wants to complicate the situation as long as possible so that he can enjoy his unprecedented prestigious status.

It is for this reason that he asks for an extravagant sum. He hopes that Avraham will refuse to pay it and that the negotiations will go on for a long time. In fact, Efron might have hoped that Avraham would become hostile, in which case the dispute concerning his land would take on a completely different character. It would turn into a much larger conflict, many more people would hear of it and Efron would become a nationally-known figure.

However, to Efron's chagrin, Avraham accepts his offer and is prepared to pay the entire sum in cash. With no other option, Efron is forced to accept. However, it undermines his very intention. No longer will he enjoy his earlier position, and his "finest hour" will be over within minutes. The children of Chet will go home, Avraham buries Sarah and Efron's name will no longer be a household word. His role as a leader and a tough, world-renowned negotiator has come to an end. Nothing could be worse.

In case our interpretation is correct, we would suggest that the Torah comes to warn us that when we confront our enemies, we should never forget that some of them may not be at all interested in peace even when they call for it. After all, they realize that once they have negotiated a true peace, they will become has-beens. Their names will no longer be on the lips of millions of people and they will fade into oblivion. No longer will they appear on the front page of international newspapers or on television. For them, that is the greatest curse. Better to keep a conflict going, even at the cost of lives, rather than live with the knowledge that one no longer plays any role in world events.

This may not only be the story of Efron but also of a modern "negotiator" known as Yasser Arafat and others like him. To overlook this would be a major blunder. Israeli leaders should take notice!

KILLING[1]

July 14, 2004

IN THIS MOST TRYING TIME for the people of Israel, during which many Palestinians have taken to the streets in Ramallah and other places in order to celebrate the killing of Jews including children, babies, soldiers and police officers in terror attacks, it is important for us to remember who we are.

While our enemies have lost all dignity by stooping to a level of unprecedented cruelty and enjoyment of those acts, the Jewish people should be reminded that the children of Avraham, Yitzhak and Yaakov would never even contemplate, let alone commit, such acts of hatred whatever the circumstances.

However, this attitude did not come to us easily. The need for revenge after a great injustice has been perpetrated is understandable. In the heat of the moment, people easily lose their minds and carry out acts of rampant destruction. They often forget against whom they are fighting and cause heavy losses to innocent people. Yet even while this is understandable, it is wrong.

When Dina, the daughter of Yaakov, was kidnapped and violated by Schechem, the son of Chamor the Hittite, the "prince of the land," her brothers were outraged, "fired deeply with indignation" that Shechem had done "a disgraceful deed to Israel" (Bereshit 34:7). They realized that had Dina not been Jewish, Schechem would not have dared to commit such an act, since none of the other neighboring nations would have let him get away with it. However, in his belief that Jews are merciful people and not interested in a real fight, he took his chances and violated Dina, thinking that

---

[1] This essay was inspired by the comments of Rabbi Zev Leff in *MD Torah Weekly* 3/19.

he would be able to use diplomacy to get the Jews not only to accept what happened but even to consent to his marrying her. When Dina's brothers said that they would be prepared to agree to the marriage on condition that all the men of Chamor's city circumcise themselves, his joy was boundless. Immediately he forced his countrymen to undergo circumcision, promising that it would be to their financial advantage. Above all, it would end the unique identity of the Jews, who would slowly vanish through assimilation.

He was badly mistaken. In no way were the brothers prepared to make any kind of deal with Schechem. Realizing very well what they were up against and with what kind of mentality they were dealing with, they planned to kill Schechem and his father. They used guile to make him believe that they agreed to his offer. The brothers would then be able to kill Schechem and his father Chamor, who seemed to have helped his son to commit the crime. Because the men were weakened by the operation, there was no danger that the brothers would be attacked. This was the brothers' plan. Yet two of them, Shimon and Levi, decided on a much larger operation without their father or brothers' knowledge. Not only did they kill Schechem and Chamor, but all the other men as well, and took the women and children captive. Their mission completed, they brought Dina home.

When they arrived home and told their father Yaakov what they had done, they thought that he would compliment them. However, Yaakov's response was very different. Accusing them of having desecrated God's name, he told them that he now anticipated a war between himself and the other tribal groups living in the country.

The brothers responded with shock. "Should our sister then be treated as a harlot?" Yaakov does not answer, and nothing more is mentioned about the incident. While his silence may suggest that he agreed with the attack, it later becomes clear that this is not the case.

As Yaakov lies on his deathbed, blessing his children, he does not mince words. He tells Shimon and Levi what he really thinks of their action. "Shimon and Levi are brothers, but are (also) instruments of violence... for in their wrath they murdered men. Cursed be their anger..." (49:5–7). He indicates that Shimon and Levi should be given a position in the nation where they will never have the power to make political and military decisions (See Rabbi S.R. Hirsch). There was no justification for their act. While

Yaakov may have fully sanctioned their attack on Schechem himself, he could not justify the murder of all the other men.

This is surprising. Were all these men not guilty by their failure to intervene? After all, they did not protest against Shechem's deed and seemed to have consented to it. Why not kill them as well? Here Yaakov seems to anticipate the halacha that one may not kill people who pose no immediate threat. One may only kill others when there are clear indications that they are planning to kill him. (However, those who pose the threat may be imprisoned or subject to other strong preventive action.)

A careful look at Yaakov's last words reveals that he is not only uttering a strong condemnation of his two sons. He is also praising them for their strong spirit, their constant awareness of their worth and their nation's pride and power. This strength needs to enter into every sphere of the whole nation and become the backbone of the ideal Jewish society. Nowhere is there any indication that Yaakov was a pacifist who advocated surrender.

> To pacifists the proper course
> Of conduct is to sit on Force.
> For in their dreams, Force can't resist
> The well-intentioned pacifists.[2]

Yaakov's point is that the nation's security must be at the center of the fight. The enemy, not those who are innocent, should be punished. A forceful attack on the enemy may sometimes involve the innocent and little can be done about it except to try to prevent it, but neither can it prevent one from attacking the enemy.

However, there is another important point that even Shimon and Levi understood. One does not rejoice in the enemy's destruction. There is no dancing in the streets, no celebration or fireworks. There is the sober understanding that killing is terrible. Even when it must be done in self defense or justice, it remains an act that people should abhor. In this spirit, Golda Meir once observed that while Jews may one day forgive their enemies for killing Israeli soldiers, we will not forgive them for having forced our soldiers to kill.

---

[2] Clarence Day, "Thoughts on Joys and Triumphs." In *Thoughts without Words*, 1928.

When Yaakov was confronted with his brother Esav and his army of four hundred men, the Torah informs us that he "was very much afraid." Rashi comments that he was not only afraid that he might be killed but also that he might have to kill. What is worse than having to take the life of another human being even when he is your enemy and even when he deserves to die?

In ancient times, when the Sanhedrin was required to take the life of an individual according to the law of the Torah, the judges did not thank God for the opportunity to perform a mitzvah or dance around his tombstone singing songs of praise. They fasted. That is the difference between us and those who celebrate in Ramallah.[3]

---

[3] The only exception where Jews celebrated their victory over their enemies was at the Red Sea. It is interesting to note that the Jewish tradition was disturbed by this. While God permitted the Jews to celebrate, He forbade the angels to join in, saying, "The work of My hands is drowning in the sea, and you sing songs?" (*Megillah* 10a). For this reason, we recite only half of the Hallel on Passover night and spill some wine from our cups. It seems as though Jews were still in need of some kind of celebration at the Red Sea, but since the angels had not gone through the hell of suffering, God silenced them. This may also be the reason why Hallel is not recited on Purim.

HATING WAR AGAINST THE ENEMY AND PR

July 8, 2004

> Perhaps one day we will forgive our enemies for killing our
> boys, but we will never forgive them for forcing our soldiers
> to kill.
>
> Golda Meir

IT IS IMPERATIVE that we do whatever we can to minimize the damage done
to our image in the eyes of the western world, now that most of it has turned
against us.

The Palestinians have intensified their hate campaign against Israel. Not
only do they manipulate and falsify the facts, but they have also shown
themselves to be masters at fabricating complete and limitless lies about our
soldiers' operations in the West Bank.

The ongoing crusade by the media and world leaders, together with anti-
Israel statements by the UN and the EU, are serious matters that cannot be
ignored. As our war with the Palestinians is first of all a media war, we must
do whatever we can to show the world that we are not just decent people
who try to prevent harm to innocent people, often taking enormous risks,
but that we suffer from the fact that we have to use weapons to defend
ourselves in this conflict which has been forced on us.

True, it will have no effect on our Arab enemies or on all those anti-
Semites who now have free rein and are proving once more how ill they
really are. But we should never forget that most people who read
newspapers or watch television are not imbued with hatred towards us.
Their dislike for us and our country is a direct result of what they hear and

watch on television and read in the papers. And this can be diminished, if not stopped entirely.

However, as we observe many of our Israeli spokespeople, we are not only astonished by their lack of proper English usage, lack of patience with those who interview them (which sometimes manifests itself in arrogance, with detrimental consequences), but also a complete misreading of the minds of their Gentile television audiences.

The element that seems to be lacking, and that is crucial for any successful pro-Israel campaign, is the need to emphasize Golda Meir's statement: "Perhaps one day we will forgive our enemies for killing our sons, but we will never forgive them for forcing our soldiers to kill." This powerful statement must be repeated and explained.

We hate having to take up weapons in order to defend ourselves. It is a nightmare to have to uproot the lives of innocent people. We abhor having to shoot people even when they want to kill our babies and mothers in suicide attacks. We take no joy or satisfaction in it. If innocent Palestinians are killed accidentally, our pain has no limit. Our hearts cry bitterly when we see young Palestinian people expressing such hatred towards other human beings. We want peace for them, which they will never achieve under the leadership of a man who cares nothing for their lives and is the arch-enemy of his own people. Our heart bleeds for all those (not so) innocent Palestinians. But we have no option other than to defend our people. It is our moral duty to fight the terrorists with every means at our disposal and we have to continue our operations on the ground until there is a decisive victory.

The continuous repetition of these and similar statements should be a matter of policy in every interview, statement and documentary made by all government members, ambassadors, army spokesmen and anyone else who speaks in the name of our country. The power of these sentiments cannot be overestimated. To deny the impact of such statements in the gentile world shows a complete misreading of the minds of millions of people who now criticize us and have begun to hate the State of Israel.

The fact that our spokesmen are not repeating these sentiments constantly should worry all of us. For a Jewish country this is the minimum that can be expected from us. It is utterly Jewish. Speaking to our spokesmen it is abundantly clear that they fully agree with this sentiment but it seems that they are reluctant to utter these words since they believe that it would be seen as a sign of weakness on our side. This is a great tragedy. Strong men can afford to be sensitive. The weak cannot.

38

THE WORLD AND THE MIDDLE EAST

May 16, 2004

WHILE IT IS DIFFICULT in these days to comprehend the ways of Divine Providence, it seems that some moments of divine revelation are granted to us when we read some biblical and rabbinical sources carefully.

When Hagar is in the desert after having fled from Avraham's home, she is told that she will bear a son:

> And an angel of God said to her: Behold, you will conceive and give birth to a son. You shall name him Yishmael, for God has heard your prayer. He shall be a wild man (*pere adam*), with his hand against everyone and everyone's against him, and in the face of his brothers shall he dwell. (Bereshit 16:11–12)[1]

> Rabbi Yochanan and Resh Lakish debated this. Rabbi Yochanan said: It means that while all people are bred in civilized surroundings, he will be reared in the wilderness. Resh Lakish said: It means a savage among men in the literal sense, for as people plunder wealth, he plunders lives. (Midrash *Bereshit Rabba* 35:9)

> *Pere adam* – what does this mean? A race of men who do not bow their necks to the yoke of other men. – Rabbi Samson Rafael Hirsch, ad loc.

---

[1] For an in-depth treatment of the following and other sources see Chapter 53 and my book *Between Silence and Speech*, Chapter 6, On the Israeli and Arab Conflict: A Biblical Perspective. Northvale, New Jersey, London: Jason Aronson, Inc., 1995.

"With his hand against everyone and everyone's against him, and in the face of all his brothers will he dwell." What does this mean? It pertains to his children, who will increase and they will have wars with all the nations. (Ramban, ad loc.)

"His hand shall be against everyone," in that he will be victorious at first over all nations, and afterwards "everyone's hand shall be against him," meaning that he will be vanquished in the end. – Rabbi Abraham Ibn Ezra, ad loc.

Although he will be a man with great potential, intellect and emotions, his hand will be against everybody and everybody's against him. Nevertheless, "in the face of his brothers he will dwell" – meaning that he will honored by the nations. (*Da'at Sofrim,* ad loc.)

At the Covenant between the Pieces, God causes Avram to fall into a deep prophetic sleep:

And when the sun was going down a deep sleep fell upon Avram and lo, dread, a great darkness fell upon him. (Bereshit 15:12)

These are the five exiles which will befall the Jews in the future: "dread" – this is Edom [the Roman Empire]; "darkness" – this is Yavan [the Greek Empire]; "great" – this is Madai [the Persian Empire]; "fell" – this is Bavel [the Babylonian Empire]. "Upon him": This is Yishmael [the Arab Empire]. Only then will Ben David, the Mashiach, come. How do we know? Because it says (Tehillim 132:18): "I will clothe his enemies with shame, but his crown will shine upon him." At the end of days, just before the Mashiach arrives, I will make the enemies wear garments of shame. Then his [the Mashiach's] crown will shine upon him [Israel and all the good nations of the world], (*Yalkut Shimoni* ad loc.).

When God blesses Avram, He says:

I will bless you and I will greatly multiply your seed as the stars of the heaven and as the sand which is upon the seashore. And your seed shall possess the gates of his enemy [*oyvav*]. (Bereshit 22:17)

Who is your enemy? The descendants of Yishmael, son of Avram and Hagar. When Rivka is asked to marry Yitzchak, her family tells her: Our sister, may you become thousands of myriads, and may your descendants inherit the gates of those that hate them [*sonav*]" (Bereshit 24:60). Who are the haters of Israel? The descendants of Esav, the son of Rivka and Yitzchak. What is the difference between enemies and haters? The word *oyev* (enemy) refers to the Arab nations, while *soné* (hater) refers to Edom, the sons of Esav (the Roman Empire, which is often identified with anti-Semitism) in the West. The enemy is more evil than the hater, since the hater will do evil but will have mercy (on himself), while the enemy's animosity is eternal, and he will not spare himself when he tries to kill Jews. Therefore, he is called *oyev* because this word is philologically related to the expression *oy va-avoy,* because somebody who falls into the hands of the descendants of Yishmael will cry *"Oy va-avoy"* [How terrible!]. (Rabbenu Bachya, ad loc.)[2]

From Tehillim 124:

A Song of Ascents by David. Had God not been with us – let Israel declare it now – had God not been with us when men rose up against us, then they would have swallowed us alive when their anger was kindled against us. Then the waters would have swallowed us alive.

You know that there are four exiles. But know that as the redemption draws closer, the Jews will have their final exile with

---

[2] This is my personal interpretation of Rabbenu Bachya's observations so as to make them intelligible. For a completely different interpretation of these verses see the Vilna Gaon's work, *Aderet Eliyahu,* on Parashat Ha'azinu.

Yishmael. This is the reason why he is called Yishmael, because the Jews will cry with painful cries and God will answer them (Yishma-El). If you ask me: Why the sons of Yishmael? I answer: Because the children of Yishmael never constituted a normal nation and were not able to dominate the West, but rather were always living in deserts. Consequently, they started to envy the other nations of the world, and at the end of days they will try to show their power and come out of their tents and try to conquer Israel and the whole world. And then we will sing: "Had God not been with us when men rose up against us, they would have swallowed us alive. Our souls escaped like a bird from the hunter's snare, the snare broke and we escaped. Our help is through the name of God, Maker of heaven and earth." (Tehillim 124) In that way, this exile will be different from all exiles before since they will try to use ways to destroy Israel as have never been tried before and God's interference will be clear." (Rabbi Chaim Vital, pupil of Rabbi Yitzchak Luria, the Arizal, in his seventeenth-century work, *Etz ha-da'at tov*).[3]

---

[3] Free translation. I am indebted for this source to Rabbi Yitzchak Bernstein *z"l* of London.

39

PRAYERS FOR THE WICKED

June 24, 2004

As THE WINDS OF WAR with Iraq draw closer, despite our understandable concern with our own security, committed Jews have a special obligation to think about what others might not wish to think about: the enormous loss of life that this war is surely going to cause among those who are or are not on our side of the conflict.

First of all there is the small Jewish community of Baghdad, which finds itself on the wrong side of the conflict and will most likely incur many losses when war breaks out. Then there are the many Iraqis who oppose Saddam and who would like to live in peace with their neighbors. Others whom Saddam silenced on pain of death or who were brainwashed and manipulated by his regime will also pay a heavy price. Finally, the lives of many innocent people – women and children, together with American and British soldiers – are at risk.

As we consider this, we would do well to listen to the words of the Netziv, Rabbi Naftali Zvi Yehudah Berlin, the last dean of the Volozhin Yeshiva, the most prestigious Talmudic institution in Eastern Europe before World War II.

In his magnum opus, *Ha'amek Davar*, the Netziv asks why the sages also called the book of Bereshit *Sefer ha-Yashar*, the book of those who are straight. His response is telling:[1]

> The reason for this is the great praise that the Torah bestows on
> the patriarchs. Not only were they righteous and pious far
> beyond the norm, but they also were uncompromising when it

---

[1] See his introduction to Bereshit.

came to straightforwardness and honesty. The patriarchs dealt pleasantly with the most heinous idol worshippers of their time and were concerned with their welfare. We see this in the case of Avraham, who prayed for the wellbeing of the wicked people of Sedom (Bereshit 18) even though he abhorred their actions, just as a man hates the wicked deeds of his son but still seeks his wellbeing. Therefore, Avraham was called Father of the Nations. We see it in the case of Yitzchak, who appeased the wicked shepherds who stole his water wells and moved elsewhere rather than fight with them (chapter 26). Likewise in the case of Yaakov, who treated his wicked father-in-law, Lavan, with mercy while the latter constantly fooled him and sought to destroy his family (chapters 29–31).

The Netziv continues that this is the very reason why the book of Bereshit is called Sefer ha-Yashar. While very few mitzvot are found in this book, the example of the Patriarchs stands out as a constant reminder of what God demands of Jews: constant concern even for the wicked. This does not mean that one should not fight wicked people when they become a real threat. Not to do so is clearly forbidden. Even Avraham fought a war against several wicked kings and killed them (chapter 14). Nevertheless, at the same time he showed unusual sensitivity for the wicked once he saw that they were no longer any real threat.

As we think about the possible war with Iraq, we should remind ourselves of the many innocent people who may be killed. While this war might be necessary in order to remove one of the most dangerous men of our time, still we should imitate Avraham and pray not only for ourselves and our soldiers but also for the many innocent people in Iraq who may lose their lives together with American and British soldiers. Following Avraham's example, we should even pray for those wicked people who are not a direct threat to us – that they repent and not be harmed.

After all, one of the great lessons of Jewish tradition is that all human beings carry the dream of God that one day they may become righteous. They incorporate the divine anticipation of great things to come. Human beings always carry the possibility of surprise and are not restricted by a foregone conclusion. Each person, even a wicked one, has the ability to change and repent.

40

TOWARD A SOLUTION

July 24, 2005

THE INTERPRETATION OF HISTORY is a delicate matter, particularly when one tries to understand the present. In his work *Clio,* Charles Péguy (1873–1914) said that it is impossible to write ancient history because we lack source materials, and it is impossible to write modern history because we have too many. This applies even more to religious people. Trying to understand the hand of God behind historical and present events is like putting one's ear to a seashell and listening to a perpetual murmur coming from waves far beyond the shore. Since the present is rolled up into countless impenetrable folds, any attempt to understand it seems to be doomed to failure from the start.

Our sages teach us that one may, with caution, use the Torah as a guide to decipher certain events. Although this undertaking carries great risks, it may give us some understanding and grant us some guidance to deal with our current challenges.

The debate about the Gaza withdrawal shows that both sides reflect competing nightmares. Opponents of the withdrawal, including top military experts, fear that the Palestinians will be encouraged to start a new, even more perilous intifada since their earlier terrorist attacks were most successful and forced Israel out. Supporters of the withdrawal are terrified that Israel will become a pariah state in which the army will be forced to violate its basic ethical standards and international pressure will grow for a one-state solution. Both nightmares are highly realistic. Each side has strong, convincing arguments. Opponents wonder how the Israeli government can prevent Gaza from becoming a terrorist state, especially when Egypt is entrusted with policing the Philadelphi corridor and the Palestinians possess a seaport and an airport. What will Israel do when rockets strike Ashkelon or even Ben Gurion Airport? Will it decide to reoccupy Gaza and northern Samaria? If so, there will be many more Israeli casualties and the withdrawal will have gained us nothing.

Those who support the withdrawal claim that it is impossible to keep millions of Palestinians under Israeli control. This will ultimately force Israel to expel them (a complete impossibility) or to continue to rule over them against their will and consequently be forced to give them full civil rights and liberties, which in the long run will sign Israel's death warrant as a Jewish state.

As such it becomes clear that the Palestinian problem has become Israel's catch-22, to which no solution seems to be possible. It seems that any solution will lead to a nightmare. From any angle, the Israeli government is confronted with a huge problem that will not go away.

In Parashat Ha'azinu (Devarim 32:20–21), the Torah discusses the severe consequences that the people of Israel will suffer if they do not live up to their religious and moral mission. God warns that in that case, He will withdraw His active and protective presence from the Jewish people. While introducing this possibility the Torah suddenly mentions the following scenario:

> And I said: I will hide My face from them,
> And I will see what their end will be.
> They are a generation of confusion [or reversals],
> Children in whom one cannot trust.
> They have aroused My jealousy
> with a non-god.
> They have angered Me with their nullities.
> *So I will cause them envy by a non-nation,*
> with a scoundrel nation.
> I will provoke them and create resentment.
> (emphasis mine)

This extraordinary, surprising text seems to suggest that when Israel fails to live up to its religious and moral commitment, it will unwittingly cause the creation of a nation – a non-nation – that, without any historical claims, will appear from nowhere. It will provoke Israel through great resentment that

Israel will not be able to escape. Only a return to Jewish values, religious commitment and a high standard of ethics will force this nation to stop wreaking havoc on the Jewish people.

Since there is little to no evidence that the Palestinians have any historical roots *as a nation,* one cannot escape the impression that the Torah may be sending a message to present-day Israel, warning it of the dire consequences it will suffer if it does not take care of its moral and spiritual condition.

The sudden and completely unexpected appearance of the Palestinian people, of which nobody had heard previously, has now become the focal point of much of the Middle East's troubles and has made the security situation in Israel complicated and precarious. Many feel that it has jeopardized the Jewish claim to its homeland and that it tries to undermine the Jewish people's capacity to live there in peace while destroying its credibility in the eyes of the world. In this new climate, any attempt by Israel to make peace is turned on its head and used to prove Israel's aggressive intentions. The absurdity is so apparent that one is forced to look for reasons beyond the scope of politics.

It is difficult to deny that as Israel's obsession to become a nation like all other nations has increased and more people have become less interested in their unique Jewish roots, its security issues have become more complex.

As calls come from Israeli officials to replace Israel's national anthem, "Hatikva," with a non-Zionist text and to remove the Magen David from its flag, as Israeli academicians teach anti-Zionist, anti-Jewish texts and philosophies and Israeli society becomes more obsessed with Western hedonist culture with its new idols of money and sex, Israel is putting its very existence at risk. It is not at all surprising to see a severe increase of crime in Israeli schools and streets (something that for years was a non-issue) as Israel loses its Jewish identity – the only reason for its existence.

Still more painful is the realization that in the absence of a strong religious inspirational Israeli leadership, Israel falls victim more and more to its own undoing, believing that the de-judaizing of its people will be its salvation. It could make no greater mistake. While we fully realize that Israelis are not going to take up a religious lifestyle en masse, throughout history the Jewish people has always respected its tradition, culture and values, and been deeply proud of its Jewishness. This respect and pride are vanishing among many segments of society and are being replaced by a hollow and cheap Israelism that, if it is not stopped, will undermine the very existence of the State.

One is reminded of the prophet Yechezkel's words:

> As for what enters your mind, it shall not be. As for what you say: We will be like the nations, like the families of the land. But I will rule over you with a strong hand. I will make you pass under the rod and bring you into the bond of the covenant. Then you will know that I am the Lord. (20:32–38)

Yet here lies our greatest reason for optimism. If our interpretation is correct, the verses cited above prove that what is now happening to the Jewish people and to the State of Israel is not the result of random forces or political turmoil. They prove as clearly as can be that God is in charge and that His providence is at work through its very apparent absence. Therefore, the solution to Israel's problems is easy to find. The people of Israel must rediscover their roots and realize that the covenant between God and the Jewish people is very much alive and must be kept. May God grant us that wisdom.

ISRAEL AND THE NATIONS
REFLECTIONS ON A WAR

August 9, 2006

When humankind ceased heeding the words of the Hebrew prophets, it invented the media.

A MIDRASH[1] SPEAKS OF SEVENTY ANGELS, also called princes, who are in charge of the seventy nations of the world. Each of these princes supervises his own nation and acts as its spokesman before the Throne of God. When the princes' respective nations are embattled, they too fight against each other, and when their nations live in peace, they are also at peace.

These princes are the symbols of various national ideologies and the contributions they can make towards the betterment of humankind. If the princes and their nations live up to these tasks, they will ascend the mighty ladder of history. If they fail and turn into dictators and dictatorships, using their power in order to nourish the illusions and deceits of a false idealism, they will fall. This will occur either in the form of lightning that flings them into the abyss of nothingness, or as gradually as a steady rain, which carries them little by little to the same end. This is the time when these princes forget who they are and what their function is. They vaunt their arrogance, each one imagining himself to be the supreme master. But the hand of their Master is over them. This is what happened to the ancient Egyptians, the Romans, the Greeks and many others.

---

[1] *Vayikra Rabbah* 29, *Pirkei de-Rabbi Eliezer,* Chapter 35.

At that time there was one nation, the Jews, which irritated them more than anybody else. This nation entered into their territories and dispersed among them, causing them infinite trouble with their moral demands and teachings. This peculiar people has a charge from heaven that makes all human beings responsible for their own actions. Its teachings oppose the egoism, illusions and deceits that these nations have adopted. As a result, the nations call for the destruction of this disturbing people. Its voice, reflecting the voice from Above, must be silenced so that these nations' consciences can rest free of guilt. Even as they resist their own destiny, they must destroy those who brought that destiny to mind.

But how can they accomplish that goal without feeling guilty about it? There is only one way: by delegitimizing them. They must prove to the world that the Jews are no better and, in fact, worse than they are themselves. Only when it can be proven that the Jews are also guilty of massacre and genocide can their voice be silenced. And so the nations look for an accusation, but do not find one easily. How can they create an impossible situation for the Jews so that they will be found guilty no matter how they respond?

They concluded that the best way would be to force the Jews into a struggle with another people against whom they must defend themselves in order to survive. But it could not be just another people; it had to be an underdog, and conditions had to be such that the Jews would have no choice but to take up arms and fight this so-called defenseless people. If such a defenseless people could not be found, it had to be artificially created.

And so it was. And the world, or at least a good part of it, fell right into this plot and consequently lost its common sense and moral fiber. In fact, it turned bizarre. With a few significant exceptions the world, governments, media and UN bureaucrats turned into an Orwellian moral universe. It stopped thinking, turned everything on its head, changed the victim into the aggressor and began to rewrite history with one goal: to delegitimize the Jews, whose very existence reminds them of their moral obligations.

Today, thousands of rockets attack the cities of Israel, every one of them designed to kill and maim. (That only dozens of people have been killed instead of thousands is a complete miracle!) Nearly two million people are forced to sit in shelters, their lives ruined and their economy destroyed, while all that the world, led by the media, does is to accuse this tiny country of "responding disproportionately" to its enemy and of deliberately killing children in the southern Lebanon town of Qana where the citizens had been warned again and again by the Israeli army (by leaflets, radio and even by phone messages!) to leave that town and others in order to avoid being harmed. (Why did the building in Qana collapse seven hours after it was attacked? Did Hizbullah perhaps detonate another bomb inside so that the building would finally collapse on the unfortunate inhabitants and the world would accuse Israel?)

The insanity of today's international outcry is that there is indeed a lack of proportion in this war. Hizbullah is deliberately trying to create many civilian casualties on both sides, while Israel does all it can to minimize them. Israel sends its ground troops into Lebanon in order to prevent the loss of innocent Lebanese lives, paying a heavy price in the lives of its own soldiers. Hizbullah deliberately hides its fighters, rockets and entire infrastructure among Lebanese civilians, risking as many Lebanese lives as possible. All that the international community can do is speak of Israel's atrocities, in some cases even comparing them to the Nazis in the Holocaust. This is in itself nothing less than anti-Semitism.

However, the cause of this madness stems from a deeper level. An unrecognized, latent hatred of biblical moral values is what makes those nations and their media turn against Israel. What many people do not recognize is that they are still unable to forgive the Jewish people for having given them Jesus and therefore Christianity. It was Jesus who, deeply influenced by the moral tradition of Judaism, brought them some of it. It is against this morality that they rebel. It is of Jesus that they are afraid. They spit on the Jews not because they killed Jesus, but because they gave him to the world. This is the root of much of Western anti-Semitism. As the proverb states: "To the eye of enmity, virtue appears as the ugliest blemish" (*Shah Nameh*).

ANTI-SEMITISM

EUROPE AND ANTI-SEMITISM

November 4, 2004

As Europe becomes more anti-Semitic and consequently more antagonistic towards the State of Israel, there is a need for a careful assessment of the nature of anti-Semitism.

In his book *Moses and Monotheism,* Sigmund Freud tried to understand Jewish history and the formation of the people of Israel and Judaism. While this work has come under heavy criticism by important scholars due to many unproven assumptions, it is remarkable that many theologians and sociologists are in agreement with Freud's understanding of anti-Semitism:

> One might say they [the anti-semitic peoples] are badly christened; under the thin veneer of Christianity, they have remained what their ancestors were, barbarically polytheistic. They have not yet overcome their grudge against the new religion which was forced upon them and they have projected it on the source from which Christianity came to them. The hatred of Judaism is, at bottom, hatred for Christianity.[1]

This is a profound observation. When we look at the history of Christianity and of Western civilization, it becomes clear that both are deeply indebted to Judaism for many of its moral values. Yet these values were not easily accepted. In fact, they were often contested, ridiculed and fought against. Millions of Christians raised in the pagan world of Rome were unable to abandon the morally questionable practices and beliefs of that

---

[1] Sigmund Freud. *Moses and Monotheism.* New York: Knopf, 1939, 145. Also see Will Herberg, *Judaism and Modern Man.* New York: Atheneum, 1973, 284.

world. As a result, Christianity became entangled in many polytheistic beliefs, giving rise to a religious society that was never at ease with the fundamental concepts of monotheism. This resulted in a complex psycho-religious condition that caught millions of Christians in an uncomfortable situation, unable to distinguish between authentic monotheism and its moral demands and pagan practices. With the exception of some of Christianity's most erudite thinkers, most of its spokesmen could not free themselves from this influence.

In 1948, the well-known Christian thinker A. Roy Eckhardt asked whether the Christian church could ever supersede the synagogue in the struggle against paganism. To this he answered "No, because the church is itself subject to pagan distortions. Against all idolatries Judaism protests: Hear O, Israel, the Lord our God is one Lord."[2]

He and others, among them the famous Protestant thinker Paul Tillich, responded that there would always be a need for Judaism to exist because Judaism is the corrective against the paganism that goes along with Christianity.[3]

Therefore, Sigmund Freud's observation is not surprising. Not only was it a near impossibility for Christians to accept the oneness of God, but the consequences were even more unsettling. The ethical demand of this God on human beings required much self-discipline and therefore encountered strong opposition. The bottom line was the awareness that Jesus was a Jew who incorporated much of Jewish ethical values into his teachings, which turned many an early Christian against authentic Christianity.

In his study of anti-Semitism, Zionist leader and author Harry Sacher wrote in 1940 that anti-Semitism is Europe's revenge on the prophets. It is because the Jew brought ethics and the concept of sin into the western world. The European Christian cannot forgive the Jew for giving him Christianity. It is not because they are good Christians that the Europeans are instinctively anti-Semites. It is because they are bad Christians – in reality, repressed pagans.[4]

---

[2] A. Roy Eckhardt, *Christianity and the Children of Israel*. New York: Columbia University Press, 1948, 146–147.

[3] Quoted by Eckhardt, op. cit. 146–147.

[4] Harry Sacher, "Revenge on the Prophets: A Psychoanalysis of Anti-Semitism." *Menorah Journal* 28/3 (Fall 1940).

It is of Jesus that the anti-Semites are afraid. They attack those who are responsible for the birth and spread of Christianity. They spit on the Jews not because they were Jesus-killers but because they are Jesus-givers. Their hatred for Jews is the result of their hatred for Jesus.

Part of the Western world has always tried to effect a divorce between the two since it could not accept that both are really one. It therefore called for the destruction of Judaism in order to obliterate the uncertainty of its conscience and the reality of its guilt. Because it wished to resist its own destiny, it needed to destroy those who brought that destiny to mind. Since the Jews spoiled the anti-Semites' lives by emphasizing the ethical demands of law and the cross, the bad Christian re-enacts the crucifixion of his savior by torturing and killing Jews, who represent for him the teachings of the Jew, Jesus.

When we look at Europe, we see an increase in pagan attitudes and a decrease of Judeo-Christian values. Therefore, it is not surprising that Europe is headed for more trouble and committed to an ongoing delegitimization of Israel. Jews need to realize that they are hated because of Judaism's stand on paganism and its unfaltering commitment to morality, and they should be proud of it. At least they should be hated for the right reasons.

WHY THEY HATE US IN THE HAGUE[1]

May 27, 2004

Some people like the Jews, and some do not. But no thoughtful man can deny the fact that they are, beyond any question, the most formidable and the most remarkable race which has appeared in the world. – Winston Churchill[2]

The Jew is that sacred being who has brought down from heaven the everlasting fire, and has illumined with it the entire world. He is the religious source, spring, and fountain out of which all the rest of the peoples have drawn their beliefs and their religions – Leo Tolstoy[3]

It was in vain that we locked them up for several hundred years behind the walls of the Ghetto. No sooner were their prison gates unbarred than they easily caught up with us, even on those paths which we opened up without their aid. – Anatole Leroy Beaulieu[4]

---

[1] Written in May 2004, when the International Court in The Hague condemned Israel for building a wall to protect its citizens against terrorist attacks.
[2] Quoted by Geoffrey Wheatcroft in The Controversy of Zion: Jewish Nationalism, the Jewish State, and the Unresolved Jewish Dilemma. London: Sinclair-Stevenson, 1996, xi.
[3] Leo Tolstoy, quoted by Chief Rabbi J.H. Hertz in *A Book of Jewish Thought.* Oxford University Press: 1966, 135.
[4] Anatole Leroy Beaulieu, French historian. *Israel among the Nations: A Study of the Jews and Anti-Semitism.* 1893. 162, 174.

The Jew gave us the Outside and the Inside – our outlook and our inner life. We can hardly get up in the morning or cross the street without being Jewish. We dream Jewish dreams and hope Jewish hopes. Most of our best words, in fact – new, adventure surprise, unique, individual, person, vocation, time, history, future, freedom, progress, spirit, faith hope, justice – are the gifts of the Jews. – Thomas Cahill[5]

One of the gifts of the Jewish culture to Christianity is that it has taught Christians to think like Jews, and any modern man who has not learned man to think as though he were a Jew can hardly be said to have learned to think at all. – William Rees-Mogg[6]

It is certain that in certain parts of the world we can see a peculiar people, separated from the other peoples of the world and this is called the Jewish people.... This people is not only of remarkable antiquity but has also lasted for a singularly long time.... For whereas the people of Greece and Italy, of Sparta, Athens and Rome and others who came so much later have perished so long ago, these still exist, despite the efforts of so many powerful kings who have tried a hundred times to wipe them out, as their historians testify, and as can easily be judged by the natural order of things over such a long spell of years. They have always been preserved, however, and their preservation was foretold.... My encounter with this people amazes me. – Blaise Pascal[7]

The Jewish vision became the prototype for many similar grand designs for humanity, both divine and man made. The

---

[5] Thomas Cahill, *The Gifts of the Jews*. New York: Doubleday, 1998, 240–241.
[6] William Rees-Mogg, *The Times*, quoted by Chief Rabbi Sir Jonathan Sacks in *Radical Then, Radical Now*. London: Harpercollins, 2000, 4.
[7] Blaise Pascal, *Pensées*. Translated by A.J. Krailsheimer. Harmondsworth: Penguin, 1968. 171, 176–177.

Jews, therefore, stand at the center of the perennial attempt to give human life the dignity of a purpose. – Paul Johnson[8]

As long as the world lasts, all who want to make progress in righteousness will come to Israel for inspiration as to the people who had the sense for righteousness most glowing and strongest. – Matthew Arnold[9]

IT IS DIFFICULT, IRRITATING AND UNCOMFORTABLE for many nations of the world to live in the presence of the Jews. The Jews put the world to shame, since they have done things that are beyond the imaginable. They have become moral strangers since the day their ancestor Avraham introduced the world to high ethical standards and to the awe of Heaven. They brought the world the Ten Commandments, which many nations would rather defy. They violated the rules of history by staying alive, totally at odds with common sense and historical evidence.

They outlived all their enemies, including vast empires such as the Romans and the Greeks. They infuriated the world with their return to their homeland after two thousand years of exile and the murder of six million of their brothers and sisters. They aggravated much of humankind by building, in the wink of an eye, a democratic state that others could not create in hundreds of years. They built living monuments such as the duty to be holy and the privilege of serving one's fellow human beings. They participated in every human progressive endeavor – science, medicine, psychology or any other discipline, out of all proportion to their actual numbers. They gave the world the Bible and Christianity its savior.

The Jews taught the world not to accept the world as it is but to transform it, yet few nations wanted to listen. The Jews also introduced the world to one God, yet only a minority wanted to draw the proper moral conclusions.

---

[8] Paul Johnson, *A History of the Jews.* London: Weidenfeld & Nicolsohn, 1987, 2.
[9] Matthew Arnold, *Literature and Dogma.* London: Smithy, Elder: 1876, 58.

Many citizens of the world realize that they would have been lost without the Jews. Even as their subconscious reminds them how much of Western civilization is framed in terms of concepts that the Jews first articulated, they do everything possible to suppress it. They deny that Jews remind them that life has a higher purpose and that human beings need to be honorable. It is simply too much to handle, too embarrassing to admit, and too difficult to live by.

Many people decided to do whatever they could in order to find a stick with which to beat the Jews. Their goal was to prove that Jews are as immoral and as guilty of massacre and genocide as some of them are. They do all this in order to hide and justify their own failure even to protest when six million Jews were murdered and to wipe out the moral conscience of which the Jews remind them.

Indeed, they found a stick. Nothing could be more gratifying for them than to find the Jews in a struggle with another people (who are completely terrorized by their own leaders) against whom the Jews have no choice but to defend themselves in order to survive. With great satisfaction, the world allows and even initiates the rewriting of history so as to fuel the rage of yet another people against the Jews. This despite the fact that the nations understand very well that peace between the parties could have come a long time ago if only the Jews had been given a fair chance. Instead, they happily jumped on the wagon of hatred so as to justify their jealousy of the Jews and their own incompetence in dealing with their own moral issues.

When Jews look at the bizarre play taking place in The Hague, they can only smile as this artificial game once more proves how the world paradoxically admits the Jews' uniqueness. By their need to undermine the Jews, they actually raise them up.

> The study of history of Europe during the past centuries teaches us one uniform lesson: That the nations which received and in any way dealt fairly and mercifully with the Jew have prospered; and that the nations that have tortured and oppressed him have written out their own curse. – Olive Schreiner[10]

---

[10] Olive Schreiner, quoted by Chief Rabbi J.H. Hertz, 177, 180.

If there is any honour in all the world that I should like, it would be to be an honorary Jewish citizen. – A.L. Rowse[11]

---

[11] A.L. Rowse, *Historians I Have Known*. London: Duckworth, 1995.

THE BIRTH OF AMALEK AND THE MAKING OF
AN ENEMY

May 12, 2004

JUDAISM'S MAJOR ENEMY in biblical times was the nation of Amalek. Symbolically, this nation is the personification of all evil, racism and anti-Semitism. Amalek was seared into the Jewish consciousness as the first enemy that the people of Israel encountered after they crossed the Red Sea. The Amalekites attacked the Jews several times, causing much disaster and destruction. It was not only that Amalek dared to fight the Israelites but also the strategy that they used that revealed its moral bankruptcy. They attacked the Israelites from the back, focusing first on the weakest and most fatigued of the people. Afterwards, they drew Israel into immoral sexual practices. Using tactics similar to later forms of anti-Semitism, they operated in secrecy (see Shemot 17:8–16).

Later in Jewish history it was Haman the Amalekite, known from the Purim story, who showed the evil intentions of this nation once again. The Jewish nation was saved from him only through a miracle.

Who was Amalek? The Torah tells us that the first Amalek was the son of Esau's son Eliphaz (Bereshit 36:2). He was the eponymous ancestor of the Amalekite people. Eliphaz had taken a concubine by the name of Timna, the sister of Lotan (Bereshit 36:12), a son of Seir the Horite who lived in the land of Seir where Esau had settled. Timna became pregnant and gave birth to a son, Amalek.

The Talmud inquires why Timna married Eliphaz and provides us with an extraordinary statement:

Timna desired to become a proselyte, so she went to Avraham, Yitzchak and Yaakov, but they did not accept her. So she went and became a concubine to Eliphaz, the son of Esau, saying: "I would rather be a servant to this people than mistress of another nation." From her descended Amalek, who afflicted Israel. Why? Because they should not have repulsed her (*Sanhedrin* 99b).

This talmudic statement is difficult to understand. After all, it is not clear why the Patriarchs would not allow her to join the Jewish people, especially when we are informed that they went out of their way to convert as many people as possible (see Rashi on Bereshit 12:5). It is remarkable that the Sages were not afraid to point their fingers at our Patriarchs. Their commitment to truth outdid their love for the Patriarchs. They could have suppressed this story or said that Timna was unworthy. The fact that they did not shows their integrity and uncompromising objectivity when truth demands it. We do not know of any other tradition that has shown such integrity when it dealt with its protagonists. Even more surprisingly, they considered the refusal by our Patriarchs to allow Timna's conversion as the reason why Israel was afflicted later by the offspring of the first Amalek.

This reminds us of a statement by the Ramban in which he discusses the reasons why the Arab nations have shown so much revulsion towards the Jewish people. After Hagar became pregnant by Avraham and began to look down upon Sarah (who was infertile), Sarah complains to Avraham about her.

"Then Avraham said to Sarah: 'See, your handmaid is in your hands, do to her that which is good in your eyes.' Then Sarah treated her harshly and she [Hagar] fled from before her" (Bereshit 16:6).

The Ramban's comment is revealing:

Sarah our mother sinned in dealing harshly with her handmaid and Avraham sinned, too, by allowing her to do so. God heard her [Hagar's] afflictions and gave her a son who was destined to be a lawless person, who would bring suffering on the seed of Avraham and Sarah with all kinds of affliction.

Later, Rabbi Shmuel Mohilever, the rabbi of Bialystok and one of the great leaders of the Hibbat Zion movement, made a similar comment when the Turkish government was about to banish from the Jewish settlements those Russian Jews who had moved to the country but had not taken Ottoman citizenship. He cried out, saying:

> It is because of "Cast out this slave woman [Hagar] and her son" (21:10) that the Muslims – the children of Yishmael – the son of Hagar, would now cast out the sons of Sarah from our land!

Once more we are confronted with an uncompromising commitment to truth. Even at the risk of putting our spiritual heroes into a compromising light, the Sages did not shrink from criticizing them. Once more we are confronted with a daring statement that because of this, Jews encounter the hostility of their enemies thousands of years later.

On another occasion, the Sages spoke once again of the injustice done to the ancestors of Haman. They stressed that much of Haman's hatred for Jews resulted from the way Yaakov had dealt with his brother Esav. On the words in the Megilla:

> When Mordechai understood all that was done, he tore his clothes and put on sackcloth and ashes. Going out into the midst of the city, he cried a loud and bitter cry (4:1–2).

The *Midrash Rabbah* dares to make the following observation:

> Yaakov caused Esav to cry one bitter cry [when Yitzchak informed Esav that the blessing originally meant for him had gone to Yaakov instead], as it is written: 'When Esau heard the words of his father, he cried an exceedingly loud and bitter cry' (Bereshit 27:34). This was paid back to him [Yaakov] in Shushan when his offspring [Mordechai] cried a loud and bitter cry [because of the great trouble that Haman, the offspring of Amalek, caused the Jews].

The Sages show that the injustice Yaakov did Esav (by stealing the blessings due the first-born) was responsible for the great pain that the Jews suffered at Haman's hands.

Why, indeed, did the Sages emphasize this injustice by our forefathers? Why not keep quiet? No doubt they did not want to justify the anti-Semitism of the Amalekites or the Arab nations. Neither did they want to embarrass the Patriarchs, knowing quite well that they were men of great spirituality.

We believe that a careful look in the Torah may provide us with the answer. In Devarim (25:19), the Torah demands that the Jews "erase the memory of Amalek from under heaven; do not forget." As is well known, this commandment seems to be a paradox. How can one erase the memory of Amalek if one is not allowed to forget what he did?

However, the Torah may be hinting not only at Amalek's monstrous deeds but also at the injustice our ancestors did to Esav and Timna. "Blot out the memory of Amalek" may mean that we are obligated to uproot from within ourselves the ways in which our ancestors dealt with Amalek's ancestors. "Do not forget that this behavior caused ongoing pain to your ancestors." In other words, the Torah teaches us to erase Amalek's memory by making sure that no such nation will ever appear again. This can only be accomplished when we do not repeat the mistakes of our great ancestors. People create their own enemies, and Jews must teach themselves and others to prevent this by all means.

However, this cannot be done once and for all. It is a constant demand that should never be forgotten. This is the meaning of "Erase the memory of Amalek; do not forget."

Therefore, our sages' earlier critical observations are crucial. While there is no way to justify any Amalekite or Arab anti-Semitism in later times, we need to understand that it all started because of injustices done to them thousands of years ago. By emphasizing the injustice that our ancestors did and the disastrous repercussions which followed, the sages gave us the means to fulfill the mitzvah of blotting out Amalek's memory by constantly reminding us not to forget how they became our enemies.

REMBRANDT, THE HOLOCAUST AND THE QUEST FOR AUTHENTICITY [1]

May 7, 2006

ON THE EVE OF YOM HA-SHOAH (Holocaust Heroes and Remembrance Day), I think of Rembrandt's superb painting, "Large Self-Portrait," which I believe is exhibited at the Vienna Art Museum. It held me spellbound when I first saw it. But on Yom ha-Shoah it invites thoughts that penetrate deep into my very being. When I try to do the impossible and imagine what happened to the members of my family and to millions of other Jews who perished in the Holocaust, Rembrandt's self-portrait wakes me up from my slumber.

On Yom ha-Shoah one can virtually smell the blood of the six million Jews, including nearly two million children, who were murdered. As I walk around at Yad Vashem in Jerusalem, I see the faces of many of them, and it is not difficult to imagine that these children could have been mine. After all, I missed the Holocaust by a hair's-breadth.

After such a moment of reflection, Rembrandt's portrait looks more powerful than ever. He was twelve when the Thirty Years' War began and completed this painting four years after the devastation of Europe ended. In those days there was no market for Rembrandt's many self-portraits. They were not painted for clients or with any hope that they would be sold. This was integrity embodied. The artist painted masterpieces without regard for what would pay or even advance a career. They were created because there was no way to suppress them in the mind of Rembrandt's genius. They represent a relentless overflow of authenticity.

---

[1] Written on Yom ha-Shoah, April 25, 2006.

At a time like this, I think of the millions who were murdered during the Holocaust and ask myself what I have done with the life that was granted to me, but not to millions of others. True, one needs to earn a living, but Rembrandt reminds us that if we want to really live, we need complete integrity and authenticity. It is all about making a real contribution to the world without regard for gain, and even being prepared to pay the price when one realizes that one's choice may seriously impede one's standing in the conventional community. At least one must make sure that one can look at oneself in the mirror at the end of one's life and say: I *lived* my life and did not just pass through it.

We live in a world where there are too many beauty parlors. We have created a world of cosmetics where the real skin of human beings is hidden and we are told that this is what life is all about. People try to convince us that we live in a world of pandemonium, that it is wishful thinking to believe in real virtue and integrity and that the only way to survive is to graft goodness onto selfishness. They say that the only way to survive is to be suspicious and that authenticity is a non-starter. We are told to be more evasive and smooth-tongued so as to make it. Because of this, human beings have engaged in a life of fear and need to believe that the ambush is the normal dwelling place of all humankind.

Rembrandt lived among the Jews of Amsterdam. Since he had a close relationship with them, surely he must have heard of the many Portuguese and Spanish Jews who were persecuted by the Inquisition or who fled Spain and Portugal because they knew that one needs to be authentic in order to live. They must have taught him that if people are not more than human, then they are less than human, and that the art of being a Jew is to know how to do more than merely live and to become more than a memory. It is our destiny to live for that which is greater than ourselves. Perhaps it was this great message of Judaism that made Rembrandt start painting without thought of gain or career. And so I stand in front of Rembrandt's "Large Self-Portrait" and realize that in the face of the Holocaust I need to create my own self with my integrity intact, without any gain and without fame, so that I will not be put to shame when millions who had no chance to live will ask me what I did with my life. God forbid that I fall silent.

BOYCOTTING ISRAEL, SUICIDE AND THE TRAUMA
OF AN ANTI-SEMITE

June 10, 2007

> Some people like the Jews and some do not. But no
> thoughtful man can deny the fact that they are, beyond any
> question, the most formidable and most remarkable race
> which has appeared in the world.
>
> Winston Churchill[1]

THE ANTI-SEMITIC WORLD has a hard time with us Jews and we should have
some pity on all those who try so hard to give us a bad name. Whether it is
those who want to boycott us in the world of academia, journalism,
European governments, in the marketplace or just in the streets of daily life,
we must admit that we are a real nuisance.

It not easy to live with us Jews. We are troublemakers and can be quite
irritating. There is no way of escaping this.

The trouble with us Jews is that we constantly do all those things that
one is really not allowed to do. Over thousands of years, we survived
empires that did all they could in order to destroy us, whether it was the
Egyptians, the Romans, the Greeks, the Germans and so on. In the
twentieth century, it looked like they had finally succeeded. The Holocaust
killed six million of us. But instead of disappearing, we Jews decided that
after two thousand years of exile, we wanted to go home and rebuild our
own country. And so we did. What took other nations centuries to build

---

[1] Quoted by Geoffrey Wheatcroft in *The Controversy of Zion: Jewish Nationalism, the
Jewish State, and the Unresolved Jewish Dilemma.* London: Sinclair-Stevenson, 1996, xi.

took us only a few. What was somehow possible we did very quickly, and what was totally impossible took a little longer. Not only did we violate the rules of history in exile, but we also became experts when we had to rebuild our four-thousand-year-old homeland. Who would deny that this is not highly irritating? What a chutzpah!

Now they want to boycott us, but how can they? It would be suicide. After all, a real boycott of Jews would mean much more than boycotting a few Israeli products or some universities. No – the anti-Semites would have to boycott many products on which their lives depend: Medications and tablets against all sorts of illnesses produced by Teva and Abic are only one example. Those who suffer from multiple sclerosis would be in particular trouble, since the Israelis discovered a blood test by which one can distinguish between mild and severe cases. Think of people who suffer from spinal injuries, paralysis, breathing problems, depression, Alzheimer's Disease, Parkinson's Disease, smallpox virus, DNA breakdown, and so on. The Jews in Israel have made major contributions towards helping people around the world, particularly those who suffer from the above-named maladies, live a more or less healthy life.

Were it not for these remarkable Jewish discoveries, most if not all anti-Semites would be seriously ill. Some would have died long ago and therefore would be unable to think of new ways to hurt the Jews and their country. So please have some pity on them. They have quite a difficult time with us!

What about Windows, voice mail, instant-messaging programs (invented by four Jewish kids!), the latest developments for the cellular phone and anti-terror systems, all developed by Jews in this awful, obnoxious country called Israel. Let us not even mention the fact that Israel produces more scientific papers per capita than any other nation and has more start-up companies per rata. It has the highest concentration of hi-tech companies in the world outside Silicon Valley. It ranks second in the world of venture capital funds. Wouldn't that make you jealous? Is there no room to pity the poor anti-Semite? *Nebbich,* without Israel they would not only be ill or dead, but they would not dare to board a plane, be able to use their computers to write their anti-Semitic diatribes or talk on the phone with their fellow anti-Semites!

And then there is this man called Jesus. He was a Jew and he introduced some very important Jewish moral stuff to the Western world. He is at center stage in the New Testament, the most admired book in the lands where millions of anti-Semites live. Not only that: he is the most admired man in the entire West, worshipped by millions as nothing less than the son of God. Imagine – a Jewish boy! And as if this were not enough, everyone knows that if he were alive today, he would not eat at an anti-Semite's home. Instead, he would ask for a kosher restaurant run by Jews with beards and sidelocks. Oy, gevalt! How do you want the anti-Semite to react?

Without some of the Jewish teachings of this man, much of so-called Western civilization would still find itself in a primitive cannibal-like stage in which anti-Semites, sipping coffee in restaurants while thinking about how to become more sophisticated anti-Semites, would have to run so as not to be eaten alive by one of their fellow human beings. But how paradoxical! Anti-Semites run scared from this very man. Why? Because he was the one who brought these Jewish ethics and moral standards, which these anti-Semites would like to destroy, to our western world! Who would not hate the Jews for giving birth to this disturbing man? Anti-Semites do not spit on the Jews because they killed Jesus, but rather because they gave Jesus to the world! They want to re-enact the crucifixion of their own savior by torturing the ones who gave them this irritating Jew. So have some mercy. These are hard times for anti-Semites!

And then, every anti-Semite knows that the USA and Britain would not be what they are today without "their" Jews. They would still look more like jungles with underdeveloped economies, bad health facilities and lack of scientific discoveries. Their laws, which are so deeply influenced by the Torah and the spirit of the great Jewish prophets – although secularized – would remain unknown, and anti-Semites would not have the freedom of speech that they now enjoy.

No, it does not make sense. Here is a country no larger than a piece of real estate in the Middle East and so small that it is nearly invisible. When one searches for it on a map, one needs a magnifying glass. Its main inhabitants, the Jews, and their brothers and sisters all around the world amount to fewer people than a standard deviation in the Chinese census! Or, as Sir Isaiah Berlin once said, "[The Jews] have enjoyed rather too much history and too little geography." And still, they are one of the oldest nations, if not the oldest, in the world. Most of the time, they lived in foreign countries without an army to protect them, and they were the poorest of the poor. Yet they contribute per capita more to the world that any other nation. Just think of it: would you not become depressed if you were an anti-Semite?

And then this: for as long as they existed, Jews had no heroes such as Julius Caesar, Titus or other men of military might. Instead, they opposed the very heroism that other nations see as their *raison d'être*. In fact, Jews could not understand what there was to admire! Instead, they loved their peace-seeking spiritual leaders such as Moses, Isaiah and Amos. Instead of desiring battles, orgies and other "delicacies," they have an unstoppable passion for learning and knowledge. They are obsessed by their Holy Book, which constantly reprimands them and gives them a hard time. So what can we expect from anti-Semites who realize that the Jews poke fun at all that they, the anti-Semites, hold dear – that they would love the Jews?

Yes – for all these thousands of years, the Jews did not really know how to fight a war (and it still seems that way!). Yet paradoxically, they manage to resist the millions of enemies who surround them. Just like the anti-Semite, everyone knows that the Jews will outlive them, just as they have for the past four thousand years. If that is not irritating, then what is? Indeed, it is as though some mysterious Power is looking after them. Who needs that Power that so many people want to get rid of so that they can "get on with their lives"? Add to this the fact that the anti-Semites make sure that the Jew, his country and his people are the most debated topics in the world, and you understand why they have such a hard time.

So who would not be on the verge of a nervous breakdown? Have some mercy on all of those anti-Semites who must deal with these terrible traumas. Understand their frustration and their need to vent. Oh, yes, and where will they end up? On the couch of a psychiatrist who uses methods developed by a Jew to relieve him of his depression! So, now do you get the picture? *Es ist shver tzu zein an anti-Semite!*[2] Boycott? Come on! Suicide, you mean!

He who laughs last, laughs best.

---

[2] Based on a famous Yiddish saying, "*Es ist schver tsu zein a Yid*" – "It is hard to be a Jew."

JEWISH TRADITION AND ISRAEL

THE SPLITTING OF THE RED SEA AND THE MIRACLE OF THE STATE OF ISRAEL

February 9, 2006

JEWISH HISTORY EXISTS of many epoch-making events. However, these events have not all made an inroad into the consciousness of the Jewish people. In order for this to happen, the event must become what the Jewish philosopher Emil Fackenheim describes a *root experience,* a moment in which the hand of God becomes most apparent through His active participation in Jewish history. Still, this alone is not sufficient to transform an event into a root experience of enduring value. It is also necessary that the experience takes place in front of the multitude, as in the case of the splitting of the Red Sea, when "even the maidservants saw what the prophet Yechezkel ben Buzi could not see." It is not the opening of the heavens but the transformation of the earth that has a decisive effect on all future Jewish generations. However, a third element is necessary above all. Later generations must have access to this vision. Only then can one speak of an actual root experience. If a vision cannot be shared with later generations, it will turn into a claim of the past and lose much of its religious value within Judaism.

In this context we must realize that it is not the conventional understanding of a miracle that is important here. While nobody will deny that the splitting of the Red Sea was a violation of the laws of nature, this is not the source of its religious power or message. The most important quality of a miracle is not that it is supernatural, or super-historical, but that it is a moment which remains miraculous in the eyes of the person to whom it occurred, even when it can be argued away in terms of science and brought into the nexus of nature and normal history. The real power of a miracle is that it is an astonishing experience of an event in which the current system of cause and effect becomes, as it were, transparent, permitting a glimpse of the sphere in which another unrestricted Power is at work. It therefore destroys the security of all knowledge and undoes the normalcy of all that is ordinary. It is the abiding astonishment that is crucial. Religious people stand in wonder; no knowledge or cognition can weaken their astonishment. Any natural explanation will only deepen their wonder. It is in this sense that a historical miracle becomes a root experience and allows later generations to have access to it through its own experience. If it is possible for later generations to relive the experience not because of what happened, but through the way it was perceived, only then can we speak of a miracle.

The establishment of the State of Israel was no doubt an epoch-making event. It is again the completely astonishing nature of this event which stands out – the transformation of the earthliness of the Jewish people into a radically different situation. While miracles no doubt took place to enable it to happen, the most important religious dimension is again the abiding astonishment with this event in terms that could be expected especially after the events of the Holocaust. Only when the establishment of the State of Israel is seen in the light of the miracle at the Red Sea will its fascination continue. And this is exactly where the greatest danger towards Israel's continued existence lies. Just as we are informed that when the miracle at the Red Sea lost its religious impact on the Israelites and normalcy became the call of the day, the Israelites complained that God had left them, so we see a similar component at work in today's Israeli society and leadership. Just as the complaints about the lack of food and water took on a new impetus after the great miracle at the Sea, so we see a mentality of psychological denial and existential dullness in the State of Israel in which many people, most of all its leadership, no longer understand the wonder of the State's very existence. And just as the Israelites in the desert paid a heavy price, so will Israeli society if it does not force itself once again to look through the clouds, see the miracle and rejuvenate itself through it.

48

THERE IS NO MASHIACH WITHOUT A SONG

May 12, 2004

WHEN WE ENTER SYNAGOGUES around the world in order to worship, we are often confronted with a lack of religious enthusiasm. In many synagogues, services are heavy and often a little depressing. It is not always the lack of concentration by the worshippers that makes synagogue services unattractive, but the absence of song and smiles. While prayer is indeed a serious undertaking, our sages teach that the opportunity to speak to the Lord of the Universe is a privilege that should bring us great joy. After all, the idea that human beings of flesh and blood can converse with their Maker has no logical basis. Who are we to speak to the King of Kings?

This is even more true when one contemplates the fact that human beings have the opportunity to praise God. As the great German poet, Johann Wolfgang Goethe, once said, "Wer einen lobt, stellt sich ihm gleich" (He who praises another places himself on the other's level). As Aristotle said, probably referring to Plato: "Everyone may criticize him, but who is permitted to praise him?"

Most interesting is the fact that one of the ways that we can identify the Mashiach is his capacity and willingness to sing. In Tractate *Sanhedrin* 94a, Bar Kappara states that God intended to appoint King Chizkiyahu as the Mashiach – the ultimate redeemer of humankind – but did not.

Chizkiyahu is known as one of the most righteous people in Jewish history. He introduced important religious reforms and was a man of outstanding devotion, committed to the highest level of morality. In fact, he was so successful in his attempt to improve Jewish education that there was "no boy or girl, no man or woman in the land who was not versed in the religious laws of *tahara* and *tuma* (ritual purity and impurity)" (ibid.).

Still, King Chizkiyahu was not even able to teach his own son, the crown prince Menashe, fear of God. The latter was known for his wickedness, and commentators observe that this was because his righteous father did not know how to sing and therefore could not inspire him. We can be sure that Menashe had been given an excellent Jewish education, yet all his learning remained academic and frigid because the warmth of a song did not accompany it.

The sages tell us that King Chizkiyahu did not even sing after he experienced a great miracle that saved Israel from the hands of the wicked Assyrian king, Sancherib (ibid.).

Not being able to sing is considered by our sages as a serious weakness that prevents one from being the Mashiach. Indeed we find that all of King Chizkiyahu's efforts to encourage Jewish learning came to an end after he passed away. Jewish learning and Judaism have no future without a song and a smile.

However, the above needs some clarification. What is there in music that the spoken word lacks and that makes it so important to Jewish tradition?

It may be worthwhile to quote an extraordinary statement by the great rationalist thinker, Maimonides. Discussing human reason and prophecy, he writes:

> I say that there is a limit to human reason, and as long as the soul resides within the body, it cannot grasp what is above nature, for nothing that is immersed in nature can see above it. Reason is limited to the sphere of nature and is unable to understand what is above its limits…. Know that there is a level of knowledge which is higher than all philosophy, namely prophecy. Prophecy is a different source and category of knowledge. Proof and examination are inapplicable to it. If prophecy is genuine then it cannot depend on the validation of reason…. Our faith is based on the principle that the words of Moshe are prophecy and therefore beyond the domain of speculation, validation, argument or proof. Reason is inherently unable to pass judgement in the area from which prophecy originates. It would be like trying to put all the water in the world into a little cup. (Maimonides, *Kovetz teshuvot ha-Rambam ve-*

iggerotav, letter to Rabbi Chisdai, 11, 23a–23b, ed. Lichtenberg, Leipzig: 1859)

Music raises the spoken word to a level that touches prophecy, giving it a taste of the world beyond. Just as there is no way to demonstrate the beauty of music to a deaf person, so there is no way to explain the difference between a spoken word and a sung one unless one sings. Song lifts human beings out of the mundane and gives them a feeling of the imponderable, which is the entrance to joy.

Some people go on a hunger strike in the prison of their minds, starving for God. It is song that will free them.

Abraham Joshua Heschel once said that prayer is our answer to the inconceivable surprise of living. To sing is to know how to stand still and dwell upon a word. While this is true for a song of the individual, it becomes more apparent when a group of people joins in communal song.

When our sages inform us that no one can be the Mashiach unless he is able and willing to sing, it should be a message to all who want to be religious that song should be an important part of their prayers and lives. We are deeply indebted to Sephardic tradition, Chassidism and people like the late Rabbi Shlomo Carlebach, who put song in the center of modern Jewish life. It is time that rabbis of synagogues gave it their full attention, teaching their followers to surprise themselves at what their souls can achieve. Prayer in song makes this possible.

49

THE MYSTERY OF THE SECOND DAY OF YOM TOV: ANOTHER LOOK AT AN OLD PROBLEM[1]

May 7, 2004

ONE OF THE MOST PUZZLING LAWS IN HALACHA is the requirement to observe a second day of Yom Tov in all Jewish communities outside Israel. This was legislated in order to ensure that biblical festivals such as Pesach, Shavuot and Sukkot would be celebrated on the correct date as required by the Torah. This was due to the fact that in ancient times, when the Jewish calendar was not yet fixed to the extent that it is today, it was not always clear which day of the month one actually had to count.

The Sanhedrin, the Supreme Court in Jerusalem, would declare a new month after witnesses had brought evidence that they had just seen the new moon in its first appearance. Immediately, the court would declare this day the first day of the new month. Since this information could not travel quickly enough to Jewish communities outside Israel, it became necessary for these communities to keep two consecutive days of Yom Tov, depending on the day on which the new month had started in Israel. Since a Jewish month can consist of twenty-nine or thirty days, there could be a difference of one day. Also, since biblical festivals always have a fixed date as stated by the Torah, a two-day celebration became necessary.

This law applies to this day. All Jews who live outside Israel must still observe two days on Pesach, Shavuot and Sukkot.

However, the difficulty with this rabbinical decree today is that since the days of Hillel ha-Nasi (fourth century BCE), Jews all over the world have

---

[1] For a short overview of this complicated issue see *Yom tov sheni ke-hilchato* by Rabbi Yerachmiel David Fried and *The Book of Our Heritage* by Eliyahu Kitov, vol. 1, Rosh Chodesh.

been using an official, fixed calendar that does not depend on witnesses. Consequently, there is no longer any doubt which day is the correct day of Yom Tov. Therefore, one wonders why the Sages did not annul the second day of Yom Tov but rather insisted that it be maintained.

The classical answer is that since this had been the official custom for so many years, it had become so well established that an annulment would no longer be possible.

In his work, *Ha'amek Davar,* the famous Rabbi Naftali Zvi Yehuda Berlin (the Netziv, 1817–1893), the last rosh yeshiva of the Volozhin Yeshiva, suggests a different approach that could be an eye-opener to many.

In Parashat Emor (Vayikra 22), we are introduced to the festivals of the Jewish year with the following seemingly superfluous words: "You shall keep My commandments and you shall do them; I am the Lord" (v. 31). After offering an interesting approach to this verse, the Netziv states that the meaning is to instruct the Sages to make a fence around these festivals and to strengthen them by ordering a second day of Yom Tov outside the land of Israel.

In his notes, called *Harchev Davar,* the Netziv quotes a statement in the responsa of Rabbi Hai Gaon, one of the greatest halachic authorities of the tenth century, that the requirement to keep a second day of Yom Tov outside Israel was already mentioned by the prophets. He concludes with the following: "Perhaps this was done since the days of Yehoshua ben Nun for those who lived outside [Israel]."

The Netziv comments that in principle, there is no reason to keep a second day of Yom Tov outside Israel even when one is not sure which day is the correct one. His argument is that Jewish law always follows the majority in all matters of halachic doubt, and since in most cases the Jewish months have twenty-nine rather than thirty days, there is no reason to keep a second day of Yom Tov.

The Netziv continues, proving his point by saying that we would otherwise encounter a serious contradiction in Judaism. Why do we not keep two days of Yom Kippur, and why do we not count the Omer, the forty-nine days between Pesach and Shavuot (see Vayikra 23:15) twice each day? After all, had Pesach started one day later, it would have been necessary to begin counting the Omer one day later. In that case, if we are outside the

Land of Israel, we should say, "Today is the thirty-first or thirty-second day of the Omer." But this is not done. In fact, it is forbidden.

The Netziv therefore concludes that the above verse, "You shall keep My commandments and you shall do them," shows us that we should be careful to observe these festivals for two days and not rely on the fact that most months have only twenty-nine days (and so keep them for only one day). Therefore, the meaning of the verse should be: "And you shall surely keep them in the best way possible and not allow for any doubt."

Still, we may wonder to what specific matter our verse refers, according to the Netziv. Why should one observe two days of Yom Tov outside Israel so as to make sure that we celebrate them properly? The answer may be found in an observation made by Rabbi Menachem Recanati, one of the great kabbalists of the thirteenth and fourteenth centuries. He tells us that outside the land of Israel, it is impossible to become as inspired by a particular festival as when one lives inside the land of Israel. Israel carries its own spirituality into any festival, and in one day one is able to accomplish great spiritual achievements. Outside Israel, however, where the spiritual environment is not conducive to such a refined spiritual state, one needs two days in order to reach the same goal. We may now understand why there is no requirement to observe two days of Yom Kippur. This is not only due to the fact that most people cannot fast for such a long time, but also because Yom Kippur, due to its extraordinary nature, offers us the opportunity to achieve the same spiritual religious experience outside Israel as that of someone who lives there. On this day the soul of a Jew can and should feel as though it dwells in the Holy Land. Thus, no second day is required.[2]

If the above interpretation is correct, we should say that it is mistaken to argue for one day of Yom Tov outside the land Israel. Instead of condemning this institution, modern interpretations of Judaism, with their emphasis on greater spiritual quality, should welcome such a rabbinical enactment since the quality of life in the Diaspora in modern times has, for all its beauty, not been conducive to greater spiritual opportunities.

---

[2] The reverse is true regarding the counting of the Omer. While Yom Kippur is able to offer us great spiritual heights even to the point that there is no need for a second day outside Israel, the counting of the Omer would be no more spiritually uplifting if a second counting were added each time the mitzvah was done.

HANUKKAH, DIVINE EMANATIONS AND THE FUTURE
OF THE STATE OF ISRAEL

November 28, 2004

HISTORY, THE STUDY OF CAUSE AND EFFECT in the annals of humankind, has been a serious hassle for honest historians. In many ways, interpreting history is conjecture. As Benjamin Franklin said, it is more a matter of what one would like to believe happened than what actually occurred which motivates many a historian. After all, how will human beings ever know the cause and effect in a specific instance? Sometimes what we believe to be the cause is actually the effect.

Our sages drew our attention to this phenomenon when they commented on the sale of Joseph and his later release from prison. On the verse "A definite period was set to the world to spend in darkness" (Iyov 28:3), the Midrash states: "A definite number of years was fixed for Joseph to spend in prison, in darkness. When the appointed time came, Pharaoh had a dream, as it says: 'It happened that at the end of two years, Pharaoh had a dream'" (Bereshit 41:1, *Midrash Rabbah*).

In his monumental work, *Ohr Gedalayah,* Rabbi Gedalayah Shorr points out that this observation differs radically from the traditional and academic way of dealing with historical events. In fact, it seems to challenge this approach, turning it on its head.

When we read the story in the traditional way, we no doubt conclude that because Pharaoh dreamed a dream that required an interpretation, Joseph, who was known to have prophetic insights into dream interpretation, was summoned to Pharaoh. After interpreting the dreams successfully he not only received his freedom, but was also raised to the position of second-in-command of Egypt. This means that Pharaoh's dream caused Joseph's release.

Yet a careful reading of our Midrash suggests the reverse. It was because Joseph had to be released and become the viceroy of Egypt that Pharaoh had the dream. The cause was in fact the effect, and vice versa. Based on the verse from the book of Iyov, "A definite period was set to the world to spend in darkness," the Midrash states that God had ordained how much time Joseph would spend in prison. Once that period had passed, God sent Pharaoh a dream so as to set Joseph free.

As mentioned before, this approach opens a completely new way of understanding history. Judaism suggests that at certain times, God sends emanations to the world so as to awaken human beings to act. Just as Pharaoh received his dreams so that Joseph's imprisonment would come to an end, so God sends divine emanations to the world so as to cause human beings to take action.

One example of this is the story of Chanuka. It was not that the Jews of those days believed that a revolt against the Greeks was possible. In fact, logically speaking, there was no way the Jews could ever win such a war, but God caused a kind of psychological upheaval within the minds of several Jews, the Maccabees, that resulted in a notion of revolt. The Maccabees' greatness was that they responded correctly to this heavenly "directive" and realized what needed to be done, however preposterous it might have seemed at the time.

Midrashic literature often compares the Greek empire to "darkness that blinded the eyes of the Jews" (*choshekh zeh Yavan*). The traditional interpretation of this is that during the time of the Maccabees, the Jews were blinded by the Greek worship of the body and followed their example. However, it may have a much deeper meaning. The Greeks are also the inventors of historical interpretation. Greek thinkers were among the first who tried to understand history in its more "scientific" form as reflected in the need to search for cause and effect. From the point of view of the Midrash, this approach blinded the Jews, preventing them from reading history in terms of emanations and the human response to them. It confused the deeper meaning of history, reversed cause and effect and "darkened" the clear insight of the Jews.

One of the most mysterious dimensions of the human psyche is the phenomenon of motivation and taste. Human beings suddenly hear an inner voice or feel a mysterious pull to do something without understanding the source. This is not only true of human actions, but also of our personal taste and preferences. History is full of examples in which human beings changed their attitudes towards particular types of art and music. Melodies that were considered superb and "irreplaceable" fell out of favor half a century later. The same thing happened regarding art, fashion and even the color of our wallpaper.

There are no proper explanations for these phenomena, various scientific suggestions notwithstanding. We would argue that all of them are the result of various divine emanations that are sent to our world. While it is difficult to explain *why* these divine messages arrive, it may be suggested that as far as music and art are concerned, their main purpose is to give human beings a feeling of renewal and an insight into the infinite possibilities of God's creation. Other messages may be the divine response towards human beings' earlier deeds or moral condition. The sudden predilections for more aggressive forms of music or art may be a warning that human beings have fallen from their previous level of dignity.

When we speak of emanations such as in the case of the Maccabees, the main problem is to hear the message, interpret it correctly and understand what it requires of us. This requires divine assistance and moral integrity.

Throughout history, Jews have experienced many divine emanations. Several indications found in the later part of Tanach allude to the coming of the Mashiach at specific times (see, for example, the book of Daniel). Some of the dates for which commentators found hints are long past, and Mashiach did not appear then.

But this should not make us wonder. Whenever Jewish sources revealed dates of the coming of the Messianic Age, they were not final statements, but rather divine signals that at these times the world would be more favorable to the coming of the Mashiach. They were not a guarantee that he would definitely arrive. Once humankind failed to respond in the correct religious and moral way, the special moment passed with no result.

It does not take much effort to recognize that now, we are confronted with new emanations from above. One cannot deny the extraordinary events that have taken place in the Land of Israel over the past several years. In autumn of the year 2000, when a Palestinian state that would have fulfilled nearly all their wishes was on the verge of being established, the Palestinians decided to undo all their achievements in favor of guerrilla warfare against the Jewish state. Their decision brought them only suffering and disaster. While politicians and journalists have offered all sorts of logical explanations, we are convinced that the Palestinians themselves are dumbfounded as to why they started this uprising when independence was almost in their grasp. (Unless they have no interest in their own state, but merely in the destruction of the State of Israel!)

The same is true for the inhabitants of the State of Israel. At the very moment that peace between both sides was as close as could be, Israelis must have wondered why everything was overthrown within moments, although many of them considered this agreement as totally misconceived. While it is not for us to suggest why this happened, we still wonder whether the utter absurdity of this situation stems from a divine emanation that demands a radical change of heart on both sides. Israelis must learn that they cannot take the State of Israel for granted and that its Jewishness stands at the core of its existence. The Palestinians must realize that without strong moral fiber and a complete rejection of anti-Semitism, their state will never become a reality, and that they themselves, and not the Jews, are to be blamed for their inability to build their own state.

51

PURIM AND THE WAR WITH IRAQ

May 16, 2004

As war between the United States and Iraq approaches (and probably has already begun by the time this essay reaches our readers), one cannot escape the fact that, just like twelve years ago in the first Gulf War, it is Purim once again, with its commemoration of the Jewish people's miraculous redemption from the hands of Haman. This should make us pay attention.

In a remarkable midrash on Proverbs, we read the following statement: "When all the other festivals are discontinued, the festival of Purim will never be suspended."

This observation seems to fly in the face of all the rest of Jewish tradition, which states categorically that the Jewish festivals mentioned in the Torah, such as Pesach, Shavuot and Sukkot, will never cease to be celebrated. The Talmud mentions this on several occasions: "The mitzvot (including the festivals) of the Torah will never be nullified, not even in the future" (the messianic era).

In his commentary *Torah Temima* on Esther 9:28, Rabbi Baruch ha-Levi Epstein cites his father, Rabbi Jechiel Michel ha-Levi Epstein, who explains this contradiction in an original way:

> The miracle of Purim is very different from the miracles mentioned in the Torah. While the latter are revealed miracles, such as the splitting of the Red Sea or the falling of the manna in the desert, the miracle of Purim was hidden. Unlike the miracles recounted in the Torah, in the Purim story no law of nature was ever violated and the Jews were seemingly saved from the hands of the evil Haman by normal historical events. Had one lived in

those days one would not have noticed anything unusual, and many secularists would have explained the miracle of the redemption of the Jews in Persia as the logical outcome of natural forces and historical facts. Only retroactively, when we look back at the story, are we astonished by all the accidents and incidents, their unusual sequence, the seemingly unrelated and insignificant human acts which led to the complete redemption of the Jews during the time of Achashverosh's empire. The discovery that all the normal events in fact revealed a miracle could only become clear after the fact.

The Torah Temima explains in the name of his father that while such miracles will never cease to exist, revealed miracles such as the splitting of the Red Sea have come to an end. Therefore, the midrash cited above does not suggest that the actual festivals mentioned in the Torah will be nullified in the future, since this would contradict the Jewish faith, but that the original reasons why they are celebrated – the occurrence of revealed miracles – have ceased. So one should read the Midrash as follows: The kind of revealed miracles mentioned in the Torah that the festivals celebrate will no longer occur, but the kind of miracles such as those of Purim will never be suspended. In other words, all the other Torah festivals will still be celebrated as great events in Jewish history, contemporized so as to make them relevant to our own lives. Yet although Purim is rooted in a historical event that occurred centuries ago, it does not commemorate any such past event but rather functions as a constant reminder that the Purim story never ended. We live in Purim times, and the Megillah was actually never completed!

Rabbi Yitzchak Hutner, *z"l*, in his work *Pachad Yitzchak,* uses this fact to explain an extraordinary halacha about Purim. As everyone knows, on every festival the congregation sings Hallel. These chapters from Psalms praise God for all the great miracles He performed for Israel in biblical times. Why then, asks the Talmud, do we not recite Hallel on Purim? Is there not even more of a reason to recite Hallel on the day when the great miracle of the salvation of Israel from the hands of Haman took place? The Talmud answers that *keriyata zu hi hillula* (the reading of the Scroll of Esther constitutes Hallel and is therefore praise). In other words, when we read the story of Esther, we actually fulfill the obligation to sing Hallel because telling this story is itself the greatest praise to God for having saved the Jews.

However, one of the most celebrated commentators, Rabbi Menachem Meiri, speculates about the need to say Hallel on Purim when one is not able to read or hear the Megillah. In this case, according to his opinion, one should recite Hallel, since one should thank God for what happened. However, Rabbi Hutner points out that no other authority agrees with Rabbi Meiri's opinion. They believe that if one is unable to read the Megillah, one should still not recite Hallel.

Rabbi Hutner explains this ruling in a most remarkable way: Hallel speaks about revealed miracles and praises God for them. It neither speaks of nor praises God for hidden miracles, which must be praised in a hidden way in order to remind worshippers that such miracles really do take place. This is the reason why we read the Scroll of Esther instead of Hallel on Purim. When we read Megillat Esther, the story of a hidden miracle, to the congregation, God receives praise in the proper manner – in a hidden way. After all, God needs no praise. Rather, human beings need to praise, and must do so in a way that corresponds to the actual miracle. Therefore, reciting Hallel is missing the point.

Without claiming any divine revelation, we dare to say that the war with Iraq will be rooted in Purim. Although it is hard to know what will actually happen (especially the day after), it will become clear that Israel, as in the previous Gulf War, has experienced a hidden miracle once again. Only in years to come will all the political and military information be revealed, and only then will people realize that a miracle occurred. This may be the reason why this war is occurring at the time of Purim, as the previous one did. By reading the Megillah, the Jewish people will be reminded of their Father in Heaven and will realize that the bizarre and exceptional circumstances under which they survive prove that the real Purim story has not yet ended.

52

THE TSUNAMI, VULNERABILITY, RELIGIOUS JEWRY AND
THE SANCTIFICATION OF GOD'S NAME

January 10, 2005

IN HIS MAGNUM OPUS, *Ha'amek Davar,* Rabbi Naftali Tzvi Berlin asks why the first book of the Torah, Bereshit, is also called *Sefer ha-Yashar,*[1] the book of the upright. In his own unusual way, the Netziv responds that this is due to the fact that the three patriarchs, Avraham, Yitzchak and Yaakov, the main figures in this book, were men of uncompromising straightforwardness. While many people are perhaps righteous and even pious, the Avot were even greater: Their concern for their fellow human beings, even those who were idolators, was almost without limit. Avraham challenged and even bargained with God not to destroy the people of Sedom, who had fallen to the lowest possible level of moral behavior. Although by Divine law they deserved to die, Avraham persisted in his efforts to save them (Bereshit 18–19).

Yitzchak showed tremendous patience with his depraved opponents, who did everything to make his life miserable. Yet in the end he did even more to appease them than what they had asked for (ibid., chapter 26). Yaakov went out of his way to avoid harming his father-in-law, Lavan, and even to please him even though Lavan broke all the rules of decent behavior towards his son-in-law and exploited him in ways that not even the pious could bear (ibid., chapters 29–31). This, says the Netziv, is the great trademark of the patriarchs and the reason why the book of Bereshit is also called *Sefer ha-Yashar.* While it is true that Judaism does not require its followers to turn the other cheek, it does demand concern for even the

---

[1] See *Avodah Zarah* 25a.

foulest among men as long it does not lead to disastrous consequences. According to the Netziv, this is because we must realize that without such compassion, humankind cannot survive.

When we contemplate the disaster that struck southeast Asia and the number of people who were killed and wounded, as well as the millions of people who lost their homes, one is reminded of the words of Rabbi Naftali Tzvi Berlin: The obligation of Jews to shower infinite mercy on the world. This is also borne out by the fact that God commands Avraham to be a father to all the nations (ibid., 17:4), which means showing great compassion for God's creatures and being always available to them for spiritual and physical help. Just like Avraham was asked to be a father to the nations, so all Jews must be.

The State of Israel has gone to great lengths to alleviate the plight of the tsunami victims. Besides sending rescue workers, medical personnel, money and food, it has asked its citizens to help financially and in any other way they can. Israelis, as real Jews, have responded and are still responding in unprecedented ways. In fact, Israel's aid works out at the highest per-capita donation of any country in the world. This is even more remarkable when we consider what Israeli Jews have been through in the last years. Whatever our own tragedies, we do not forget the world at large, although a good part of the world, including those who now are in need of our help, seems to forget us.

However, what is missing here is a massive, nationwide religious response. As a nation committed to the commandment to sanctify God's name, the religious establishment, including the chief rabbinate, heads of yeshivot and other religious institutions should feel obligated to call on their people to pray for all those who are still missing as well as for the sick and the poor.

Synagogues should add special prayers to the daily service. Yeshivot should organize special study sessions dedicated to the victims, and their leaders should invoke feelings of deep compassion through their talks and *mussar* (ethics) sessions. A public fast day should be seriously considered[2] and

---

[2] When Rabbi Yisrael Meir ha-Cohen, the Chafetz Chaim, was informed on September 1, 1923 that an earthquake had struck the Kanto Plain in Japan and more

calls for an increase in our moral and religious obligations should be heard around the country. Statements of sympathy should be published and large prayer gatherings should be organized throughout the land. This is the minimum obligation of the religious community of the people of Israel.

After all, what happened was not just a local event but a global disaster that will be felt for many years to come. In many ways, it has already transformed our basic notions about our lives. For one, our belief that we are secure in our homes and that nature is a reliable companion has been utterly shattered. There is no way we can be assured that we will still be alive in the next five minutes. A veil has been ripped away and we stand bare in front of ourselves. Ultimately our faith has been challenged, but also enhanced. Now we realize that we live by Divine mercy only. Therefore, we are able to re-discover why many of us have chosen a life of religious observance. Religion, after all, is the art of living in wonder. It is a call to protest against taking matters for granted.

The fact that the world community has shown unprecedented concern for the well-being of all the victims is even more reason for world Jewry and those who stand for the Jewish religious tradition's highest values to stand up. That this has not yet (fully) happened is disappointing, and we call on all those in power to turn the tide.

Religious Jewry cannot permit itself the slightest impression of indifference even when it concerns those who have little in common with us and are no lovers of Israel. Religious Jews should be at the forefront of humanitarian concern without regard to the attitudes of the people who need our help. Just as it would have been easy for Avraham to turn his back on the upcoming disaster in Sedom and even argue that it would be wrong to interfere in God's plan concerning those wicked people, religious Jews could give the impression of making a similar mistake by arguing that since the disaster was an act of God, it is not for human beings to interfere. Just as Avraham never considered such an attitude as an option, religious Jewry should do everything in its power to fulfill its religious duty to help and show compassion in every way possible. To do anything else is contrary to authentic Jewish teachings.

---

than one hundred thousand people had died, he began a personal fast and called on his fellow Jews to repent.

Yet besides all this, Jewish religious leaders should send a message to all of the people of Israel and to all humankind that it is time we realized that the world is a different place from what we imagine it to be. While there are moral and religious values worth fighting for, we often focus on our physical pleasures, our need for honor and comfort, our hates and loves, which occupy millions of us, yet are not worth the time and energy that we spend on them. In times of vulnerability, we mature and realize what is important and what is not. As father to the nations, it is our task to make ourselves and others aware of this.

Instead of trying to discover textual hints for this disaster in biblical or kabbalistic texts (which is mostly fanciful speculation and wishful thinking), religious Jewry should act responsibly, showing that they have not forgotten their duty towards all of humankind. This would create respect for Jewish tradition throughout the world and accomplish the greatest possible sanctification of God's name.

PART II

STUDIES

ON THE ISRAELI-ARAB CONFLICT:
A BIBLICAL PERSPECTIVE[1]

IMPARTIAL OBSERVERS OF THE MIDDLE EAST will realize that these are extraordinary times. Tens of thousands of Jews from many different countries are returning to their national and historic homeland after thousands of years. Arab states are beginning to reconsider their attitude towards Israel now that they realize that after more than fifty years, the Jewish state is here to stay.

Many gentiles throughout the world are showing a new and keen interest in the Bible, proclaiming fulfillment of the old biblical prophecies. The continuous conflict between the Israelis and the Arabs, especially the Palestinian Arabs, is a constant focus of world attention, allotted more broadcast hours and newspaper column space than any other conflict. It is the most discussed issue at the United Nations and the perceived root of international tension. It is believed to have the potential to cause a large-scale conflict in the Middle East and even a global confrontation.

However, the truth is more prosaic. The conflict between the Israelis and the Palestinians is something of a local affair. Looking on the world map, many larger hotbeds can be identified, with even greater issues at stake. For the religious mind all this presents a great challenge. What is the spiritual secret behind the conflict?

From a religious perspective, it seems that another, more profound point is being made. History is not made up of social, political, or economic

---

[1] This essay, with slight differences, originally appeared in my book *Between Silence and Speech* (Jason Aronson, 1995) and is reprinted here with the permission of the publisher.

factors alone, but also of spiritual forces that have far-reaching moral implications. As always, religious people will turn to the Torah and Jewish tradition, the blueprint of all history and reality, to seek deeper insight. It is the author's hope that this essay might serve such a purpose.

The Israeli-Arab Conflict

The Torah relates a remarkable sequence of events toward the end of the life of Avraham, the patriarch and founder of monotheism. "Avraham grew old, and God blessed Avraham with everything" (Bereshit 24:1).

After the death of his wife, Sarah, only one dream remained to be fulfilled: to find a wife for his son, Yitzchak, in order to fulfill God's promises of continuity. With that accomplished, Avraham would finally be able to close his eyes and be "gathered to his fathers."

And so we read that Avraham sent his faithful servant, Eliezer, to find a wife for Yitzchak. After a long, eventful story, Yitzchak marries Rivka.

> The servant related to Yitzchak all the things he had done. Yitzchak brought her to the tent of his mother, Sarah, and he married Rivka. She became his wife, and he loved her, and only then was Yitzchak comforted for the loss of his mother" (Bereshit 24:66–67).

Now, finally, Avraham can die peacefully. His life's work is accomplished. His great mission – to introduce monotheism and justice into the world – has been achieved, and the future of that mission has been guaranteed through the establishment of Yitzchak's family. We now anticipate the moment when the Torah will inform us of the patriarch's death. However instead of Avraham dying, we read:

> Then Avraham took a wife whose name was Keturah. She bore him Zimran, Yokshan, Medan, Midian, Yishbok and Shuach (Bereshit 25:1–2).

Does this not surprise us a little? We may be justified in asking why Avraham, a tired, old man, should think about getting married again, not to mention fathering another six children.

If this is not perplexing enough, the Midrash identifies Avraham's new wife: "Who is Keturah? Hagar!"[2]

It will be recalled that years before, Hagar had been Avraham's second wife after Sarah (Bereshit 16). But after Hagar bore Yishmael, God forced Avraham to send Hagar and her son away (Bereshit 21). This occurred after many episodes of friction between Sarah and Hagar (Bereshit 16) and after Yishmael threatened to kill Yitzchak.[3]

At this point we are right to be puzzled. Why, after a long time of separation, would Avraham remarry Hagar, the very woman who had been the cause of so much trouble in the past? Hagar represents a tragic and somber moment in Avraham's life, a tremendous setback accompanied by intense feelings of failure. What could be worse for any man, let alone one who epitomizes benevolence and justice, than having to send away his wife and child? It might be argued further that in remarrying the very woman he had exiled many years earlier, Avraham was only courting disaster and conflict anew.

In its perplexity, the Midrash asks: Who suggested this match? To our surprise, we are told that it was Yitzchak. Commenting on Bereshit 24:62, the *Midrash Rabbah* observes that Yitzchak had been searching for Hagar and brought her to Avraham for possible re-marriage.[4] Why would Yitzchak make such a suggestion? What was his motive in raking up the past? After all, he had suffered bitterly from the whole episode with Hagar.

The Birth of Yitzchak

In order to gain an understanding of these complex questions, we need to examine the history of the relationship between Avraham, Sarah and Hagar, and between these protagonists and Yishmael. We read much earlier in the narrative:

> Sarai, Avram's wife, bore him no children; and she had an Egyptian handmaid whose name was Hagar. Sarai said to Avram, "See now, God has kept me from bearing. Please go to

---

[2] *Bereshit Rabbah* 61:4.
[3] Rashi on Bereshit 21:9.
[4] *Bereshit Rabbah* on Bereshit 24:62.

my maid; perhaps I shall be built through her." And Avram heeded Sarai's voice (Bereshit 16:1–2).

Rabbi Yitzchak Arama, the great fifteenth-century Spanish commentator, is perplexed by Sarai's suggestion. "Why did Sarai not ask for children as Rivka did (later on)? If she recognized that it was He who denied them to her, than it would only be logical to turn to Him." In other words, did Sarai not have enough trust in God that she would become pregnant and bear Avram a child? Was it not obvious that all the promises God made to Avram that he would have a child and become the progenitor of a nation meant that Sarai would be the mother? "I will make you a great nation; and I will make your seed as the dust of the earth" (Bereshit 15:5).

At the time of this promise, Sarai was Avram's sole wife. Therefore, it would be reasonable to assert that only she would be the mother of Avram's child and future generations. So why did she ask Avram to marry Hagar?

Rabbi Yitzchak Arama argues that Sarai had sound reasons for not invoking divine mercy. In referring to the verse (Bereshit 18:11), "It had ceased with Sarai to be after the manner of women," he argues that it would have been a mistake for Sarai to ask God to allow her to become pregnant since this would have involved the violation of the laws of nature. Sarai's postmenopausal condition made it impossible for her to have children unless an open miracle was performed. Based on the principle that "*ha-olam be-minhago holech*" (the world runs its course in a natural way; the laws of nature are created as a fixed reality), Sarai reasoned that asking God for pregnancy would be out of order. Miracles occur only when there is no alternative, but in Sarai's mind there was a ready alternative in Hagar. Moreover, Hagar had been raised and educated by Sarai and therefore was, in many ways, her adopted child and pupil. This, reasoned Sarai, was enough to allow Avram to marry Hagar. The child born of this union would be Sarai's child for all practical purposes and would be educated to continue Avram's great mission. (The very fact that Sarai was prepared to agree to such a compromise shows her greatness and profound faith. She was prepared to give up on her own motherhood for the sake of a higher divine value.)

On a deeper level, it may be suggested that Sarai argued that for the Jewish people to be effective in the world, they had to be born within the boundaries of the laws of this world. The child had to be born in a natural way, without any surprising or unprecedented occurrences.

Avram, however, looked beyond. He had been informed that his progeny will have to represent the "beyond." It will have to present the divine truth, and that truth is not entirely of this world.

> He [God] took him outside and said, "Look towards the heavens and count the stars, if you are able to count them." And He added, "So shall your offspring be" (Bereshit 15:5).

On this the Midrash comments:

> Did He then lead him forth to the outside of the world?... But He showed him the streets of heaven, He lifted him above the vault of heaven; hence He tells him, "*Habet*" – Look now towards heaven; "*Habet*," signifying to look down from above (*Midrash Rabbah*).

This Midrash clearly implies the metaphysical aspect of the nation to be born: its root is above the normal and logical.

Only from a heavenly perspective can one understand the Jewish people's essence, mission, and remarkable capacity of survival. "Look towards heaven" implies the understanding that there is no end to heaven. The world "beyond" is the root where the foundation of Israel may be discovered. Avram is asked to elevate himself above the finite world.

For this reason, Avram cannot agree with Sarai. He waits for the unprecedented, the unusual, and because of all this, he is convinced that Sarai may still become pregnant. More than that, because the nation of Israel must hold the potential to become a meta-historical people, it has to be born from the supernatural and the unprecedented. Therefore, from this perspective, Sarai was the most obvious mother-to-be!

If so, why did Avram not refuse Sarai's request to marry Hagar? The answer given by Ramban, who posed this question, is that he agreed to Sarai's request only in order to give her the satisfaction of fulfilling her maternal feelings. Nevertheless, Avram did not believe for one moment that Hagar would give birth to the child he had been promised.[5]

> Avram heeded Sarai; and Sarai, Avram's wife, took Hagar, the Egyptian, her maid…. She gave her to Avram, her husband, to be his wife. (Bereshit 16:3).

Then something happened that caused unexpected complications: "When she [Hagar] saw that she had conceived, her mistress lost value in her eyes" (Bereshit 16:4). In describing her characteristics, Rabbi Samson Raphael Hirsch notes that the name Hagar connotes being bound in, restrained. Hagar is therefore a limited woman with little insight into the spiritual and metaphysical world of Avram. She believes that her immediate pregnancy is a sign of personal divine favor and therefore she, and not Sarai, is the truly righteous woman.

Hagar's philosophy is simple. She does not understand that only through trial and hardship does one become a righteous and great personality. An easy life does not produce people of significance. This is the reason why many women in the Torah suffer from infertility. Only after great effort and spiritual struggles do they give birth to children.

Since Hagar is solely of this world, rooted in the natural order of things, she misreads her own story and that of Sarai. We may add that Hagar is a descendant of Cham, the second son of Noach and the father of Canaan. The Torah tells us that after emerging from the ark, Noach planted a vineyard and became intoxicated, and uncovered himself in his tent. Cham saw his father's nakedness and reported the incident to his brothers, Shem and Yaphet (Bereshit 9:20–29). One can see in this incident a most important and illuminating fact. Cham, the "heated" one, sees the world from an intoxicated position. He cannot see the deeper meaning of this life. He does not understand that human beings' physical appearances are only external and that the real human being is within.

In many ways, Hagar is a descendant of Cham. Since she sees the world through Cham's prism, she does not grasp Sarai's trial and concomitant greatness. She identifies material success with divine approval, displaying

---

[5] Bereshit 16:2.

little appreciation for the higher, heavenly world. Due to this misperception, she looks down on Sarai.

Sarai's Mistake

Aware of the deep-rooted conflict, Avram gives Sarai carte blanche in her treatment of Hagar:

> Sarai said to Avram, "… I gave my maid unto your bosom and now that she has conceived, I have lost value in her eyes."… Then Avram said to Sarai: "See, your maid is in your hand. Do to her that which is good in your eyes." Then Sarai afflicted her and she [Hagar] fled from her (Bereshit 16:5–6).

In his careful reading of the text, the Ramban makes a most remarkable and disturbing observation. Instead of trying to justify Sarai's behavior, he condemns her for having mistreated Hagar:

> Sarai, our mother, sinned in dealing harshly with her handmaid, and so did Avram by allowing her to do so. [Therefore] God saw her affliction and gave her a son who was destined to be a lawless person who would bring suffering on the seed of Avram and Sarai with all kinds of afflictions.[6]

According to the Ramban, Sarai not only violated the principles of general morality but also profoundly misunderstood the situation that she herself had created. Rabbi Samson Raphael Hirsch explains:

> What she [Sarai] had forgotten is that she had wished an impossible thing… that a woman who had become wife to Avram and mother to his child could not, on the other hand, be a slave. Avram's proximity and Avram's spirit would break the

---

[6] Ramban on Bereshit 16:5.

feelings of slavery, awaken the feeling of the equality of all human beings, arouse the urge for freedom and break all chains.[7]

Taking this argument one step further, we may suggest that Sarai not only misunderstood Hagar's personality, but also failed to realize that the child born from Avram's union with Hagar could only be a highly complex personality.

Many of this child's qualities were rooted in Avram's spiritual world. Yet at the same time, he would also inherit many of Hagar's characteristics – in other words, of Cham, the "heated one." This created a complex situation with a great deal of tension and contradictions. The child would be pained by his inability to identify totally with either Avram's world or Hagar's, always on the run, never at peace with himself. Sarai did not realize that Yishmael would taste from the wellsprings of Avram's world but would never be completely included in it because of the Chamite mentality that he had inherited. Sarai was playing with fire.

What would have happened if Sarai had allowed herself to care for Yishmael properly and to nurture him? It is likely that his personality would have developed differently and that he would have had the strength to overcome the inherent tensions within his being. Rabbi Hirsch postulates that the Arab nation would have become a great asset for the cause of the monotheistic and religious-ethical life and would have worked hand in hand with the people of Israel.

> The nation descended from Avraham and Hagar is half-Jewish. God has given us, the Jewish nation, a mission, which has a dual aspect: 1) *emunah,* theoretical truth that we must accept and that our minds must develop; and 2) the Law, the commandments, which in harmonious agreement with these truths shape our whole lives in accordance with the dictates of the divine Will. On the one aspect, the theoretical, the Arabic nation holds a high place in the ranks of mankind. It has developed the Arabic thoughts of God with such fine acuteness that the thoughts of

---

[7] Rabbi Samson Raphael Hirsch, *The Pentateuch, Translated and Explained.* Trans. Isaac Levy. New York: Judaica Press, 1971.

the unity of God in the works of Jewish theological philosophers, as far as they are developed philosophically, rest predominantly on the works of Arabian writers. These have the emunah but not the mitzvot. It is not sufficient to have spiritual thoughts of the unity of God, [but it must include] that practical submission of all forces and efforts [to daily life] and for that it is not sufficient only to be begotten and brought up by Avraham; for that one must be born from Sara. The specific people of Avraham is not given the mission to be the theological philosophical herald of the Unity of God, but *"lishmor derech Hashem la'asot tzedaka u-mishpat,"* "to preserve the way of God and do righteousness and justice." This requires the submission of all one's forces, and above all, all one's sensuous forces, urges and impulses, that demand the dedication of the body. One only begins to be Jewish with the dedication of the body.[8]

Had Sarai cared for Yishmael, then the great Arab nation would have had an easier task in fulfilling itself, and history would have unfolded much differently.

Sarai's treatment of Hagar left a permanent rift between the two women even after Hagar returned home and gave birth to Yishmael (Bereshit 16). This sense of hurt and bitterness undoubtedly became imprinted in the mind of the child Yishmael who, thereafter, could only have felt a stranger in the home of Sarai. He nurtured his hard feelings against Sarai over the many long years of his difficult life until, as Ramban seems to suggest, they became indelibly marked on the souls of his descendants and developed into implacable hatred for the children of Avraham and Sarai.

However, the Ramban's observation has its problems. How does he reconcile his claim that Sarai was wrong to afflict Hagar and send her away when we read later (Bereshit 21:12) that God agreed with Sarai, telling Avraham to send Hagar and Yishmael away?

After Yitzchak's birth, tensions intensify between Yishmael and his younger half-brother, eventually reaching such a point that Sarai tells Avraham, "Cast out that slave-woman and her son" (Bereshit 21:9).

---

[8] Ibid., Bereshit 16:14.

Avraham is greatly distressed "for it concerned a son of his." Clearly, Avraham does not want a second tragedy. No father willingly spurns his own son, however wayward he may be. He has learned from the past. Therefore he refuses to act on Sarai's wish until God surprisingly indicates His own agreement: "Whatever Sarai tells you, heed what she says" (Bereshit 21:9).

So it appears that Sarai is right after all. The act of sending Hagar away has God's blessing. Yet if Sarai is correct in this instance, then what was wrong in driving out Hagar earlier by afflicting her? Did God not afflict Hagar further by making Avraham send her and her son away?

The answer to this question is clear. God tells Avraham that the first expulsion was wrong. It has wrought terrible damage, evoking in Hagar and Yishmael an eternal hatred. But one cannot turn back the clock. To keep Yishmael in the home of Avraham and Sarah after all that has happened will only lead to further complications. Now it is too late. Avraham must learn that there is no way back.

Avraham's Repentance

Now we may begin to arrive at an understanding of our earlier dilemma – namely, why Avraham married Hagar at the end of his life. Avraham now realized the enormity of the injustice that had been inflicted on Hagar. Her earlier sufferings and her expulsion together with Yishmael continued to torment Avraham. In setting his affairs in order before his death, he wonders how he – the embodiment of kindness – could have permitted such a thing to happen. How can he meet his Maker without having resolved this problem of his own making? How can he make amends?

Yitzchak sees his father's anguish and understands that this matter has the potential to become Avraham's downfall. All that he had lived for – his devotion to acts of kindness, his piety and all his acts of righteousness – are of little consequence as long as this one matter remains unsettled. Yitzchak's suggestion that his father remarry Hagar is therefore understandable. By giving her a happy family life and security, Avraham may be able to make amends, look himself in the face, and meet his Maker with equanimity.

Therefore, it is not surprising that on several occasions, Avraham sought out his son Yishmael and advised him whom to marry. However wayward and unruly he may have been, Yishmael was still Avraham's son and entitled to his support.[9]

Pere Adam

While Hagar is in the desert after fleeing from Sarai the first time, God appears to her and reveals to her the qualities of her unborn child: "He will be like a *pere adam*" (Bereshit 16:12). The rabbis struggle with the exact meaning of these last words. The classic rendering is "a wild ass," a disturbing translation.

> Rabbi Yochanan and Resh Lakish debated this. Rabbi Yochanan said: It means that while all people are bred in civilized surroundings, he would be reared in the wilderness. Resh Lakish said: It means a savage among men in its literal sense, for as all people plunder wealth, he plunders lives. (Bereshit Rabbah 35:9)

Rabbi Hirsch adds: "He will not be merely an *adam pere,* a free man, but he will be *pere adam,* the *pere* among mankind... such a race of men who do not bow their necks to the yoke of other men."[10] God continues:

> His hand against every man, and every man's hand against him, and in the face of all his brothers will he dwell. (Bereshit 16:12)

This could mean that he will stand up against his own brothers and cause instability in the Arab world. It may also refer to his constant struggles with the nations of the world. Da'at Sofrim on Bereshit 16:12 explains the prophecy further: "Although he will be a man with great potential, intellect and emotions, his hand will be against everybody, and everybody's against him. Nevertheless, in the face of all his brothers he will dwell – he will be honored by all nations." Ramban expands the argument: "The subject pertains to his children, who will increase, and they will have wars with all the nations."

---

[9] *Bereshit Rabbah* 61.
[10] *Ad loc.*

Such prophecies and interpretations do not imply that Yishmael must become as they describe, nor do the earlier observations justify the Arab animosity toward Jews in our days or at any other time. The injustice of Sarah toward Yishmael cannot be used as a precedent for ongoing hatred toward the children of Avraham and Sarah.

These observations and visions draw attention to the roots from which these feelings stem. They indicate that these prophecies will come true if Yishmael yields to this disposition instead of fighting it. The chief goal of people in life is to become human and to protect their humanity against these kinds of tendencies. Had Yishmael understood this and fought his inclinations or channeled them appropriately, he could have become an eloquent and highly civilized man, perhaps more civilized than all those who did not have to go through such challenges.

The above-quoted prophetic descriptions are made from a combination of dispositions that make up the personality of Yishmael. On the one hand, they are rooted in the world of Avraham, while on the other, they stem from the world of Cham.

Perseverance, courage, and independence are the very qualities that Avraham developed in order to fulfill his mission to teach all humanity about God. Once, however, these qualities become misdirected and absorbed by the world of Cham, they start to serve external and physical purposes such as military power and willful stubbornness. The very propensity for domination found within the Arab world, combined with the vast financial resources at its disposal, is the result of the qualities inherent in Avraham's spiritual mission having been misdirected. When these qualities are used for earthly causes, as is the case with the Chamite philosophy, they become dangerous and destructive. The Arab will to dominate, with its bold, daring and often self-destructive courage, combined with autonomous philosophies, is therefore a misdirected quality inherited from Avraham.

World Domination

At this point it would be pertinent to investigate another feature of our global question. From the verses cited above we can deduce that the descendants of Yishmael would like to dominate the world and create an independent world power. We may ask how an entity becomes a world-dominating power. In other words, how does one possess the world? How does one seize the very powers by which this world is set in motion?

Jewish tradition believes that a kind of spiritual and moral domination is accomplished by possessing the land of Israel, specifically Jerusalem which, we are told, is built on the *even shetiyah,* the world's foundation stone. The Talmud, in *Yoma* 54b, states that it was called so because "from it the world was established." In his commentary to this statement, Rashi adds, "Zion was first created, and then around it other clods and rock formations. Continents were formed until the earth was complete."

The Ramban, commenting on the first verse of the Torah and reflecting kabbalistic teachings, writes, "Jerusalem is the preeminent place, for the life of the world starts there, its potential is developed therein, its climates and species of all orders appear in it."

Therefore, Jerusalem is seen as the root of all places. The land of Israel, the first extension of Jerusalem, is the "soul" of the world. It is the Holy Land, sanctified and set apart from the rest of the world. It is the world in microcosm, in which all the components of the greater world are represented. It is the "*kav emtza'i,*" the medium line, the "inner, spiritual bolt that contains everything that connects all points of the world among themselves to the original point."[11]

This is the reason the nations of the world have always maintained their focus on Jerusalem and Israel. Subconsciously, they have been aware that, somehow, possession of this city and this land meant "controlling" the world. The essence of this world is virtually contained in Jerusalem. Obviously, this means that Jerusalem and Israel are the center of this world in the *spiritual sense.* It is from there that the teachings of the Torah will come and transform the world. However, the many nations that once occupied the land of Israel translated this inner knowledge into terms of purely physical occupations, without understanding the spiritual implications.

In the case of the Arab nations, this matter is even more apparent. As children of Avraham, they regard the status and ownership of the land of Israel as a vitally important matter. Their longing for this land is not just bound up with their ambition to become a world power. It is the consequence of Avraham's mission to transform that makes the impetus to

---

[11] Rabbi Menachem Recanati, Bereshit, 8a; Va-yetze, 28a–29a.

possess this land so powerful. As explained above, it is this mission, albeit misdirected by Chamite influence, that makes the Arab world seek ways to inherit the land and overpower the world. It is this matter that makes the Israeli-Arab conflict so complex.

What are the conditions by which one can permanently secure the Land of Israel and thereby really inherit it? Such a matter is not decided on the basis of history or political force alone.

According to biblical thought, the matter depends mainly upon the spiritual and moral condition of the tenant. The country itself, as the center of the world, is like Jerusalem, which is also called "Sha'ar Shamayim" (the gateway to heaven). Jerusalem is a heavenly city. The Sanctuary with the Holy of Holies, in which there is no limitation of time and space, is located there; it is *le-ma'ala min ha-teva* (beyond the laws of nature). It is heaven reflected on earth. Consequently, only a nation that is rooted in and lives by the norms of heaven is capable of possessing this land and this city.

In its discussion of the mitzvah of making pilgrimage to Jerusalem in order to celebrate the festivals in the Temple, the Torah states, "No one will covet your land when you ascend to appear before the Lord three times a year" (Shemot 34:24). The implication of this verse is that if all Jews go the Temple on Pesach, Shavuot and Sukkot, the borders of the Land of Israel will be in grave danger. The pilgrimage will be an open invitation for Israel's enemies to cross the border and force the people of Israel out of their homeland. Nevertheless, the Torah states that not only will the enemies not enter the land but they would not even consider making such a move. This is an unusual, unnatural promise and goes against our general experience. Why should Israel's enemies not consider such an option? Why would they not even consider coveting the land?

According to our observations, we may understand what the Torah is driving at. When the Jews ascend to "appear before the Lord" – in other words, when their lives are built upon the principles that the Temple represents, only then will it be clear and undisputed who holds the title to this land. When Israel views its national life from beyond and lives up to its mission, it will have peace on its borders. This land can only be possessed by those whose lives are in accordance with its spiritual nature. Otherwise, other nations will claim it. Only when the Land of Israel's spiritual standards are met will other nations no longer aspire to possess it.

This, then, is the prophecy behind the above-cited verse. *Only the people of Israel, adhering to the Torah of Israel, hold title to the land of Israel.* This may be the biblical message behind the Israeli-Arab conflict.

HEARING AND SEEING
AND THE FUTURE OF ISRAEL

Introduction

In Pirkei Avot 3:9, we encounter an unusual and puzzling statement by the sage Rabbi Yaakov:

> If a person is taking a walk while he is learning [Torah] and interrupts his studies and says: How beautiful is this tree, or how beautiful is this field, it is as if he is liable of a mortal sin.

This Mishna seems to contradict a fundamental concept within Judaism. The need to be amazed by our surroundings, to be impressed by the beauty of nature, is a vital condition for genuine religious life. King David makes this most clear when he says: "The heavens declare the glory of God; the skies proclaim the work of His hands" (Tehillim 19:2).

Jewish law requires that we recite a blessing whenever we enjoy food, drink or a pleasant aroma. Indeed, there is even a special blessing over the sight of new fruit trees in the month of Nissan. A blessing, which expresses a sense of amazement at God's world, is in many ways a protest against taking that world for granted.

So why it is that when a person interrupts Torah study to fulfill precisely this halachic requirement – praising God for a beautiful tree or field – he or she "is guilty of a mortal sin"?

Rabbi Yaakov

A second question needs to be asked. Who was Rabbi Yaakov, the author of this mishna? After all, it is not for nothing that the sages who made important aggadic or halachic statements are mentioned by name. Each statement, such a practice seems to suggest, reflects a particular belief or experience central to the life of its author. "*Hu haya omer*" means "He constantly said." So why was Rabbi Yaakov constantly saying that a person is liable of a mortal sin when he praises the beauty of a tree or field?

Commentators identify Rabbi Yaakov as the grandson of Elisha ben Abuyah (c. 140 CE), one of the most disturbing, yet equally fascinating, figures in Talmudic history. Notorious for his heretical views and refusal to live in accordance with halacha, Elisha became known as Acher, "the other one," for his betrayal of Jewish tradition. In many ways he is the forerunner of all later Jewish heretics, from Spinoza in seventeenth-century Amsterdam to our own times. Elisha renounced his heritage, adopted Greek culture and spent the rest of his life in a gentile environment. The question we must ask ourselves is whether his apostasy has any connection with the subsequent observation of his grandson, Rabbi Yaakov.

The Two Mountains

To complete the picture, we must address a third and final question. As everyone knows, there are two mountains that play a vital role in Jewish history. One is the Temple Mount, where the Temple used to stand and where – hundreds of years earlier – Avraham very nearly sacrificed his son Yitzchak. The other is Mount Sinai, where God revealed His will to the entire Jewish nation, giving them the Ten Commandments and all of the Oral Torah.

The halachic difference between these two mountains is extraordinary. There is a long list of laws pertaining to the Temple Mount's sacred status. Many authorities believe that it is absolutely forbidden to cross the threshold of the mountain, even after the destruction of the Temple, because of its immense sanctity. Some opinions even hold that one should not touch the Wailing Wall for the same reason. These and other prohibitions distinguish the Temple Mount and strengthen its position as the holiest place in Judaism.

The halachic status of Mount Sinai could not be more different. Not only do we not know where it is but, even if we did, the site would possess no halachic significance whatsoever. One would be permitted to ascend Mount Sinai with absolutely no prohibition. One could even conduct one's day-to-day affairs on the very spot where Moses received the tablets! This is astonishing. We would have expected that this mountain, which saw the Jewish people's finest hour, would carry so much sanctity that any ascent to its top would constitute enormous sacrilege. How can it be that the Temple Mount, where nothing of the magnitude of the Sinai revelation took place, is considered a place of such great sanctity while Mount Sinai plays no lasting role in Judaism?

Torah and Homer

Two radically different thinkers have attempted to answer these questions: Rabbi David Cohen (1887–1972), known as the Nazir, who was a close disciple of Rabbi Avraham Yitzchak Kook, in his book *Kol ha-Nevua*; and German literary theorist Professor Erich Auerbach (1892–1957) in *Odysseus' Scar*.[1] Both scholars posit a fundamental difference between early Greek prose and the biblical narrative, comparing the prose of Homer (the greatest Greek poet, author of the *Iliad* and the *Odyssey*) with the Bible. In Homer's epic poems there is an emphasis on detailed descriptions, on the "delight in physical existence," on the external beauty of human beings – their garb, weapons and surroundings. There is an excess of "fully externalized description," with never "a form left fragmentary… never a lacuna, never a gap, never a glimpse of unplumbed depth."[2] The battles, passions and achievements of the Greek heroes are described in dazzling detail; Homer leaves nothing half-illuminated.

One finds a very different world in the Torah. The text provides little to no information about people's physical appearance. At times, events are related in fragmentary form. Indeed, it seems as if, unless warranted by a

---

[1] *Mimesis: The Representation of Reality in Western Literature*, chapter 1.
[2] Ibid.

moral-religious need, externalized narrative is left out of the Torah altogether. Instead, there is an emphasis on humanity's existential condition, its moral struggles, its challenging encounter with an invisible God. Homer's heroes of the battlefield are replaced in the Torah by heroes of godliness and righteousness. This visual obscurity opens the biblical narrative to a myriad of diverse interpretations, allowing for the consequent development of the oral tradition (of which Auerbach does not seem to be aware).

This textual distinction has far-reaching cultural implications. The Greek world of Homer, the forerunner of Western civilization, is primarily a visual world, the one in which art, architecture, sculpture, theatre and other visual arts are deeply rooted. It is the world of artistic brilliance and sensual splendor – very different from the world of the Torah, which has almost no graphic imagery.

Writing about the Binding of Isaac, Professor Auerbach claims the following:

> We now turn to the other person in the dialogue, to Avraham. Where is he? We do not know. He says indeed: "Here I am," but the Hebrew word means only like "Behold me" and in any case it is not meant to indicate the actual place where Avraham is, but a moral position in respect to God…. Where he actually is, whether in Beer Sheva or elsewhere, whether indoors or in the open air, is not stated, it does not interest the Narrator. And what Avraham was doing when God called him is left in the same obscurity.

> To realize the difference, consider Hermes's visit to Calypso, for example, where command, journey, arrival and reception of the visitor, situation and occupation of the person visited, are set forth in many verses.

> Here, however God appears without bodily form, yet He appears, coming from some unspecified place. We only hear His voice…. And of Avraham too nothing is made perceptible, except the words in which he answers God – *hineni*. A most

touching gesture expressive of obedience and readiness is suggested, but it is left to the reader to visualize it.[3]

Later on, Auerbach adds: "All of the stories are fraught with background."

Herein lies the essential difference between the Greek world, represented in Homer's prose, and the Hebrew world, embodied in the Torah. While seeing and visualization stand at the heart of Greek culture, it is hearing that plays a central role in the Torah.

This division found its way into the respective languages of the Greeks and the Jews. Most western languages are rooted in the Greek tradition. Take the English language, for example. When we speak about understanding we often mention insight. We use words like "foresight," "hindsight" and "observation," and phrases like "people of vision." All these expressions, which have nothing to do with actual seeing, convey a certain mentality, a view of the world, that implies the predominance of sight. The same is true of words like "idea" and "video."

Conversely, when we examine Hebrew, we encounter a world view based on audibility. If Greek uses the idiom "I see" to signify understanding, classical Hebrew has coined the phrase *ani shomea* – "I hear." The Talmudic expression introducing a new concept or law is *ta shema,* "Come and hear." When one draws a conclusion, one uses the word *mashma* or *shema mineh*; and when one cannot agree, one says *lo shemia leh*. In fact, the entire oral tradition is referred to as *mi-pi ha-shemuah,* "from the Mouth that is heard" (referring to the Revelation at Sinai).

To summarize: the Greek world (and, by extension, Western civilization) is one in which matters are grasped in an external, superficial way. By contrast, the Torah maintains that real life takes place on a hidden, more profound level – that the deeper meaning and purpose of life must be heard rather than seen. This is also the difference between idol worship and monotheism. For pagans, the medium of the eye is crucial. They must see their god represented in nature. Jews, on the other hand, perceive their God as being outside nature, above and prior to it. The Divine manifests Itself through the medium of the ear. At Sinai one hears God; one does not see

---

[3] Page 13.

Him. The pagan beholds his god, while the Jew hears his God and apprehends His will.

Elisha ben Abuyah

We may now begin to understand the mishna quoted above and its personal connection to Rabbi Yaakov. When a person interrupts his Torah study to exclaim "How beautiful is this tree, how beautiful is this field," he is doing something radical. Such a person is guilty of a mortal sin because, symbolically, he has abandoned the world of hearing in favor of the world of sight. The whole of the Oral Torah, of which this Mishna is a part, is to be learnt through hearing, not through sight. Indeed, in earlier times it could not be seen at all, since there was an explicit prohibition against writing down the oral tradition. It could only be heard from one's teacher.

It is in this distinction between the Greek culture of sight and the Jewish tradition of hearing (represented, as we have seen, in Homer's prose and the Torah, respectively) that the story of Rabbi Yaakov's grandfather becomes revealing. Elisha ben Abuyah replaced the world of hearing with the world of sight. He was no longer prepared to heed the words of the Torah, but turned to the Greek world – the world of the eye – instead.

Having witnessed the catastrophic consequences of his grandfather's tragic choice, Rabbi Yaakov warns us against making the same mistake. In a world where sight rules supreme, there can be no real morality. There can only be an inadequate, superficial understanding of the meaning of life.

This is not to say that Rabbi Yaakov forbids paying any sort of attention to the visual world. The Jewish tradition doubtless appreciates the perceptible beauty of this world – allocating, as we have seen, special blessings for various pleasant sights. However, when one is learning Torah – involved in the act of hearing the Divine Voice – then turning to the beauty of this world becomes a liability. In Judaism, what the eye observes must always be subordinated to the human being's inner ear.

The Mountains

Let us return to the question of Mount Sinai and the Temple Mount. Why is Mount Sinai divested of any kind of sanctity while the Temple Mount is considered to be the apex of holiness?

A reading of the Sinai narrative reveals a remarkable fact: "All the people saw the sounds and the flames and the tone of the shofar and the mountain smoking. And the people saw and they trembled and stood at a distance" (Exodus 20:15).

How extraordinary! It was the faculty of sight that stood out at the time of the Divine Revelation! Smoke, thunder, lightning – the Sinai phenomenon seems to be primarily visual. Even the tone of the shofar was seen, not heard! Hearing was only in the background, a secondary experience. And when the Divine Voice was actually heard, the frightened People of Israel turned to Moshe and said: "You speak to us and we shall listen; let God not speak to us, lest we die" (Exodus 20:16). Clearly, the Israelites were not yet capable of hearing God's voice *a priori* (the definitive form of hearing). In many ways, their lives were still rooted in the world of the eye and they could not fathom the experience of hearing. It is thus understandable that after the Sinai revelation they made the golden calf, which they could at least see and touch. The statue represented a world which they could grasp and feel comfortable with.

It is for this reason that Moshe decided to break the original tablets. After the incident of the golden calf, he was obviously afraid the Israelites would come to worship the tablets themselves. Since the tablets were tangible and perceptible, the people would not listen to their message but would treat them as an object of idol worship, merely observing their shape and beauty.

The Sinai experience, anchored in the superficial faculty of sight, could not function as a permanent source of inspiration. Unable to last within the minds of the people even briefly, it quickly waned – note the immediacy in which the people fell into sin. Hence, Mount Sinai could not become a place of lasting sanctity. As a place of sight, it lacked the internal, profound experience that only hearing can offer.

By contrast, the Temple Mount is a place of hearing. When God appeared to Avraham at its peak, there were no spectacular visual effects, smoke or lightning. There was only a voice. When Avraham was asked to sacrifice his son Yitzchak, it was above all an act of hearing to which he responded. There was little to see. Avraham understood the faculty of hearing as few have ever done. He was the man who had completely broken with the world of idol worship, the world of sheer visuality. Therefore, he was the man to whom God could speak in terms of untainted Judaism.

Sinai Premature?

We are now confronted with another major problem. Why Did God choose to give the Torah under less than optimal conditions? After all, it is clear that the Israelites were not yet ready to receive the Torah. Unversed as they were in the art of hearing, they were unable to reach the level of pure monotheism (since, as we have mentioned, the monotheistic God is outside nature and cannot be seen).

This was certainly the result of many years of slavery in Egypt. The idolatrous Egypt was in many ways the forerunner of ancient Greece, the world of the eye. With the Israelites still under the influence of their four–hundred-year sojourn in Egypt, during which they had all but descended to the lowest level of spirituality, it was virtually impossible to make them reach the highest levels of sanctity within so short a period as seven weeks (from Pesach to Shavuot). It would take far longer before they could attain such a level. Why then was the Torah given at such an early, if not premature, stage? Why not wait until the Israelites were duly prepared to receive the Torah in all its glory?

Shem and Yaphet

An insight made by Rabbi Samson Raphael Hirsch, the great spokesman of Judaism in the nineteenth century, may be of help here. Discussing the relationship between the three children of Noach after the flood, Rabbi Hirsch quotes the blessing which Noach bestowed upon two of his three sons, Shem and Yaphet: "God will open the mind of Yaphet but it will dwell in the tents of Shem" (Bereshit 9:27).

His commentary on this unusual verse reads as follows:

When we look around in historical facts, we can say: The stem of Yapheth reached its fullest blossoming in Yavan, the Greeks Ever; that of Shem, the Hebrew, Israel, who bore and bear the Divine Name of God, through the world of the nations.

To the present day it is only these two races, the descendents of Yaphet and Shem, the Greeks and the Jews, who have become the real educators and teachers of humanity. For all the spiritual treasures, which the world has required, these two have to be thanked, and everything, which, even today, works at the culture and education of mankind connects with that which Yaphet (the predecessor of the Greeks) and Shem (the predecessor of the Jews) brought to the world.

The spiritual gifts of the Romans too, were only a gift of the Hellenes. Yaphet has ennobled the world aesthetically. Shem has enlightened it spiritually and morally, Hellenism and Judaism have become the great active forces in the educational work on mankind, and the rest of the world has been merely the passive material on which they worked.[4]

But what are the future and the purpose of Yaphet?

For Rabbi Hirsch, Yaphet is the bridge between Shem, the carrier of the Hebrew tradition, and Cham, Noach's third son, who took advantage of his father's intoxication and left his naked body uncovered, and who represents sensuality and raw materialism. It is Yaphet, the aesthetic world of the Greeks, which needs to bring about the transformation from the hedonistic world of Cham to the spiritual world of Shem.

But he (Noach) sees that this goal (of bringing the world of Cham to the one of Shem) will not be achieved at once. Between Cham and Shem there is Japhet. A Cham is not immediately responsive to the teaching of the God of Shem. Out of the raw,

---

[4] Rabbi Samson Raphael Hirsch, *The Pentateuch, Bereshit*, trans. Isaac Levy. New York: The Judaica Press Inc., 1971, ad loc. Isaac Levy's translation is highly problematic.

a cultured man has first to be made. The demand which the God of Shem makes is not a small one. A person must first acquire the taste of something higher than he is in his raw, even if this something higher is at first also something that appeals to the senses.... The culture of the beauty and grace of Japhet's schooling is a precursor of the semitic mission, a preparatory school for teaching the people the loftier concept, the still greater beauty which lies in a harmonious joining all the aspects of life under the single idea of the devotion to God.[5]

Sinai as a Preparatory School for Hearing

Herein lies the secret of Sinai. Just as the world of Yaphet is a prerequisite to attaining the exalted level of Shem, so the Sinai visual experience had to precede the more profound acceptance – the hearing – of the Torah. The Divine Revelation had to first involve the eye. Although this may not have been the best mode of revelation, it was absolutely necessary. Yet once the Israelites experienced the Word of God through the medium of sight, through the thunder and lightning and smoke, did it become possible to begin to hear its inner meaning. Without the help of sight, there could have been no hearing. As Jewish history would subsequently show, sight continued to play a role throughout the many upheavals of the Jewish people, although that role decreased with time. Step by step, the faculty of sight made room for the art of hearing – diminishing, yet never disappearing entirely. Only in messianic times, once the Jews reach the level of their ancestor Avraham, will they no longer depend on sight.

The Jews: The People of the Ear

We must always remember that ideally, the Torah should be taught by hearing, not by sight. Although the Jewish people are often referred to as "the people of the book," this is not so. They are the people of the ear. They heard the Divine Word at Sinai. The original Torah was spoken, not written. It was only later, out of necessity, that it became frozen, regrettably, in

---

[5] ibid.

writing. Even then, God established a great tradition of oral interpretation in order to ensure the constant "defrosting" of the written text.

Western Civilization and the State of Israel

Modern Western civilization is to this day engrossed by the faculty of seeing. "Seeing is believing" is still the prevalent attitude amongst most people of the West. People are still incapable of hearing. What, after all, are the main concerns of Western civilization? The visual sciences – physics, biology, technology and economy. While we teach all these disciplines in our universities, we have yet to develop a discipline of hearing.

Judaism does not reject the visual sciences. On the contrary, it has much to say about them. A great deal of halachic literature is dedicated to these fields. At the same time, however, Jewish tradition tells us that if we want to build a better world, we must rank the art of hearing above the visual sciences.

This lesson is particularly pertinent to the State of Israel today. Many of the state's contemporary problems are a direct result of its pervasive use of Greek concepts, its inability to practice the art of hearing. The campaign to open shopping centers on Shabbat, for example, is disturbing. It is not so much the desire to buy, but the desire to see, that motivates the campaign. This is more than a religious problem. It is a psychological one. Many people are not at peace with themselves. Beset by unconfessed feelings of boredom and frustration, they escape their inner selves, desperately seeking diversions in the external world. They can no longer spend quality time with their families, sharing meaningful conversation with their children or spouses. Nor can they concentrate on books or any other form of intellectual stimulation. Hence the desire to open shopping centers on Shabbat. It is a reflection of the inner poverty of a large part of Israeli society. We have created a culture of denial, visual diversions, hiding places in the form of cheap entertainment – all of which prevent us from acknowledging our tragic loss of the art of hearing. We no longer search for the deeper, more refined meaning of life that is so necessary for our inner happiness. We strive for joy, yet we settle for pleasure instead, not realizing that joy can only be found in the passage from a lesser to a greater form of perfection.

Seeing the Shechina

Let us now return to the story of Elisha ben Abuyah. The Talmud in Tractate *Chagiga* describes the origin of Elisha's moral corruption: a mystical voyage in which he, together with three other great sages (Ben Azzai, Ben Zoma and Rabbi Akiva), entered the Pardes – the esoteric world.

> There were four who entered the Pardes.... Before they entered, Rabbi Akiva told them: When you approach the pure marble stones [which resemble the Divine Presence], do not say: There is water here, there is water here [do not look, for your eyes will trick you into thinking they are like pure water], but just continue. Still, Ben Azzai looked and consequently died. Ben Zoma glanced and became mentally unstable. Acher [after watching] chopped down the saplings [his misperception inspired him with a perverted notion of Judaism which led him, and many others, astray]. Only Rabbi Akiva [who did not look] emerged unharmed. (Chagiga 14b)

Here again we have the tragic consequences of the misleading faculty of sight. It was the attempt to see the Divine Presence which brought about the downfall of the three sages. Only Rabbi Akiva, who did not look, emerged unharmed – realizing, as his friends did not, that the eye can grasp no more than a deceptive appearance, an external shell that has nothing to do with the true essence of things. Rabbi Akiva understood that God's Shechina cannot be observed, but only listened to. In this sense, it is revealing that Elisha, whose ruin was instigated by his desire to see, eventually became part of the Greek world, the world of the eye.

Halacha and Aggadah

Judaism is not immune to Greek influences. After all, it is in many ways a religion of external acts. But a deeper look into its *weltanschauung* reveals, as Franz Rosenzweig so correctly argued, that Judaism possesses a profound understanding of the human condition, of our need to hear in the deed. Through the external observance of a mitzvah we may begin to grasp its exalted meaning, to hear its inner voice. Contemplation about the mitzvot without actually fulfilling them makes one deed-deaf. We can understand the profound meaning of a mitzvah only by experiencing it.

Nevertheless, one should never content oneself with the technical observance of the mitzvot. The hearing of a mitzvah's inner voice does not come automatically. It is for this reason that the study of aggadah, the non-legal part of Judaism, is so important. Halacha may instruct us on how to act in a given situation, but it does not provide insight into the quality of a given act or the spiritual elevation which it achieves. For that, one needs the aggadah. Aggadah, in fact, has been Judaism's answer to all those who have accused it of behaviorism. In the words of Yeshayahu, speaking in the name of God: "The people draw near with their mouth and honor Me with their lips, while their heart are far from Me and their fear of Me is a commandment of men learned by rote" (Yeshayahu 29:13).

Unfortunately, the prophet's condemnation resonates strongly in today's Jewish world. In many religious communities, outward compliance with the mechanics of the law has taken the place of authentic engagement with the living God. Observance has been reduced to superficial conduct. Contemporary Jewish education provides students with an incomplete halachic understanding, since the description of an action is divorced from its ultimate intention. We often perceive the mitzvot through the eye of the Greeks, seeing only their external form. David Hartman calls this "the Akeda consciousness" – an act that becomes totally unintelligible once it is divorced from its Divine meaning. While it may have been necessary in the case of Avraham sacrificing his son, it is definitely not what the Halacha is all about. Divine meaning is an integral part of halachic observance. And, while it may be true that the final word of the *Shulchan Aruch* was sufficient for our forefathers, whose deep religious feeling enabled them to hear the sublime music behind the text, it is no longer the case today. Today, we must have aggadah in order to hear. The current proliferation of halachic works, listing the intricate technicalities of the halachot without ever allowing us to hear their meaning, is in fact a very Greek way of approaching Jewish law. It turns the word of God into little more than a mechanical act.

JEAN PAUL SARTRE, ANTI-SEMITISM AND
JEWISH IDENTITY[1]

IN 1946, THE FRENCH EXISTENTIAL PHILOSOPHER, Jean Paul Sartre, published his famous treatise entitled "Anti-Semitism, Anti-Semite and Jew." In this study, Sartre analyzes anti-Semitism and tries to illuminate the depths of its ugliness. The essay directly attacks anti-Semitism and offers a "cure" for mankind to rid itself of this disease. Indeed, Sartre identifies anti-Semitism as a sickness of the human soul that requires surgery.

The central concept in this study is that of "authenticity." According to Sartre, the root cause of anti-Semitism is that people lack authenticity, which he defines as the ability to be oneself and accept oneself for what one really is, with all one's positive and negative character traits. Anti-Semites are people who are unable to feel comfortable in their own skins, and then accuse others of causing their failures and shortcomings. They cannot accept what they see when they look in the mirror, and thus constantly focus their attention in the direction of others. In their search for a group whom they can easily identify as the source of what they lack, they look for an underdog, for those who cannot defend themselves. And so they become anti-Semites, since Jews, over the thousands of years, have been a small nation, most of the time living in exile under very difficult circumstances that made it virtually impossible for them to protect themselves. Consequently, argues Sartre, once the gentile becomes authentic and no longer needs to project his fear and discontent on others, he will cease to be anti-Semitic.

---

[1] From my book *Crisis, Covenant and Creativity*. Jerusalem: Urim Publications, 2005.

But what about Jewish authenticity? To this question Sartre responds with a forthright definition: "This is for the Jew to live to the full his condition as a Jew."[2] At first, one cannot but agree with Sartre. For the Jew to live his life as a Jew and not to hide or deny it seems indeed to be the only way to achieve internal authenticity. Once the Jew respects his own traditions and is proud of his highly unusual history – once he makes a deep commitment to Judaism – then one can indeed speak of Jewish authenticity. However, this is not at all what Sartre has in mind.

As we read on, we realize that Sartre has an all together different understanding of what it means for a Jew "to live to the full his condition as a Jew." Instead of calling on Jews to respect their own traditions and live according to the Torah, he calls for a radical re-assessment of what it means to be Jewish, and in doing so, he offers the bleakest analysis, offering a concept of jewishness that stands in total opposition to every authentic Jewish interpretation.

To introduce his theory, Sartre makes the following disturbing observation: "Jews have neither community of interests, nor community of beliefs. They do not have the same fatherland, they have no history."[3] Sartre argues that it is not Judaism, nor Israel, nor Jewish history which defines the Jew. If anything, these are by-products – the associated sub-cultural accoutrements from a prior Jewishness. But what then do Jews have in common? What makes the Jew Jewish?

"The sole tie that binds them is the hostility and the disdain of the societies which surround them. Thus the authentic Jew is the one who asserts his claim in the face of the disdain shown toward him."[4] In other words, to be Jewish is to be the object of anti-Semitism and to face this fact unflinchingly. Once Jews realize this fact, they are authentic and true to themselves. For Sartre, this is the essential definition of the Jew. The Jew's existence depends on the hatred of others. Indeed, it is out of the gentiles' primordial hostility that the Jew is formed.

---

[2] Jean Paul Sartre, *Anti-Semite and Jew*, translated by George J. Becker, New York: Schocken Books, 1965.
[3] Ibid., 91.
[4] Ibid.

Sartre's observation requires our careful consideration. When he argues that Jews have no community, no fatherland or history, Sartre knows full well what he writes. Sartre does not deny that there is Judaism, that Jews have a most unusual history. As Leo Baeck once said, "More history has been assigned to these people than other people."[5] But this history of the Jews, their longing for their land and even their religion, is not the result of their own endeavors, but of the hatred of others. Jewish history, argues Sartre, is merely the history of anti-Semitism. What glues the Jews together and what has made them a unique and eternally enduring people is that they are singled out for hatred. Their unique and unprecedented history and power to survive against all odds is not the result of a genuine inner strength, but merely an ability to resist external abhorrence. Sartre's is a geological metaphor. The intense pressure from without melds the Jews together, turning them into an indestructible nation.

Gentle Liquidation

That Sartre contradicts himself does not seem to worry him. In the case of all other nations, authenticity means to be oneself and not to allow others to determine one's very being. For the Jew alone, this is different. The Jew's authenticity is to recognize and accept that he is essentially inauthentic. Thus Sartre calls for the gentle liquidation of the Jewish people, not out of hatred, but in fact out of love. Since anti-Semitism is a great injustice, we should hope and pray for its end. But of course, this ipso facto will bring an end to the very existence of the Jewish people. Indeed, this is the only logical outcome. Interestingly, the anti-Semite now finds himself in an unusual paradox according to Sartre: in order to destroy the Jews, all he must do is stop wishing and working for their destruction!

"Thus, the authentic Jew is one who thinks of himself as a Jew because the anti-Semite has put him in the situation of a Jew is not opposed to assimilation any more than the class-conscious worker is opposed to the liquidation of the classes.... The authentic Jew simply renounces for himself

---

[5] Leo Baeck, *This People of Israel*, 402.

an assimilation that is today impossible; he awaits the radical liquidation of anti-Semitism for his sons."[6]

That Sartre comes to this conclusion out of genuine concern for the Jewish people, and as an outgrowth of his ongoing battle against the evil of anti-Semitism, does not take away from the fact that his conclusion – although for totally different reasons – comes out identical to the ideology espoused by Hitler and the Nazi-regime: a world without Jews is a better world.

Sartre's idea that anti-Semitism has provided the life-force behind the Jews' survival throughout history is not entirely new. In the seventeenth century, Spinoza made a similar observation in his *Tractatus Theologico Politicus*.[7] Nor can one deny the fact that the Jewish tradition itself hints in this direction.[8] Indeed, God always seems to find a way to send an enemy to make it impossible for Jews to assimilate completely. Yet Sartre's contribution is of such great significance because a great number of scholars, including Jewish scholars and thinkers, adopted his approach. While early generations of Jews would never have seen their destiny and identity in Sartre's terms, there is much evidence to suggest that since the emancipation of the Jews in the nineteenth century, more and more Jews have accepted his theory.

After the Holocaust, the question "who is a Jew" became one of great urgency. For many centuries, Jewishness had been determined according to Jewish tradition. A Jew was a person born of a Jewish mother or who converted according to Torah law. It meant that one belonged to a nation with a deeply religious and moral message. Jewishness was understood in purely Halachic terms, and no Jew would even consider questioning these definitions. But with the radical shifts of the nineteenth century, attempts were made to secularize even the definition of the Jew, which ultimately led to great confusion and a myriad of conflicting interpretations. This was caused by the desire to become part of European culture, to be accepted by the gentile world, and to be able to interact with that world on a completely

---

[6] Ibid., 50.

[7] Spinoza, *A Theologico-Political Treatise*, translated by R.H.M. Elwes. New York: Dover, 1951, 55.

[8] See Amos 3:2 and commentaries.

equal basis. As long as Jews continued to eat kosher food, observe the Sabbath on Saturday instead of Sunday, to pray in Hebrew, and to circumcise their sons, it would be hard to integrate into the European gentile's world.

Judaism: Hereditary Illness?

In Israel, this issue continues to burn, robbing many Israelis of their sense of identity. Chief Rabbi Sir Jonathan Sacks quotes a young Israeli who was once asked what it meant to him to be Jewish: "Judaism is a hereditary illness…. You can get it from your parents and also pass it along to your children. And why call it an illness? Because not a small number of people have died from it."[9]

It is not difficult to understand how this young Israeli came to such a grim conclusion. When the "old" religious definition of Jewishness was challenged and undermined, there was no new adequate one to replace it. Earlier generations saw their Jewishness in the light of their universal ethical-monotheistic mission to bring God-consciousness into the world. It was a great privilege and an honor to be a Jew and to live by the commandments of the Torah and its oral Tradition. But when the mission was removed from the heart of being Jewish, Judaism turned into a burden without a rational *raison d'être*. In their quest to come up with a new meaning for Jewishness, scholars and thinkers groped for and suggested a hodgepodge of definitions, but none could be maintained with any degree of intellectual honesty. In the eyes of many Jews, Jewishness lost much of its beauty and its accompanying feeling of pride. Gone were the mission and the awareness that one lived by a divine covenant of high responsibility and dignity. And since there is no alternative definition of Jewishness, because Jewishness is just about our special relationship with the Creator of the Universe, Judaism for the uninitiated became a negative burden.

---

[9] Jonathan Sacks, *Radical Then, Radical Now: The Legacy of the World's Oldest Religion.* London: HarperCollins, 2000, 2.

Holocaust Obsession

The preoccupation with the Holocaust as a source of identity in many Jewish assimilated circles throughout the world, which in some cases approaches the level of an obsession, is a clear manifestation of this trend. While no one would deny the need to study, discuss, and remember the Holocaust in all its dimensions and ugliness, it is clear that on a deeper level Holocaust memorialization has replaced classical Judaism as a new form of quasi-religious worship. Holocaust memorial centers have proliferated in nearly every part of the Jewish world in ways that are frequently problematic. Building memorials is not in itself such a problem, except that they tend to exist in the absence of other Jewish centers that could provide a highly positive understanding of what it means to be a Jew. Memorial centers are visited by thousands of young Jews who would never enter a synagogue, take part in Jewish learning sessions, or participate in any other form of uplifting Jewish life-experience. The result is obvious: Jewishness becomes synonymous with suffering. We also find that Holocaust programs dominate the Jewish Studies departments in many universities and that the Holocaust is the primary theme explored by modern Jewish literature.

Although the Holocaust provides the secular Jewish community with an identity, it is a horribly negative and distorted image of our people. We are not merely a nation that suffers, but sadly this idea is what unites an otherwise divided community and provides the logic for secular Jewish survival. They persist in order to spite Hitler, and in so doing have unwittingly become Sartre's Jews. They are Jews only because of gentile hatred. It is perfectly understandable why young Jews would view their Judaism as an affliction they contracted from their parents and which they may or may not wish to pass on to their children.

One is reminded of the well-known Jewish philosopher, Professor David Hartman, who observed that we cannot build the future of the people of Israel on the ashes of Auschwitz. Indeed, such an approach ultimately leads to a disaster the consequences of which we can already see. Judaism as protest against Hitler produced a generation of young people that despises and disregards its Jewishness. The Holocaust scholar Lucy Davidowicz warned us when she wrote, "If we are a people that gets murdered, the young people will flee from us."[10]

The preoccupation with the Holocaust, particularly in America, may serve as a subconscious escape route from a positive identity of Jewishness and Judaism. Once a person no longer wants Judaism to be at the center of his life, but desires instead to release himself of its responsibilities and mission, he is left in a precarious situation. Unless he is willing to turn his back on his heritage completely, he must find a justification for identifying himself as a Jew. In the absence of a constructive, positive motivation, he is forced to look for a negative root cause. In the Holocaust, he finds his tunnel out, but it is a dark and ugly passageway devoid of the joy and stimulation that real Jewish content provides.

The younger generations must come to learn that Judaism and Jewishness live on *despite* Auschwitz and not because of it.

Pride in Israel

Still, this is not the whole picture. After all, it cannot be denied that the establishment of the State of Israel created a completely different spirit within our nation. The emergence of a Jewish state became, after all, a source of tremendous pride for Jews wherever they found themselves. In contrast to the victimization of the Holocaust, the Jewish people suddenly felt a renewed sense of destiny. With the creation of our own state, our people's suffering drifted into the background of our identity, to be replaced by a feeling that Jews working together can accomplish the impossible. The feeling that Jews were re-entering history in an unprecedented way stood in total opposition to the experience of the Holocaust. A nation that after losing six million of its members found its way home after nearly two thousand years of exile and built a state from scratch while defending itself against several mighty Arab armies was something that, for many, radically changed the meaning of Jewishness.

In fact, many scholars and Zionist leaders believed the establishment of the State of Israel would finally solve the problem of anti-Semitism. Israel

---

[10] Quoted by Jonathan Sacks, *Traditional Alternatives: Orthodoxy and the Future of the Jewish People*, London: Jews' College Publications 1989, 107.

would normalize the Jews, who would be considered a nation like any other. No longer playing the underdog under Diaspora conditions, Jews would consequently be accepted and embraced by the international community. Israel thus became the "baby" of even the most assimilated Jews and produced a groundswell of nationalistic spirit.

Above all, Zionism became the sought-after substitute for authentic Judaism. It was not Jewish tradition that would keep Jews alive and together, but Zionism. Many Zionist thinkers declared that while Judaism had undoubtedly kept the Jews alive in the Diaspora, it had now become obsolete and could respectfully be dropped. Zionism became the new *raison d'être* of the Jews. The Jews found a new mission and a new definition to guarantee their future.

However, a careful examination of Israel's history shows that the Zionist ideal started to become untenable in 1967. While Israel had been an unprecedented success story in its early days, the cracks in its walls started to show once winning its wars became more challenging. Slowly but surely, Israel's existence came under threat, to the point that the war in 1967 was seen by many as a potential new Holocaust in which the Jewish people for the second time would run the risk of being exterminated completely. Although Israel was miraculously saved from destruction, the later wars proved to be extremely traumatic for world Jewry and especially so for Israel's citizens.

With an increase in Arab hostility, terrorist attacks, more wars, and more loss of life, many Israelis became convinced that there was no escape from the eternal condition of Jewish suffering. With the outbreak of the Intifada, with its continuous stream of suicide bombings, this feeling of hopelessness became even stronger. Simultaneously, Israel lost its credibility and admiration among large parts of the world community when it was forced to defend itself against the Palestinian populace, using last-resort tactics it had hoped to avoid. An outbreak of anti-Semitism in Europe came shortly afterwards. As if it were just waiting for an opportunity to turn its back on the Jews, Europe used Israel's self-defense as a provocation for anti-Semitic attacks on its own Jewish communities and on Israel. Comparing Israel's army to the Nazis, European countries accused Israel of stealing land from the Palestinians and managed to rewrite the history of the Middle East in radically anti-Semitic ways.

Israel as a Source of Anti-Semitism

The State of Israel, which was supposed to serve as a beacon for the Jewish people, suddenly seemed to be the source of its undoing. Jews had always been taught that the State of Israel was the solution to anti-Semitism, and now Israel was being used throughout Europe as the reason to justify anti-Semitic hatred. What was supposed to normalize the Jewish people only increased their utter otherness. Therefore, many Israelis became more and more convinced that the original Zionist program to rescue the Jewish people from this status as Other had failed miserably.

On a deeper level, the ramifications were even more radical. The perceived failure of Zionism to bring about an end to anti-Semitism robbed many Israelis and Jews of their recently acquired sense of Jewish pride. Israel was seen as a source of shame. Once more, Jews had to face their vulnerability. The international press made it virtually impossible to rely on the State of Israel to provide the foundation for a positive Jewish identity.

Neither the Holocaust nor the State of Israel yielded a meaningful definition of Jewishness. What the early Zionist leaders did not realize, or perhaps did not want to realize, was that a state cannot create its own meaning. The state's role is to secure and make tangible a prior set of values and history that exist independent from it. No political entity can provide the sole meaning in the lives of its citizens. At best, states can create the conditions under which a population can flourish. The State of Israel can do no more than to make sure that Jews are able to uphold their Jewishness, to increase their commitment to Jewish values and, if necessary, defend our people against attack. To call upon the state to provide our Jewish identity, independent of Judaism, is a naïve and self-destructive dream.

The *"Signon"* Problem

> "And it came to pass in the morning watch, that God looked down to the camp of the Egyptians through a pillar of fire and cloud and brought the camp of the Egyptians into confusion." (Shemot 14:24)

This verse, which describes the moment when the Jews stood at the edge of the Red Sea with the Egyptian army in pursuit, is of great importance to us in our quest to uncover the deeper meaning and purpose of "identity." Rashi in his commentary is particularly taken here by the concept of confusion. In what way did God confuse the Egyptian camp?

"He befuddled them and took away their reason."[11] In other words, God denied the Egyptians the ability to use their faculty of reason, and that ultimately brought about their defeat. They were, seemingly, no longer able to think clearly. Their lack of mental clarity caused them to pursue the Jews into the parted sea despite the clear signs that God Himself was guiding and protecting them. And so they drowned when the water came crashing down upon them.

However, there is more to Rashi's observation than meets the eye.[12] In Hebrew, Rashi uses the word *signon,* which is conventionally translated as "reason," but this word implies much more than just logical thinking. To understand Rashi fully, we must turn to an intriguing passage in the Talmud (*Sanhedrin* 89a) in which the rabbis try to offer a clear methodology for unmasking a false prophet. The legitimacy of a prophet, it turns out, depends on a special quality that the Talmud calls *signon,* the same word used by Rashi: "One *signon* is revealed to many prophets, yet no two prophets prophesy in an identical *signon.*"

In this case, the conventional translation of *signon* is "communication" or "phraseology," but this translation fails to resonate with the Talmud's deeper intention. Again Rashi comes to our aid in his commentary on this passage, throwing light on his earlier observation about the confusion of the Egyptian camp.

He explains that when God communicates with several prophets, He uses a single phraseology and also expresses the message with one kind of "intonation." This is the meaning of "One *signon* is revealed to many prophets." In other words, God's style of communicating does not vary when He speaks to different prophets. God apparently has a very specific and personal way of doing things. When it comes to communicating with

---

[1] Ad loc.

[2] I am indebted to my *mechutan* and friend Rabbi Chaim Walkin, *mashgiach ruchani* at Ateret Yisrael Yeshiva, Jerusalem, for making me aware of this insight.

His prophets, God expresses His message in a form that is innate to Him and no other.

However, when prophets pass God's word on to the people of Israel, each does so in his own way. Each has his own *signon*. When conveying God's words, each prophet uses his own style and intonation, since each prophet is unique in his nature and psychological composition. This fact is essential to understanding prophecy: all prophecy is filtered through the personality of the prophet, and therefore always carries an element of the prophet's distinctive individuality.[13] Thus the prophet as medium becomes part of his prophetic message, which ultimately enables him to convey God's word to the people in the most powerful and effective way. But since (and this is crucial to Rashi's argument), two prophets are necessarily two separate individuals, each with his own style, it is impossible for them to use identical phraseology or intonation. If they do, it is a clear indication that something is wrong and that one or both of them are false. One is imitating the other and therefore lacks authenticity.

This is the deeper meaning of Rashi's statement concerning the confusion of the Egyptians. The confusion which the Egyptians experienced at the time they pursued the Jews at the Red Sea was a severe identity crisis. God took away their sense of identity and purpose, and this became their undoing. The Egyptians no longer knew who they were. They became confused about their essence and lost their distinctive *signon*.

They lost all direction, even to the extent that they could no longer deal rationally with their earlier hatred for Jews. As Sartre predicts, their hatred for Jews increased because of this lack of authenticity.

Man is only Himself

In an enlightening essay, the famous *Mashgiach* of the former Mir Yeshiva, Rabbi Yerucham Leibovits, discusses the importance of having a clear sense of identity:

---

[13] The only exception to this rule is Moshe, who on certain occasions became the direct vehicle through which God spoke, as if God Himself were speaking. See, for example, Rashi and many other commentaries on Devarim 30:1. See also BT *Megillah* 31a.

Man is only himself, i.e., his inner life. Every move he makes against his inner essence, particularly when he focuses on his appearance (i.e., what kind of impression he likes to make) he becomes a stranger to himself and will deny his very self.

Because man is able to move out of himself without end and thus can lose himself completely, he will wander around without a place and without recognizable surroundings and will not be able to hold on to anything.[14]

This indeed is the greatest evil that can befall a human being; the loss of selfhood. One is reminded of Sartre's observation that we only become what we are by the radical and deep-seated refusal of that which others have made of us. The constant desire of most men to be something other than what they really are is one of the greatest tragedies of our times. To be authentically oneself in a world that strives night and day to mold us into something Other is perhaps the greatest battle that man needs to fight if he wants to stay sane and significant. Once one has lost one's *signon*, one has basically lost everything, because a man's *signon* is what makes him into an individual whom he can recognize as himself – as a being that has no equivalent. A man's *signon* is the foundation of his self-awareness and self respect.

Moshe's Identity Paradox

Surprisingly enough, it was Moshe Rabbenu who had to deal with the problem of *signon*-identity more than any other. As we look at his life, we are struck by the fact that it was he who became Israel's greatest teacher. While we would have imagined that such a leader could only emerge from a strong Jewish background, the story of Moshe shows us otherwise. Moshe is brought up in a non-Jewish, perhaps even an anti-Jewish, environment after Pharaoh's daughter rescues him from the river. Growing up in Pharaoh's house, he was utterly disconnected from his people, hardly aware that he was

---

[14] Rabbi Yerucham Leibovits, *Da'at Chochma U-Mussar.*

a Jew. Years later, as a grown man, he encountered his true self, which led to one of the most heroic moments in Jewish history.

While still part of Pharaoh's household, Moshe suddenly decides to go see his brothers, the Jews. This confrontation with Self proves to be perhaps the most crucial moment in all of his life.

> "It came to pass in these days that Moshe grew up and went out to his brothers. He saw their burden and he saw an Egyptian striking a Hebrew, one of his brothers. He looked left and right and he saw that there was no man, and he struck the Egyptian and buried him in the sand." (Shemot 11:2)

This whole episode is concealed in mystery. What made Moshe suddenly decide to go and see his brothers? How did he know that these were "his brothers" in the first place? What caused him to take the side of the Hebrew instead of the Egyptian? What is the significance of first "looking left and right" and only then striking the Egyptian?

Moshe, once grown up, somehow felt that he was different from the other men in Pharaoh's house. Something deep within him must have told him that the slaves living at the other side of the fence were related to him, and he was compelled to have a look. This led to an encounter with something he could not have anticipated: anti-Semitism and his own authenticity! Once he saw the Egyptian officer strike the Jew, Moshe experienced a most intricate dilemma. On whose side was he going to be? It would have been entirely natural for him to take the side of the Egyptian. The Egyptian belonged to the culture with which he was familiar. This was his world, and he certainly must have heard a lot about "those Jews" who refused to adopt the Egyptians' ways. These were a people who had their own religion and a culture removed entirely from the world of Egyptian polytheism, and this created a strong feeling of hatred amongst Egyptians for their Jewish slaves.

For Moshe, this must have been a moment of profound identity crisis. Where do I belong? Who am I? For a moment Moshe does not know what to do.

And He Looked Left and Right

Suddenly these words: "And he looked left and right" take on a much deeper significance. He looked one way and he saw the world of Egypt; then he looked the other way and saw the world of the Israelites. And he realized that there was no man, i.e., that he himself could not claim to be a man as long as he remained caught between two worlds. It is utterly impossible to be a man in this world unless one has a clear identity. In that split second Moshe decides. "He struck the Egyptian and buried him in the sand." In a moment of violence and total clarity, Moshe resolves his identity crisis and buries the Egyptian within himself, determining once and for all that his lot should be with the Israelites.[15]

Moshe's choice created a revolution in his own life and radically transformed the whole of Jewish history. In a split second Moshe found his *signon,* and only then was able to start his real life. It is from that moment onwards that the greatest revolutionary movement in all human history starts to take place. Moshe's becoming an authentic Jew heralds all the other great revolutions that continue to shape world history. It was the moment that led to the foundation of mankind's liberty, and through which it became possible for God's ethical message for humanity to become part of our physical reality. Once man becomes aware of his identity and accepts his mission as a free moral being, then his real story begins.

Speech Impediment

However, identity formation does not usually happen overnight. It is a process that requires great effort and struggle. To give birth to identity is to experience moments of utter despair and also great victory. But the most crucial moment is the one when human beings make up their minds to discover their identities and own their lives. This matter is borne out in an episode that follows from Moshe's authentic Jewish awakening. Still far from certain what his identity is really all about, Moshe meets God at the burning bush. Here God commands him to return to Egypt to challenge Pharaoh and to liberate his people. Moshe is overwhelmed and shocked by this divine

---

[15] This unique interpretation was orally transmitted to me. The author is unknown.

demand. Nothing is further from his mind than to lead this people, with whom he never had any real connection, to freedom. As a result, a surprising and unprecedented dispute between man and God takes place.

> God said, "I have seen the suffering of my people… and I have heard their cries… and I have come down to save them from the clutches of the Egyptians… and take them up… to the land flowing with milk and honey…."

> "So now come, that I may send you to Pharaoh and take My people, the children of Israel, out of Egypt." Moshe said to God, "Who am I that I should go to Pharaoh and that I should take the children of Israel out of Egypt?" [God] replied, "I will be with you, and this is the sign that I have sent you."

> "Also, when you take the people out of Egypt, you [all] will serve God on this mountain." Moshe said to God, "When I come to the children of Israel and tell them, 'The God of your forefathers has sent me to you,' they will ask, 'What is His name?' What shall I answer them?" God said to Moshe [to tell them]: "I am whoever I am…."

> Moshe said to God, "Please, O Lord, I am not a man of words – not yesterday, not the day before… for I stammer and have difficulty speaking." *(Shemot 3:7–4:10)*

Moshe's objections are intriguing. How can he argue with the Creator of the Universe? Although this divine encounter must have come to him as a complete surprise, it is not that fact per se that he cannot accept. What seems to bother him is that he himself is not able to speak well, and certainly not to Pharaoh! Moshe claims that he is not a "man of words," yet nearly everything else we know about his life demonstrates his unusual talent for public speaking (nearly the whole book of Devarim is a single lengthy speech he gave before he died). We clearly need to investigate the deeper meaning of this supposed inability to speak.

It is possible that Moshe's refusal to speak was not born out of a physical speech impediment but rather from his lack of a clear identity from which he could form a coherent position. Just because a person recognizes that he is a Jew does not mean that he understands the content of his identity. This was Moshe's situation, so that he doubted his ability to complete the mission that God gave him. How can I stand in front of Pharaoh and argue that he should let the Israelites go, if I do not yet fully realize what an Israelite is? No doubt Pharaoh will realize that I am not really, fully one of them. I may belong to their tribe but I have not yet become one of them in spirit, and this will make my argument weak. My authenticity is not yet well established. A man cannot fight for something unless he knows what it is he's fighting for! After all, it is not the physical liberty of the Jews that You, God, most desire. Primarily what You want is to liberate the Israelites spiritually, and so how can I confront Pharaoh when it is not clear to me what that means?

But Who Are You?

Then, suddenly, in the middle of the debate, Moshe turns the argument around. Instead of responding to God's questions, he asks God a question, one that may very well be seen as the ultimate chutzpah. You want me to tell the Israelites that the God of their fathers has sent me to them, but they will ask me, "What is His name?"

What difference would it make whether Moshe knows God's name or not? If he tells the elders of Israel that God appointed him to lead the people out of slavery, does he really think they won't be interested in what he has to say because he does not know God's official name? On a deeper level, this projected question of the Israelites is in fact Moshe's own question, and at the heart of the issue is a question of a most profound nature.

I do not know who I am, but even so, tell me who You are. What is Your identity? When we read this question for the first time, we get the impression that Moshe does not know to Whom he is speaking. Since when can a human being ask God about His identity? Is it not extremely arrogant to think that God has to explain Himself to human beings? Nevertheless, God understands Moshe's inquiry. By asking who God is, Moshe is really looking for a way to understand his own identity fully. Only when we understand our source can we understand ourselves. Jews are particularly defined by the special relationship that they have with their Creator. If I am essentially part of a relationship with God, then only when I understand this relationship and the being to Whom I am relating do I really attain self-knowledge as a Jew. Only when human beings acknowledge and experience in their innermost core that they are created in God's image can they know who they are. But that means that they must have some idea of what that Image is all about. Only then does self-knowledge become possible.

Therefore, it is only Moshe's consciousness of God that enables him to understand his mission. Only consciousness of his Creator can give him the strength to confront Pharaoh and fulfill God's commandment.

In fact, since everything else in this world is affected by external forces and subject to change, the only stable source of identity is God. God's identity is by definition absolute. God's response now resonates to us in a beautifully simple and harmonic way: "I am whoever I am." The secret to identity is authenticity. Nothing from without which is not part of My essence affects My being. I will surely influence outer forces, but they will not change My essence. In fact, it is My essence that gives Me the power to affect the world around Me. And so you, Moshe, must try to develop a similar attitude. Once you have tapped the root of your inner self, which is so inherently connected with My image, you will be able to achieve full authenticity, and then the faculty of speech will be yours. When you are no longer swayed by external forces, your deepest essential being will reveal itself.

Gentile Reminders

Jewish continuity and survival depend upon Jews recognizing that their identities spring from thousands of years of carrying out a divine mission. Neither the Holocaust nor the State of Israel will provide them with a solid identity. If we want to survive, and if we believe that it matters whether or not there are Jews in the world, then we must look into our traditions, re-evaluate them, and come to understand ourselves as essentially Jewish selves.

In a world in which Jews have lost their sense of Jewishness, it seems that God sometimes comes to remind them of who they are through the wise words of the gentiles. Sometimes it is *they* who recognize the Jews as the instrument through which God's divine plan for the world is to be realized.

The Russian novelist Leo Tolstoy wrote the following:

The Jew is that sacred being who has brought down from heaven the everlasting fire, and has illumined with it the entire world. He is the religious source, spring and fountain out of which all the rest of the peoples have drawn their beliefs and their religions.[16]

In our own time, it was Thomas Cahill who wrote, in his own admirable way:

The Jews gave us the Outside and the Inside – our outlook and our inner life. We can hardly get up in the morning or cross the street without being Jewish. We dream Jewish dreams and hope Jewish hopes. Most of our best words, in fact – new, adventure, surprise, unique, individual, person, vocation, time, history, future, freedom, progress, spirit, faith, hope, justice – are the gifts of the Jews.[17]

This, indeed, is the real identity of the Jew. Over vast regions of space and time, Jews have carried the word of God, and by doing so became the natural representative of this Word, influencing their fellow human beings in every generation. Once they rediscover this mission, they will rediscover their identity, and then their problems, and those of the world, will be resolved. Because it is only through the word of God that humanity can hope to find redemption.

---

[16] Quoted by Chief Rabbi J.H. Hertz, *A Book of Jewish Thought*. London: Oxford University Press, 1966, 135.

[17] Thomas Cahill, *The Gifts of the Jews*. New York: Doubleday, 1998, 240–241.

COUNTING JEWS:
MORTAL DANGER AND JEWISH ETERNITY

VERY FEW PROHIBITIONS in the Torah are as mysterious as the one forbidding us to count Jews. Very few mitzvot in all of the Torah penetrate as deeply into the essence and identity of the Jewish people as this prohibition does.

In Shemot (30:12) we read: "When you take census of the Children of Israel according to their numbers, every man shall give God 'atonement money' for his soul when counting them, so that there will not be a plague among them when counting them."

This means that counting Jews is basically *sakanat nefashot,* mortally dangerous – it could cost people their lives. When for reasons of security or taxation one needs to know how many Jews there are, the only way that one may count them is to do so indirectly. Thus, each Jew was asked to offer a half-shekel to the Tabernacle or the Temple. These half-shekels were counted, and in this way one would know how many Jews there were. The same *shekalim* were afterwards used as a contribution to the upkeep of the Tabernacle or Temple. Furthermore, we are taught that these contributions also functioned as an atonement for counting the Jews in the first place.

Later, King David violated this rule and had the Jews counted directly. The consequences were dreadful; many died (2 Shmuel 24).

Commentators have tried to understand the reason for this prohibition and its severity. Many struggle to find a satisfying answer. What is wrong with taking a census of a nation? What moral or religious principles are violated that could warrant the death of so many people? No nation can survive without knowing its numbers; its economy, army and security depend on this information.

Yet counting the Jewish people is so detrimental that it seems as though the Torah would have preferred not to allow for a census at all, since counting even indirectly requires atonement. Out of sheer necessity, the Torah permits taking a census by way of *shekalim*, but only in this roundabout way and only for the benefit of the Temple.

In order to grasp the significance of this issue, we must look into the very nature of the Jewish people. It is clear from the very inception of this prohibition that to count Jews would do the understanding of the nation's essence a great injustice and would be entirely missing the point of its existence.

Jerusalem and Caesarea

To help us unravel this mystery, we need to delve into a remarkable observation that the Talmud makes concerning Jerusalem and Caesarea:

> Regarding Caesarea and Jerusalem: If somebody tells you that both places are laid to waste, do not believe it. When people tell you that both are settled [doing well], do not believe it. However, if somebody says: Caesarea is laid to waste but Jerusalem is settled, or Jerusalem is laid to waste and Caesarea is settled, you may believe it (*Megillah* 6a).

What is the meaning of this obscure observation? We believe that the Talmud is trying to make readers aware of a fundamental principle in the philosophy of history: One can read history through the eyes of Jerusalem – through the lens of Judaism – or through the eyes of Caesarea – the Roman or Western perspective. This is especially so when one tries to understand the history of the Jewish People. When we read Jewish history through the eyes of Jerusalem, we read it through a Jewish, religious and moral *weltanschauung* that may include metaphysics. Therefore, it will convey a specifically Jewish message. However, when one reads it through the perspective of Caesarea, one must draw completely different conclusions. After all, the Talmud sees Caesarea as a symbol of the Roman perspective –

in other words, Western civilization – and the Roman Empire gave birth to a secular understanding of history. An island of Rome inside the Land of Israel, Caesarea often clashed with the worldview of Jerusalem. Caesarea's presence symbolized the fact that Rome's views had infiltrated the *weltanschauung* of the Jews, even in the Land of Israel, and consequently the door was open for many Jews to read their own history by the criteria of Rome.

The Talmud's message here is that the Jewish view and the Roman view are mutually exclusive. They have no common ground in their understanding of Jewish history. One can read Jewish history from a Western perspective and try to understand it by the criteria of Western philosophical thinking and academia, or one can read it is as an integral part of a religious Jewish experience, which sees everything in a completely different light. While Yerushalayim is the symbol of Jewish sovereignty, Caesarea symbolizes exile and all that is foreign to Judaism. When one is "settled," the other is "laid to waste." The Talmud, then, tries to get to the root of what exactly makes Jewish history uniquely Jewish.

Jewish Self-Understanding: Exile and Redemption

It is here that we become involved in the question of Jewish self-understanding. What is it that makes Jews aware of who they are? Two concepts that are fundamental to this self-understanding can be categorized as exile and redemption, *galut* and *geulah*. These two existential experiences shape Jewish history and make Jews special.[1] While much has been written about these concepts in terms of history and sociology, little has been said about their religious-philosophical meaning.

Geulah is the belief that ultimately the Jewish people, and humankind at large, will be redeemed in the Messianic Age. This belief is of primary importance when one wants to understand the psychological makeup of the Jew. No matter how long the exile may last, the Jewish people will return to the Land of Israel and find redemption there. Yet this belief is problematic; in fact, it is bizarre. How can a nation that has lived in exile for thousands of years continue to believe that it will ultimately be redeemed? This is nothing

---

[1] See Eliezer Berkowitz, *Crisis and Faith.* Sanhedrin Press, NY: 1976, Chapter 11.

less than irrational and wishful thinking. The entire course of world history contradicts it. The longer an exile lasts, the more absurd belief in redemption becomes.

Nevertheless, we see that throughout Jewish history, at least until the Enlightenment, Jews throughout the world were absolutely certain that the Redemption would arrive one day. In fact, the longer the Exile lasted, the more their belief that the Redemption was imminent increased. Jews kept this belief throughout the years of exile even though the reality that generations had lived and died without seeing the Geulah would seem to contradict it.

Even more absurd than their irrational belief in redemption is the experience of exile itself. Jews had more than sixty exiles, both major and minor. The fact that they survived them all as a distinct nation is one of the greatest miracles in human history. Historically, when other nations were exiled from their homelands, they disintegrated and eventually disappeared entirely. But the Jews stubbornly remained. Even in exile they built vibrant communities, much of the time under difficult circumstances, surrounded by anti-Semitism and hostile environments. Although one might argue that faith in redemption gave them the strength to endure exile, this actually complicates the phenomenon because, as we have said, faith is irrational. One cannot solve a puzzle with an enigma.

What gave the Jews the strength to survive exile, to accomplish what no other nation could? How did they continue to believe in the dream of redemption when no evidence was at hand to justify that belief?

Jewish Time

To understand this issue better, we must address another Jewish marvel: the Jews' unusual and nearly absurd relationship to time. This relationship finds expression in the way Jews deal with both past and future. They relate to both in ways that are unknown to the rest of the world. The way that Jews relate to time is closely related to the way that they experience mourning and joy.

Jews have a strong connection to grief. To the outsider it looks as though Jews are obsessed with it since they seem to do anything they can to keep themselves in a state of mourning even when the cause occurred thousands of years ago. The most famous example of this is their ongoing mourning over the destruction of the Temple, which took place almost two thousand years ago. One might argue that the day has come to forget about this national tragedy. What other nation still mourns an event that occurred even one hundred years ago, let alone two thousand? Still, the Jews mourn every year for the destruction of the Temple as if it had happened this very day. On the ninth day of the Hebrew months of Av for nearly two thousand years, they have been sitting on the floors of their synagogues, fasting and reading the Book of Lamentations by the prophet Yirmiyahu, who was witness to the destruction.

If one were to ask a Jew why he does this, the Jew would respond that this tragedy did not happen several thousand years ago. Rather, it is something that happens every year on the anniversary of both Temples' destruction. Somehow it is in a Jew's blood. The catastrophic experience of destruction and exile threw all of Judaism into turmoil and was so overwhelming that it rooted itself into the deepest root of every Jew's soul for all the thousands of years to come. Therefore the issue of time was, and continues to be, completely irrelevant. For Jews, it is as if the destruction occurred this morning.

Mourning and Joy

Jews deal with the inescapable experiences of the past in ways that negate the traditional, linear concept of time. They draw the past to the present, making it come alive as if it were new. Jews themselves undergo some kind of metamorphosis and find themselves in their own century, yet in the company of the prophet Yirmiyahu! Together with him, they watch in horror as the Temple goes up in flames. They relive the experience without giving any thought to the fact that this is a tragedy long past. Time is annulled and the past becomes the present.

A similar phenomenon occurs when Jews deal with the future. Instead of waiting patiently for the moment when the future will actually take place, the Jew decides to live it in the here and now. The most outstanding example of this is Shabbat. This day is traditionally called *me'ein olam ha-ba* – reminiscent of the future world. *Olam ha-ba* refers to either the Messianic Age or to the afterlife. The way in which the Jew experiences his Sabbath is by relaxing, not working or worrying, and focusing on matters of the spirit. This is what the future world is all about. Shabbat is "holiness in time," as Abraham Joshua Heschel once described it, a moment of total tranquility in a world of stormy events. On Shabbat, Jews live in the future. To live in a time frame that has not yet arrived is certainly wishful thinking and unrealistic, but it is exactly what the Jews have done for all these thousands of years, and because of it they became an eternal people. Their attitude was clear: Why not enjoy *now* what any way is going to happen in the future? Why not borrow something from the future?

Seder in Auschwitz

Another incredible example is the fact that Jews continued to celebrate festivals such as Pesach in the concentration camps. Countless Jews risked their lives to hold the Seder behind the backs of their Nazi oppressors. They recounted and celebrated their ancestors' exodus from Egypt and escape from Pharaoh, eating makeshift matzoth and declaring, "Last year we were slaves in Egypt but now, on this very night, we are free!" Psychologists have been astonished by this. "But *now, on this very night,* we are free"? The situation in the concentration camps was much worse than anything that ever happened in Egypt! How could anyone celebrate freedom in Auschwitz, where freedom was the farthest thing away? The astonishing answer is that Jews could feel free even in the concentration camps. Even when their bodies were enslaved and tortured, their souls were already living in the future. They believed in a redemption that might take place only in the far future. So why not celebrate it now? Why not even in Auschwitz? This constituted the Jewish mindset throughout the generations.

Mourning and consolation, past and future, exile and redemption ultimately unite in the now. Precisely for that reason, the distinctively contemporary does not exist. The present is made up of past and future, and it is in this world that the Jews live. They never lived in the same kind of contemporary as the Romans or the Greeks. For the Romans and the Greeks, the here and now is all there was. Not so for Jews, who experience time on a different plane. They cannot be trapped in the present, since they are still living in the past or already living in the future. Therefore, they become untouchable and eternal. This is why the anti-semitic world has such a hard time coping with the Jews. Whenever anti-Semites look for Jews in order to destroy them, the Jews are not there.

I suggest that this is the deeper meaning behind the Talmudic saying cited above. From the perspective of Rome and Caesarea, the Jews cannot escape time. That would be contrary to the historical evidence of every other nation in the world and would violate the very premises on which history is built. But from the perspective of Jerusalem, this transcendence of time is not only possible, but is at the root of Jewish existence and testifies to Israel's destiny.

Anomaly

The ordinary and universal rules of history are constantly violated when it comes to the Jews. Where other nations would have succumbed, Jews managed to survive in ways that are hard to explain logically. Always on the edge of death, the Jewish people stayed alive by creating a future that had not yet arrived. The Jews were a dying nation that never actually died. Outliving their enemies became their trademark. The Egyptian, Greek, Roman, Persian and German empires could not destroy them. Instead, the Jewish people miraculously stood at the tombstones of all these empires, poking fun at all its enemies.

Jewish Influence

Not only is the mere survival of the Jewish people not natural, but also its influence on the world has been overwhelmingly out of proportion to its size. This small nation should have vanished, never to be heard of again, yet it stood and continues to stand at the center of world history, making one major contribution after another. There is no field in which Jews have not played a crucial role, whether in the religious world or in the temporal one. Not only did Jews give the Ten Commandments to humankind, but they also gave it the entire Bible, including the New Testament. They gave birth to a man called Jesus, who for millions of people is no less than the messiah. On him – a Jewish boy! – the entire structure of Christianity is built. His birthday and the anniversary of his circumcision are celebrated every year by billions of people on Christmas and New Year's Day.

Jews brought ethics and higher meaning in life to the world, which is partly why they are so hated. Judaism became a revolutionary movement in which humanity refuses to accept the world as it is. Jews taught the world that the pain of injustice, violence and oppression are not inevitable, but can be overcome. Jews have brought to the world the awareness of a higher Authority and the idea that human beings must pay a penalty for immoral acts. When human beings accept that they have a higher calling and are not free to do whatever they wish, the world can be repaired and mended.

The Wrath of the World

Jews have managed to provoke the wrath of the world by staying alive without a homeland, an army, or proper finances, while making the most remarkable discoveries in science, psychology and medicine. In the course of time they have shaped not only their own history but also that of all Western civilization. They gave the world a new language by introducing concepts such as freedom, progress, commitment, justice, and spirit. They also gave humanity a dream to hope and pray for: the Messianic Age.

As Sir Isaiah Berlin said, the Jews "have enjoyed rather too much history and too little geography." It was under these peculiar circumstances that they experienced the Holocaust, history's most devastating genocide. In the expectations of much of the world, including even many of the Jews' greatest sympathizers, it was clear that the Holocaust would end Jewish history once and for all. The Nazis seemed to be finally accomplishing the goal that our other enemies had failed to accomplish in thousands of years: the destruction of the Jewish people. But it was not to be. Although the Jewish people suffered dreadfully, losing six million of its people and enduring unspeakable cruelty, it overcame even this tragedy of unparalleled hatred.

Return to the Land

Not only did the Jewish people survive, but it also managed to make a dramatic recovery that no one in the world, friend nor foe, ever expected and that surprised even themselves. Throughout history, great and powerful nations tried to destroy the Jews, but neither the Roman Empire, Nazi

Germany, nor any of the other nations stopped the Jews from returning to their homeland after thousands of years. This return has no parallel in all of human history.

In every way, the Jewish nation is one of anomaly. It has turned the philosophy of history on its head, confronting scholars and philosophers with a phenomenon that to this day remains unexplained in secular scholarship. The world sees Jews as a mysterious people with an even more puzzling religion, filled with bizarre rituals and outlandish customs. They also see the Jews as frighteningly obsessed with justice, even at the cost of their own well-being – in short, a peculiar and eccentric nation that constantly did all those things that reason could not allow and Caesarea could not accept.

Zionism

At this point we must discuss one of the greatest spiritual tragedies in modern Jewish life. Since the days of the Enlightenment more and more Jews have called for the "normalization" of the Jewish people. This call was born of the conviction that if the Jews would behave and think like the nations of the world, Jewish suffering would come to an end and world Jewry would be accepted like any other nation. Once the non-Jews recognized that Jews are a nation like any other and are willing to rid themselves of their specific, peculiar Jewishness (resulting from their religion, customs and, above all, their claim of exclusiveness), anti-Semitism would vanish. To achieve this goal, secular Zionism came into existence. Its adherents believed that once the Jews had their own country, managed their own affairs, created their own financial infrastructure and even possessed an army they would prove beyond all doubt that they belong and must be welcomed into the community of nations. According to their way of thinking, Zionism was the solution to anti-Semitism.

But it was not to be. To the shock and disappointment of many Jews and Israelis – and above all the Israeli leadership – the State of Israel did not end anti-Semitism. In fact, it is now argued that the state is the major cause of anti-Semitism. Since the Yom Kippur War, Israel has been accused of carrying out a deliberate plan to steal land from its Arab neighbors and from the Palestinians. While Israelis try desperately to refute this argument, they are unsuccessful. To their astonishment, they are witnesses to the deliberate rewriting of history.

The argument is that Israel was born in sin. Zionism is referred to as a curse. Now people argue that Jews should never have returned to Israel. Had they only stayed in the Diaspora, goes the claim, they would have been accepted and anti-Semitism would have vanished.

The Israeli Trauma

Millions of Israelis find the ongoing attempt to fight the State of Israel on all fronts – denying its very existence, calling for its destruction, boycotting its universities and its products – mind-boggling. Suddenly they see that they are more isolated than they ever imagined. For many Israelis this has led to a traumatic realization: Whatever we Jews do, we will always be the exception to the rule. We will always be condemned. This is our fate.

Together with this recognition goes the knowledge that Israel stands at the center of world politics. This country, which is so tiny that it is almost invisible on the world map, occupies more space in the newspapers of the Western world than any other nation. Although millions of people are tortured and killed throughout the world, Israel was internationally held up and condemned as the most dangerous threat to world peace when it constructed a security wall in order to protect its citizens. Israel holds the highest record of condemnations in the United Nations's history. Nothing seems to be more scandalous than a few million Jews trying to survive among three hundred million Arabs. This alone bears witness to the utter anomaly of the Jewish people.

Normalization

What Israelis are slowly realizing is that the "normalization" of the Jewish people is a non-starter and wishful thinking. What was true of the past is true of the present and the future. The Jews are exactly what Bilaam, the anti-semitic prophet in the days of the Torah, said when he watched the Israelites: "A people that dwells alone and is not counted among the nations" (Bamidbar 23:9). There seems to be no escape from this fate and no solution to this idiosyncrasy. Yet that is only a problem for those who look at Jewish history through the lenses of Caesarea.

Jerusalem and Heilsgeschichte

For Jerusalem, however, Bilaam's observation names the very essence of the Jewish people and is not a burden to be cast off. Rather, the whole purpose of the Jewish people is to be a nation that dwells alone. Only as a nation apart can it contribute to the future of humankind. As we have mentioned before, the Jewish nation has a great mission: to bring humankind to the recognition of God and His ethical demands. Its task is to protest and irritate until mankind hears the voice of God. Therefore, it must dwell alone.

Israel seeks to change the world through actions. This is the only way that humankind's destiny can be fulfilled. Therefore, it incorporates a kind of Heilsgeschichte, a redemptive history.

Universal ideas are impersonal, and if redemption came about through ideas alone, then there would be no need for Israel's solitude. Yet, as Judaism teaches, redemption comes about through personal relationships and actions. Therefore the world can only be redeemed through the personal and the concrete. Only when a nation feels that it has been called and rises to its calling can it make an impact on its surroundings. This is at the root of Jewish self-understanding. In order to send a universal message, one must be motivated by an individual and particularistic task. Jewish history is a particular history, but it is not only the history of the Jewish people in the way that other nations have their own individual histories. Jewish history is the history of the world, because the nation of Israel is God's unique instrument for bringing about world redemption.

The Failure of Categorization

The Jewish nation is a sociologically unique phenomenon that defies all attempts at classification. It cannot be grasped in the categories of sociology or ethnology. Although one might try to place it into thousands of categories, it fits into none of them. Sometimes it is a nation, sometime less, sometimes a religion and sometimes more, even to the point of obsession. This fact alone frustrates the world's need to categorize. Israel becomes a frightful phenomenon. It is *sui generis,* an unprecedented existence. This fact lies at the root of anti-Semitism. It creates a kind of fear of ghosts. This nation that looks so sinister to those who hate them, groups of nomads walking the world and planting themselves in every corner of the globe, represents the impossible. This is especially true now that it has returned to its homeland after nearly two thousand years and after its greatest tragedy, the Holocaust. The Jews did exactly what history had never allowed before.

Two Israels

Israel has been a country once again since 1948. That is, *also* a country but *not only* a country, as the other descriptions continue to apply – a people, a religion, an obsession. Although the nation of Israel continues to fall outside all logic, it continues to exist. The world used to have one Israel which was a scattered but distinct nation. Now that people continues to exist, but there is also a second Israel, the State of Israel, and the world now has two Israels to deal with. Until recently, the State of Israel seemed to respond to the criteria of Caesarea and the normal foundations of history, such as territory and economics. But now we see that it is on its way to becoming as mysterious as the "first Israel," the nation of Israel.

Now we are forced to see that the State of Israel is also well on its way to defying categorization. In fact, it already does, and shows all the signs of a metaphysical entity. How does it continue not only to exist but to flourish despite the surrounding animosity and calls for its destruction? How and why does it hold the key to world peace in the eyes of millions, when its small physical size and population should have rendered it unknown?

The Israeli leadership and its people must deal with this fact: Israel's utter and ongoing anomaly is inescapable. Israelis must make up their minds as to how they will see themselves and the State of Israel. Whether they like it or not, they will be forced to recognize and take pride in their uniqueness and build the country accordingly. If they do not, they will continue to live with the dream of normalization that will destroy their lives. They will have to realize that there is no Israeli claim to the land, only a Jewish claim. Either we return to the Holy Land or there is no land to return to.

In this great conflict between Jerusalem and Caesarea, there are no compromises.

Yet there is more. The only way to understand this phenomenon called Israel is through faith. From any viewpoint other than faith, the inability to fit Israel into a category is unacceptable and intolerable. But through faith and only through faith, this inability gives evidence to the meaning and mission of Israel's uniqueness. Israeli society must come to terms with this. It is part and parcel of its self-understanding.

Counting Jews

We now may return to our original question. Why prohibit the counting of Jews? Why is it so dangerous that Jews have died because of it? What can be so dangerous about taking the census of a nation? Why may it be done only through the counting of the donated half-shekel to the Tabernacle and the Temple?

The well-known Jewish sociologist, Milton Himmelfarb, provided the answer to this question when he wrote, "The total population of the Jews throughout the world is smaller then a statistical error in the Chinese census."

Nothing could be more dangerous than judging and defining Jews by their numbers. Though it was tiny in numbers, this ever-dying nation survived against all odds. We could make no greater mistake than to believe that the survival of the Jews in this world has anything to with its numbers. To this day, it has outlived all its enemies despite them. This is exactly what Moshe referred to in his farewell speech when he said: "Not because you are more numerous than any other people that God desired you and chose you, for you are the fewest of all people" (*Devarim* 7:7).

How, then, should one count Jews? Our verse at the beginning of this essay answers: By requiring them to give a contribution to the Temple. Jews are counted by what they contribute, not by how many they are. Their uniqueness, their separateness, their commitment to God and ethics, and their obsessive concern with the wellbeing of humankind made them the eternal contributors to the world. They gave humanity their God, the Bible, the institution of Shabbat as a weekly day of rest, the dream of the Messianic Age, the awareness that all human beings are equal and created in the image of God, the possibility of repentance, the belief that human beings are not alone and the understanding that behind all absurdity there is meaning.

The Jews gave the world some of its greatest scientists, physicians and psychologists. They had a hand in nearly all revolutions to promote the wellbeing of humankind. All this was totally out of proportion to their numbers at any time in their history. If the Jews were counted by numbers, nobody would ever have heard of them. Yet if we count them by their gifts to humankind, they are the largest nation in the world.

In order for Israel and the Jews to continue this holy work, they must assume the burden of their uniqueness. They must assume the yoke of the kingdom of God. This is their call of the hour.

PART III

TWO LECTURES

JEWISH TRADITION AND THE INTIFADA

July 11, 2001

DEAR FRIENDS,

It does not take much wisdom to realize that since its establishment, the State of Israel has never faced as many difficulties as at this moment in time. Israel has undergone many wars, lost many of its soldiers and lived from crisis to crisis. Still, the latest conflict with the Palestinian people is of a very different kind. While all previous conflicts were wars with Arab countries which took place on the battlefield, this time the war is taking place on the home front and Israel has to deal with daily terrorist attacks in the center of its cities in which Palestinians blow themselves up, killing tens of Jews and injuring hundreds.

Over the many years the Israeli army withstood mighty hostile armies and succeeded in defeating them. While it paid a heavy price, it was always victorious. This time, the Israeli army is confronted with a group of terrorists that are no match for it at all in terms of numbers or power. Therefore, it seems to be child's play. It would not take more than a few hours for the Israel Air Force to end this Palestinian mini-war entirely without one Israeli soldier being killed or wounded. But while other armies have done exactly that – killing thousands of people, including women and children, in the process – the Jewish nation has no such option. Since its Jewish conscience does not permit it to kill people who are innocent (or even not so innocent), Jews pay a heavy price for being decent. At the same time, it is clear that no other nation would restrain itself under similar circumstances.

There is much more. We all feel that there is something else going on that we are unable to verbalize. Somehow it is clear to Israeli Jews and to many Jews who live outside Israel that this time the situation is unusually serious. Not only is the army having difficulty coping with the enemy, but there is also a realization that the rules of the game have changed – the sand is shifting, the Jewish people are more vulnerable than ever since the establishment of the state, the Jews are losing their nerve and the Jewish state may be losing the very ground under its feet. There is an uneasy feeling that we Jews are not what we used to be, and that our four thousand years of survival capacity seem to have become exhausted.

We realize not only is our army being forced to reveal its weak spots, but that we are also dealing with a government led by one of the most experienced men in the history of modern Israel, but which seems nevertheless to be at a loss as to what it needs to do and what governing is all about.

While we were once a strong-minded people, capable of standing up against the largest empires in the world, today we seem confused. We have exchanged self-confidence for limited hysteria and we do not even know what has happened to us. We do not know where to turn and how to start finding answers.

It is in the light of these facts that I humbly offer the following observations. Yet before I do so, I should make it clear that interpreting current events is a very risky undertaking. After all, who knows why things happen the way they do? Studies show that the interpretation of history is built on much speculation and little consistency. We are not prophets and we do not have enough knowledge to understand the problem fully.

As religious people we are asked to look for the deeper meaning of world history, since one of the foundations of our belief is that God has a hand in the unfolding of history. In order to do so, we are used to consulting biblical and Talmudic sources, examining them and drawing conclusions. However, this is not done without serious danger.

Often, these texts are open to a great many interpretations that frequently contradict each other, leaving us in confusion. To apply these texts and to declare that we have unraveled "the ways of God" is not only dangerous but presumptuous. It could backfire on us with disastrous results.

Almost nothing is more dangerous than claiming to have definite insights into the mind of God. This is arrogance and impudence of the first order, something to which religious people have frequently fallen victim, bringing religion into disrepute.

On the other hand, these texts were given to us so that we could make them relevant. If they are not, they become meaningless and ultimately lose their reason for existence.

Therefore, we are left with only one option. We must study these texts as if they are relevant. Above all, we must try to discover the moral lessons from these texts that inspire us to be better human beings and Jews. In other words, it is our obligation to learn from these texts those matters that increase our moral consciousness without stating that they are unique or even an authentic interpretation. It may be that these texts were deliberately written in such a way that they can apply to several circumstances, yet remain open to various interpretations without a definite meaning.

With this in mind, let us ask some questions. What could possibly be the reason why we find ourselves in this terrible crisis? Remember: as religious people we must look beyond politics for a deeper reason. What are the moral and religious implications? In other words, what can God be trying to tell us? What can we, as individuals, do about it? What are our obligations?

Before we try to answer these questions, we should realize that the observations we will make could easily be misunderstood and even misused. It is for this reason that I beg my listeners to be extremely careful with the words I offer. My words are those of a humble man who wants nothing more than to help his people. As in every other case in which certain claims are made, the speaker must take risks, knowing that he may play into the hands of those who harbor bad intentions. We can be sure that as far as our discussion is concerned, there are many who belong to that camp. Nevertheless, honesty demands that we speak up even when doing so may make us unpopular with some of our listeners.

Let us first look at a Talmudic story found in Tractate *Sanhedrin* 91a that tells about a legal claim brought by the descendants of the Canaanites – the earlier settlers of Israel in the days of Yehoshua – in the International Court of Alexander the Great.

When the Bnei Africa – thus called because the Canaanites' descendants lived in Africa at that time – came to plead against the Jews before

Alexander the Great of Macedon, they said: "The land of Canaan belongs to us! As it is written [in the Torah of the Jews]: "The land of Canaan with the coast thereof [Bamidbar 34:2]. Canaan was the ancestor of our people. So we are the legitimate owners of the land and consequently we want it back!" After Alexander had told the Jews about this, a Jewish ignoramus by the name of Geviha ben Pesisa came to the sages of Israel and said: "Authorize me to go and plead before Alexander in favor of the Jews. Should they defeat me, you can say: 'You have defeated one of our ignorant men,' but if I defeat them, then tell them: "The Law of Moshe has defeated you."

They authorized him, and he went and pleaded with them. He asked: "From where do you derive proof that the land is yours?" And they said: "From your own Torah!" He said, "I, too, will bring you proof from the Torah, for it is written in the story of Noach [after Noach became drunk and undressed himself and his son Cham, also called Canaan] witnessed his nakedness and told his two brothers, Shem and Yaphet, about it. Yet instead of relishing the secret with Cham, they covered their father's nakedness. On waking, Noach cursed his son Canaan and said: "Cursed be Canaan. He shall be a servant of servants unto his brothers." Continued Geviha ben Pesisa: "So you are our slaves, since we are the descendants of Shem. Do we not have a rule that states that whatever slaves acquire belongs to their master, since the slaves themselves belong to the master? Consequently, the land belongs to us even if your claim is correct! Moreover, you have not served us for many years."

Then Alexander told the Canaanites, "Answer him. The Jews seem to have a strong claim." "Give us three days," they pleaded. So he gave them a respite. They sought a response but could not find one. Immediately they fled.

The Maharsha, one of the most important commentators on the Talmud, analyzes this Talmudic passage (ad loc.) very carefully and asks some penetrating questions.

He asks: how could the Canaanites turn to the Torah as their proof text when, if they had only turned the page, they would have seen that although the land may have belonged to them once, God gave it to Avraham and his descendants, the Jews? Were they not guilty of selective reading and ignoring those facts that were not to their liking?

Even more difficult to understand is Geviha ben Pesisa's response. Why did he cite the story of Noach and his curse against Canaan to defend the Jewish claim? Why did he not use all the obvious biblical passages such as the promises to Avraham? Why was he using an argument which is a little far-fetched and circumstantial?

The Maharsha's response is revealing: In no way were the Bnei Africa guilty of selective reading. They knew of all the passages in the Torah in which God promised the land to the Jews, but they claimed that these passages were no longer relevant. They understood that their unethical behavior, which included violence and corruption, was the reason for their expulsion. Therefore, when the Jews came to take possession of the land in Yehoshua's time, it was indeed the fulfillment of God's promise to Avraham, Yitzchak and Yaakov. At the time, it was legitimate.

Yet, they argued, the claim no longer applied since God gave the land to the Jews on condition that they live by the Torah's laws and ethical values. The Jews were no longer living by these values and, just like the Canaanites before them, were guilty of unethical behavior. Since they had desecrated the land, they had lost the right to live there. Therefore, the land should be returned to the original owners, the Canaanites. The Maharsha continues that this is also the reason that Geviha ben Pesisa could not use the verses that mention the promises to Avraham. Since he realized that their statements were somewhat justified, he could cite only a (problematic) proof from the story of Noach.

My dear friends, we have a great society that does a lot of good. Nowhere in the world is so much chesed – kindness and charity – done as in our country. But must I elaborate? And who I am to do so? Still, let us be honest. However painful it may be, we have an obligation to ask ourselves whether this story does not reflect our situation today as well. Could we perhaps be losing this beautiful land because we are not living up to the conditions under which it was given to us? Could a foreign nation that lived sporadically in this country before the State of Israel was established perhaps be reminding us that we need to improve ourselves if we want to hold on to this country? Although we cannot know for sure, do we not have an obligation to take this story seriously and at least draw the conclusion as if it relates to our case?

❧   ❦

Let me quote a statement made by Rabbi Naftali Zvi Yehuda Berlin (the Netziv), the last dean of the Volozhin Yeshiva. Commenting on the verse: "The Rock is perfect in His works; righteous and straight is He" (Devarim 32:4), he writes:

> The meaning of this verse is to vindicate the judgment of God with the destruction of the Second Temple in a generation that was perverted and twisted. While the people in those days were righteous and pious in their religious obligations, they were not honest in dealing with their fellowmen. They suspected anybody who did not agree with them in the way they served God, calling them *apikorsim,* heretics and Sadducees. Because of this, there was bloodshed and the nation became divided, which ultimately led to the destruction of the Temple. So Divine judgment came and allowed the Temple to be destroyed, since God is honest and does not tolerate such "righteous people." He protects only those who are straight and not crooked, even when their motivations are in their eyes done "for the sake of Heaven." The main reason for this is that such behavior and attitudes destroy our social structure and our successful settlement in the land and the world. (from the introduction to his commentary, *Ha'amek Davar,* on Bereshit)

My dear friends, take notice. The Netziv warns us not so much about the violation of religious obligations such as Shabbat and kashrut (however important they are), but about the way we treat each other and how our infighting will ultimately lead to the destruction of our society. Should all of us – including myself – not be obligated to take these words seriously, especially now when we see our society so shaken?

❧   ❦

Let us speak for a moment about the Palestinians. Who are they? Why are they suddenly making our lives hell? Is it not most remarkable that until only a short time ago, nobody had ever heard about a Palestinian people, and suddenly they have become a major issue in world politics? They appeared out of nowhere with no real historical roots, yet instantly the world accepted them as a nation with considerable power.

Is it not peculiar that after the Palestinians joined the stage of world politics, the Jews surrendered to them the very first cities in Israel that God granted them in Avraham's time and later under Yehoshua's leadership in an attempt to make peace with them? These cities include Shechem, Hebron and Jericho, and even Judaism's most important city, Jerusalem, is not far behind. It seems that we are losing the land in the same order that we received it. The first cities we inherited are the first ones to go. How bizarre!

In an unusual passage in Devarim 32 called Haazinu, we read the song that Moshe sang at the end of his life. It is one of the most difficult parts of all of the Torah to understand. Nevertheless, some of the verses speak for themselves. Among many important subjects, it discusses the Jews' misdeeds and includes God's warning of the consequences.

> I [God] said: I will hide My face from them and I will see what their end may be. They are a generation of confusion, children in whom one cannot trust. They have aroused My jealousy with a non-god [they have trusted in powers other than God]. They have annoyed Me with their nullities, and I will provoke them with a non-nation. Through an unwise nation I will provoke them to rage and resentment.

Once more we must ask ourselves if these verses do not speak about our own condition in which a non-nation – a group of people without historical roots or cultural identity – heaps terror attack after terror attack upon us, driving us to panic while bringing its own people to ruin.

It also reminds us of Rashi's observation regarding a section of Moshe's farewell speech in which he reminded the Israelites of one of their enemies, the Emorites:

> The Emorites went out... and pursued you as bees do. They struck you in Seir, all the way to Chorma (Devarim 1:44).

Rashi questions the meaning of the simile, "like bees," and answers that just as a bee dies immediately after stinging a person, so did the Emorites. Normally, no nation contemplates attacking an enemy whose retaliation leaves no survivors. Only the most vicious, fanatical hatred makes people carry out suicide attacks with the intent of taking as many of their enemies with them as possible.

Hatred can become so powerful that it goes totally out of control, to the point that the one who hates can no longer explain the reason for his hatred. His hatred now rules him; he has fallen victim to it. In such a situation there is no point in offering him any favors or compromise. Not even total capitulation to his wishes will help. By this time his hatred has been completely disconnected from its original motive. It has become hate for hate's sake.

It seems that hatred has overrun the Palestinian people. Just like bees, they attack, bringing disaster and death on themselves. We are now witnessing this psychological condition in a people whom we tried to help and to whom we offered a large portion of our country. But hatred seems to blind them so completely that they can no longer see the potential for their own future.

Now let us understand this hatred not only from a psychological but also from a religious perspective. Again we are reminded of a verse in the Torah that may relate to our circumstances.

In Shemot 34:24, we read concerning the obligation of each male to come to the Temple on Pesach, Shavuot and Sukkot:

> Three times in the year shall all your males let themselves be
> seen close to the presence of the Lord God, the God of Israel.

When you do so – in other words, when you not only come to the Temple three times a year but also live up to the moral and spiritual condition of that holy place, then – as we read one verse later:

> No one will covet your land when you go up three times a year
> to the Temple.

This verse is remarkable. How can it be that when all Jewish men stand in the court of the Temple on these days, the country will not be overtaken by the enemy? When no soldier guards the country's borders, how can the land be secure from its enemies? Not only is this impossible in normal human experience, but actually suicidal. Therefore, this biblical promise seems to be absurd.

As we look at these verses carefully, we see that their message is not that when our enemies come to our borders, God will stop them from invading. It says that the enemies will not even covet the land and will show no interest in entering or occupying it!

This is extraordinary. We are being told that the psychological condition of our enemies will change once we behave the way we should. It seems to suggest that our behavior influences their psychological attitudes not only on a social level but also on a metaphysical one. I am not prepared to comment on this other than to say that the issue is striking.

However, let us not make the mistake of thinking that this frees our enemies from their responsibility. It does not say that they will lose their ability to decide between right and wrong and that they are compelled to attack our country like preconditioned robots. It means that it will be harder for them to resist those subconscious elements calling for our downfall, just as in the case of God's hardening of Pharaoh's heart in Shemot.

To return to our earlier thesis, we must understand that most of these verses and their rabbinical interpretations emphasize the need for the highest standards of ethical behavior on the part of the Jewish people. While the observance of religious laws such as Shabbat and kashrut are very important, it is clear, as we see particularly in the Netziv's observations, that the *mitzvot bein adam la-chavero,* the laws governing human social behavior, seem to be vital when the land needs to be secured. The message should be obvious.

One may live a so-called religious life without being truly religious. If we observe Shabbat, kashrut and other ritual mitzvot but fail to treat our fellow human beings properly, society will not be able to function properly and will eventually disintegrate.

☙ ❧

We are reminded of a profound observation made by the great sage Rabbi Meir Simcha ha-Cohen of Dvinsk (1843–1926) in his commentary on the Torah, *Meshekh Chochma*. In his commentary on Shemot 14:29, Rabbi Meir Simcha draws our attention towards a problematic statement in the Torah about the cause of the Flood. In Bereshit (6:11) we read:

> The earth was (*tishachet*) corrupt before God and the earth was filled with (*chamas*) violence.

Rashi, ad loc., comments: Corruption (*hashchata*) refers to sexual immorality and idol worship, while violence (*chamas*) refers to robbery.

He continues, making the following comment based on the Talmud (Sanhedrin 108): "The divine decree [to bring the flood] was sealed because of robbery." In other words, robbery – rather than sexual immorality or idol worship – was the cause of the flood.

Rabbi Meir Simcha argues that this is a bizarre assertion that contradicts Jewish law. According to the Torah, robbers are liable to fines and punitive damages, while those who commit idol worship and sexual immorality incur the death penalty. So how could God have brought the Flood on all humankind merely because of robbery?

If anything, the reasons for the Flood should have been sexual immorality and idol worship. This idea is intriguing because one of the great principles of Judaism is that God is obligated to act according to His own rulings (see the Jerusalem Talmud, *Rosh ha-Shannah* 1, 3a). So how could He mete the death penalty to humankind when the crime was robbery? This violated His own law!

Rabbi Meir Simcha responds by revealing an extraordinary concept within Jewish law, laying down a major principle that has far-reaching consequences.

He argues that although individuals are subject to the death penalty for sexual immorality or idol-worship, this is only true when the vast majority of their fellow human beings are not. In such a case, individuals should know better since their surroundings make it abundantly clear. Almost no one else practices these immoral acts since they consider such behavior unacceptable.

But what happens when all of humankind engages in these practices? Rabbi Meir Simcha argues that in such a case, the death penalty no longer applies. The reason is obvious: when everyone commits such acts, no one knows better. Once the practice becomes the accepted norm, no one can be made liable. To make an individual liable in that case would not be justified. How would the individual know that such practices are forbidden when all of humankind accepts them as legitimate?

However, this is only true concerning laws that deal with the relationship between human beings and God, such as idol worship or sexual immorality (in which both parties consent to the relationship and are not harming society). In these cases, God may waive His personal honor and forgive the offenders.

This is not true in the case of robbery. One cannot argue that since all people are robbers, robbery is consequently permitted since the offender knew no better. After all, everyone sees the result of robbery – the breakdown of society. No one can argue that he did not know that robbery is wrong and thought that it was a norm.

In fact, Rabbi Meir Simcha argues, the more people engage in robbery, the worse the transgression. While one or two robbers can do only limited damage, in a case where all of society starts stealing, the damage is much greater. Consequently, the customary monetary penalty will not be enough. After all, it is no longer robbery of which people are guilty, but the total destruction of society. Such a collective sin requires a much stronger punishment, since it undermines all that society stands for.

According to Rabbi Meir Simcha, this is the reason why the generation of the flood became liable to capital punishment because of robbery rather than idol worship or sexual immorality. They had destroyed their society completely. It was as if they had committed social suicide. If they had broken the laws of idol worship or sexual immorality, God would not have brought the Flood upon them, since they would not have known better. Such behavior would have been considered the norm.

A statement in the Jerusalem Talmud (*Peah,* chapter 1, mishna 1) can serve as proof:

> In the generation of King David there were only righteous people, but because there were informers among them, they –

the righteous people – fell and died in war. In the days of King Ahab, many were involved in idol worship, but because there were no informers among them, they were victorious.

In the latter case, the verse "He [Divine providence] will [still] dwell among them in their contamination" (Vayikra 16:16) applies, but in the case of the informers the text reads: "He will be lifted above the heavens" (Tehillim 57:6). In other words, the Divine Presence will no longer be among them. In the first case, people violated the moral code as far as their fellow human beings were concerned. Therefore, God was no longer prepared to remain with them even though there were many righteous people among them. In the second case, even though the people were idol-worshippers, they behaved properly to each other. Consequently, the Divine Presence stayed with them despite their great sin.

The sages made a similar point when they asked which of the destructions was worse – that of the first Temple or the second. The answer is striking: the second. While the first Temple was destroyed because of idol worship and sexual immorality, the second was destroyed because of *sinat chinam* – groundless hatred – even though many people studied Torah then. The fact that the construction of the second Temple took only several years shows that the punishment for idol worship and sexual morality is limited. Yet once the second Temple was destroyed two thousand years ago, no third one has yet been built. This shows us that God considers groundless hatred between fellow Jews much worse than idol worship or sexual immorality (*Yoma* 9a, b).

In other words there is overwhelming evidence that on a national level, the commandments dealing with the relationship between fellow human beings are vital.

While we cannot be sure that the various biblical and rabbinic texts apply to Israel's current precarious situation, we should at least conclude that we have a duty to inspire ourselves and our fellow Jews to take these texts to heart and try to build a better Jewish society. It is widely known that there are few places in the world where so much kindness is done as in Israel. We are blessed with charitable organizations of every kind, of a scope unheard of in other countries. As Operation Defensive Shield demonstrated, Israeli soldiers follow standards of moral warfare that no other nation in the world would contemplate. In their frustration, these nations have turned against us because they cannot bear the knowledge that their leadership and armies are so far removed from our soldiers' moral standards. This is our fate and we should be proud of it.

Still, there is much to be done. Israel should start a national campaign to promote the commandments between human beings. National outreach programs that use radio and television broadcasts, websites, email, CDs and educational videos could reach hundreds of thousands of people. We should flood Israeli society and the Jewish world at large with uplifting literature, presented in an attractive way in order to inspire people to show the highest sensitivity to the feelings of our fellow human beings. Advertisements on billboards at bus and train stations and in shopping centers sponsored by major industries, should call on readers to be more patient with each other, greet passersby with a smile, show courtesy, help wherever possible and make it a matter of honor and pride to be a real *mensch*.

This can be done in effective ways without preaching, appearing pietistic or too agreeable.

Because Israelis have been through so many wars, they are reluctant to show their emotions lest they be thought weak or compromising. Nevertheless, anyone who knows Israeli society understands that inside all Israelis are delicate Jewish souls looking for ways to help and serve their fellow human beings.

Religious Jews have an important task in all this. They must be able to strike a light inside the hearts of other Jews by setting a good example. They need to realize that they must be a light to their own nation before they can be a light to other nations. There can be no mediocrity. This requires that religious schools, seminaries and yeshivot devote more time to teaching and discussing the commandments between human beings. There is no point in suggesting stringencies in the laws of Shabbat and kashrut if they are not accompanied by similar, if not stricter stringencies in our relationships with our fellow human beings. This is the great challenge that now faces religious Jewry and its leaders.

Dear friends, I want to reiterate that while the verses I cited above may apply to our crisis, there is no guarantee that they actually do. Nobody really knows. Nevertheless, I think we agree that we should draw the necessary conclusions and act as if they did. Nothing is more uplifting than having an even better society.

In fact, we should realize that if these verses do indeed discuss our situation, then they carry a message of great hope. After all, what do they suggest? They submit that our future is first of all in our own hands and not in the hands of our enemies. This, I might suggest, makes the problem easier to solve. All we need to do is put our house in order. It is not our foreign policy that will solve the problem, but our conduct. This is possible. There is little doubt that with a lot of effort, we can change Israeli society for the better. This is especially true because our society carries the seeds for excellent behavior, as Israel's brief history has shown again and again.

The unprecedented feeling of unity at this hour is striking. We see how the religious and non-religious are able to work hand in hand. We can testify that there is a common recognition of brotherhood between Sefardim and Ashkenazim, between rich and poor. This should wake us up. Every crisis is also an opportunity. Without denying or belittling in any way the terrible tragedies in which so many people have been killed and injured in the past several months, this crisis may one day turn into a blessing and function as a catalyst towards a better future. Let us work and pray that it will.

May the God of Israel grant us mercy, and may we soon see the day in which tranquility will return to this great country.

I thank you.

FOR GOD'S SAKE, WHOSE LAND ARE WE OCCUPYING?[1]

(First presented in 1983 as a lecture at Congregation Poale Zedek,
Pittsburgh, Pennsylvania, USA)

THE JEWS LIVING DURING THE REIGN of Emperor Napoleon Bonaparte, one of the most influential leaders of the European continent during the eighteenth century, benefited greatly from his patronage. While it is true that Napoleon was responsible for a lot of unrest within the European Jewish community, his most famous decision as far as the Jews were concerned was to free them from the ghettos where previous monarchs and empires had confined them.

This is why they honored him with a Hebrew name, calling him "Chelek Tov," literally meaning "good part" (a literal Hebrew translation of Bonaparte).

A lesser-known decision of Napoleon's – perhaps because it did not succeed – was his attempt to establish the State of Israel. In 1799, Napoleon found himself in the Mediterranean port of Acre, having arrived there with his army after his Eastern Expedition. While he was there, Napoleon sent a proclamation to all Jewish communities of France in which he urged the Jews to return to their ancestral homeland:

General Headquarters, Jerusalem

1st Floreal in the year 7 of the French Republic (April 20, 1799)

---

[1] I am indebted to many sources for this lecture/essay. Special mention should be made of *Israel: An Echo of Eternity* by Abraham Joshua Heschel (New York: Farrar, Straus and Giroux, 1974). In certain parts of the essay I have used Professor Heschel's idiom, which is very beautiful.

Bonaparte, Commander-in-Chief of the Armies of the French Republic in Africa and Asia, to the rightful Heirs of Palestine:

Israelites, unique nation, whom, in thousands of years, lust of conquest and tyranny were able to deprive of ancestral lands only, but not of name and national existence! Attentive and impartial observers of the destinies of nations, even though not endowed with the gifts of seers like Isaiah and Joel, have also felt long since what these, with beautiful and uplifting faith, foretold when they saw the approaching destruction of their kingdom and fatherland: "… that the ransomed of the Lord shall return and come with song unto Zion, and everlasting joy upon their heads; they shall obtain gladness and joy, and sorrow and sighing shall flee away" (Isaiah 35:10).

Arise then, with gladness, ye exiled! A war unexampled in the annals of history, waged in self-defense by a nation whose hereditary lands were regarded by her enemies as plunder to be divided, arbitrarily and at their convenience, by a stroke of the pen of Cabinets, avenges her own shame and the shame of the remotest nations, long forgotten under the yoke of slavery, and, to the almost two thousand-year-old ignominy put upon you; and while time and circumstances would seem to be least favorable to a restatement of your claims or even to their expression, and indeed to be compelling their complete abandonment, it [France] offers to you at this very time and contrary to all expectations, Israel's patrimony!

This young army with which Providence has sent me hither, led by justice and accompanied by victory, has made Jerusalem my headquarters, and will, within a few days, transfer them to Damascus, a proximity which is no longer terrifying to David's city.

Rightful Heirs of Palestine!

This great nation which does not trade in men and countries as did those who sold your ancestors unto all peoples (Joel 4:6) hereby calls on you not indeed to conquer your patrimony, nay, only to take over that which has been conquered and, with that nation's warranty and support, to maintain it against all comers.

Arise! Show that the once overwhelming might of your oppressors has not repressed the courage of the descendants of those heroes whose brotherly alliance would have done honor even to Sparta and Rome (Macc. 12:15), but that all the two thousand years of slavish treatment have not succeeded in stifling it.

Hasten! Now is the moment, which may not return for thousands of years, to claim the restoration of your rights among the population of the universe which had been shamefully withheld from you for thousands of years, your political existence as a nation among the nations and the unlimited natural right to worship God in accordance with your faith, publicly and most probably forever (Joel 4:20).[2]

This is one of the most moving appeals ever made to the Jews. It is true that Napoleon had his political reasons for such an initiative, but it cannot be denied that he had a keen understanding of the unusual relationship between the Jews and their homeland.

The Temple Was Destroyed an Hour Ago

There is an anecdote which may throw some light on his attitude. Some years before this episode, Napoleon and his entourage found themselves riding through Paris on the Hebrew date of the Ninth of Av – the date on which the first and second Temples were destroyed and on which many tragedies in Jewish history took place. When Napoleon entered the city's Jewish quarter, he found all the streets deserted. Puzzled, he came into a

---

[2] Quoted by Franz Kobler, *Napoleon and the Jews*. New York: Schocken Books, 1976, 55–57.

synagogue and saw all the Jews sitting on the floor, weeping and reciting Lamentations.

He decided to ask one of the rabbis about this unusual scene. Why did all the Jews look so distressed? Had an accident happened? Had one of the leaders of the Jewish community just died? Had there been a pogrom about which Napoleon had not heard?

"Much worse," the rabbi answered. "Our Temple was destroyed, and we were exiled from our homeland."

"But that happened nearly eighteen hundred years ago!" Napoleon said.

"No," said the venerable sage. "It happened an hour ago."

When Napoleon wondered at this bizarre answer, the rabbi answered that as far as the Jews were concerned, the event had just occurred. It was as if Jewish history had not moved from the moment of the destruction. Jews still lived the experience as if it had happened that very morning.

Once Napoleon grasped the profundity of this answer, he declared that if the Jews felt so strongly about their Temple and their homeland, they would no doubt rebuild the Temple, and no power in the world would stop them from returning to their homeland.

While it may be argued that Napoleon became one of the first gentile Zionists, he was not the only one. Throughout history, other powerful non-Jews supported the Zionist dream. Among them was John Toland, a disciple of the famous English philosopher, John Locke. Another was Lord Anthony Ashley Cooper, the Earl of Shaftesbury in the nineteenth century. Others were Lord Byron, John Thomas, William Blackstone, George Eliot (Mary Ann Evans), author of *Daniel Deronda,* and Alexandre Dumas.

All these people saw it as their task to encourage their governments to sponsor and help the immigration of Jews to the land of Israel. They seemed to realize that this was a legitimate right of the Jews. As far as they saw it, no serious reader of history would doubt the legitimacy of such an aspiration.

For just a few moments, let us try to understand what moved all these people and the Jewish community at large.

We conjecture that no other nation has had such vibrant arguments for its claim to its ancient land than the Jews. One could even argue that nations such as the United States of America, France or Great Britain might well be envious of the people of Israel if they were to realize how weak and problematic their claims to their own lands are compared to the Jews' claim to their ancient land. And who would doubt the legitimacy of their claims?

The Chutzpah of Survival

To begin with, let us dwell for a moment on the nature of the Jewish people. Only then will we understand the unusual relationship between the Jews and the land of Israel.

First, we must realize that the very existence of the people of Israel is a historical mystery. The Jewish people are nearly four thousand years old. If that does not make the Jewish people the oldest nation in the world, at least it makes it the most peculiar. It is a nation that has spent more time living in exile than in its own country. It is a nation that survived for nearly two thousand years without its homeland, without an army, without its own government, without finances and without friends. It has been tortured for thousands of years, constantly attacked and repeatedly on the brink of total annihilation. No nation has witnessed so many attempts to destroy it. No nation has outlived its enemies against all historical odds. Yet the Jews have survived the impossible. They outlived six empires whose chief aim at one time or another was to destroy the Jewish people. There were the Egyptians in the days of the Bible, the Babylonians, the Persians, the Greeks, the Romans and, recently, the Germans.

Although the tiny Jewish nation has been the victim of inquisitions, pogroms, massacres and holocausts, it survived them all.

The British historian, Professor Arnold Toynbee, called the Jews fossils and denied them the right to exist since they violated the rules of history. Others felt that they were the lowest of all human beings. Yet although the Jews lingered on the brink of extinction, they never perished. Who would ever have believed that a small nation that was invaded by the largest army of the world at the time, the Romans, would outlive its arch-enemies? Who would have believed that the Romans would vanish utterly from the earth while this small nation survived? This is *chutzpah* of the first order!

Just over fifty years ago, even the best friends of the Jews believed that the complete annihilation of the Jewish people had finally happened. After the Nazi extermination of six million – in which nearly two million Jewish children were brutally murdered – most people believed that this time the

Jews could not possibly survive. They believed that Hitler had succeeded in doing what the Romans and so many others throughout history had not been able to accomplish. Who could survive such devastation? Yet we did. Against all logic and historical precedent, the Jews outlived Hitler as well.

The Most Irritating People in the World

It is understandable that Jews constantly annoy the rest of the world with their ability to outlive everyone, including Hitler. The most honest and fitting way to define the Jews might well be as the most irritating people in the world.

Throughout history, when anti-semitic individuals and nations tried to destroy the Jews, they discovered that the Jews thrived as never before. If this was not enough to make the world feel uneasy, there were other troublesome things to consider: no other people had such an influence on Western civilization. While the Jews were smaller in number than some of the lesser-known tribes in Africa, they contributed towards every form of human knowledge, totally out of proportion to their size. By normal standards, no one should ever have heard of the Jews! But the facts show that the world has heard more about the Jewish people than about any other nation. This is fairly irritating.

Nevertheless, the most irritating thing about the Jews is their miraculous return to their homeland. Despite the seeming loss of hope that the Holocaust represented and the predictions of even the most sympathetic onlookers that the Jews would soon vanish completely, the next event in Jewish history was the establishment of the State of Israel in 1948. This was too much for some anti-Semites to handle. Not only had the Jews endured throughout the thousands of years, contributed out of all proportion to humankind and Western civilization, but now that they had survived their worst calamity at the hands of Hitler, they had the unparalleled *chutzpah* to return to their homeland after two thousand years – three years after the Holocaust!

Israel as an Embarrassment

It is against this background that we have to understand why the Jewish people and the State of Israel are constantly attacked and criticized. People simply cannot deal with the unprecedented. Israel's return to its homeland is unparalleled. It is a breakthrough, a creation *sui generis* that requires a new and daring way of understanding and explaining the impossible.

This is why the State of Israel has become an embarrassment to the world. Our conventional way of thinking does not allow for surprises of this magnitude. Our mental habit is to think in terms of sameness and to ignore uniqueness.

On a deeper lever, the State of Israel represents a metaphysical reality about which people do not want to hear. It is a manifestation of the ultimate, the *mysterium magnum,* that forces itself into the daily lives of human beings. Nowhere has it become clearer than in the Jewish people's survival against all odds and in the establishment of the State of Israel that a higher force is at work in human history. Human beings' confrontation with this Force is often too much for them to bear. Secular people do not want to be confronted with this higher power, which urges them to recognize a higher morality that they did not create. Israel's existence forces human beings to confront God. It is therefore not surprising that many people have turned against the State of Israel. Once we recognize this, we are able to understand more about the Jewish people, its connection to its land and its unique position in the world.

Protest for Two Thousand Years

From the time that the Jewish state was destroyed by Titus approximately two thousand years ago until it was reestablished in 1948, it never became the homeland of anyone else or an independent state. In all these years it was simply conquered and re-conquered by various nations, fourteen times in all. It was populated by a hodgepodge of nations coming and going, and all its conquerors saw it as occupied territory to be ruled from outside.

Not once did any of them claim the land of Israel as their new homeland. The only people who saw it as its homeland for nearly two thousand years were the Jews, and only the Jews reestablished it as their old/new homeland in 1948.

It is essential to realize that the Jews never left the land willingly. Although they were forced out by Titus, the Roman emperor, they made it clear that they considered the land of Israel as their eternal homeland. They never ceased to assert their right and title to this land. It is a most important Talmudic dictum which reminds us of a common rule in jurisprudence: "If an object is taken by violence but the owner does not abandon his hope of regaining it, nobody ever has any claim to the object except the original owner" (*Kiddushin* 52b).

The moment that Titus exiled the Jews, the Jews spoke about the possibility of return. They refused any other homeland. While individual Jews considered other countries their homeland, the nation of Israel did not.

One may argue that the Jews never protested against Israel's occupiers in the public squares or in the political establishments. It is true that throughout history, their voices were not heard in the international courts. The reason is obvious. Jews were not heard because their tongues were cut short before they could speak. Thousands of years of anti-Semitism did not allow Jews to utter a word in the public forum. Nevertheless, within the Jewish community, within the walls of the ghettos and the synagogues, the protest was forceful.

Every Jewish prayer over the past two thousand years was steeped in longing for the land of Israel. These prayers were emotional pleas to return to a place that the Jews in fact had never left. While the Jews mourned the loss of their land, they never renounced it. The more distant the land became, the more it lived in their hopes and prayers. At length an overwhelming fire took hold of their souls, leading them to actualize in 1948 what they had dreamed of for nearly two thousand years.

Jews Never Lived Outside Israel

How many times did the Jews ask themselves: Where do we live? Where is our home? The answer is clear: Jews never lived in Poland, Spain or Russia. They may have stayed in those countries, but they never settled there. Human beings do not live where their bodies reside, but rather where their souls dwell. The Jewish soul always lived in one place: Jerusalem and the land of Israel.

On a deeper level, we need to realize that the State of Israel was not established in 1948 but rather in the year 70, the day after the Romans exiled the Jews. In the very instant that Titus forced the Jews out, they were busy contemplating how to get back.

One look at the prayer book of the Jews reveals their uncompromising attachment to the land. Every morning, afternoon and evening, for two thousand years, they have prayed for their return to the land. "God, may You rebuild Jerusalem in Your mercy." "Have mercy, O God of Israel, on Jerusalem, Your city on Mount Zion, the habitation of Your glory." "May it be Your will, O God, to cause us to return to our land."

For two thousand years, millions of Jews made these prayers an ongoing priority. Such a commitment has no precedent in the history of any other nation.

Jerusalem: City of Titus, Godfrey or Saladin?

For decades, the international community has been saying that Jerusalem should be internationalized. The Roman Catholic Church, through the office of the pope, has told the people of Israel that it is necessary. Yet is there really anything to be discussed? To whom does Jerusalem belong? To the descendants of Rome? To the Christian Church? To the Arab world? Is it not true that Jerusalem was always named the City of David even by Israel's enemies? Was it ever called the City of Titus, the City of Godfrey of Bouillon or the City of Saladin? For all these thousands of years, it bore the name of a Jew called David.

Which nation mourned for Jerusalem for two thousand years? Do the descendants of Titus, Godfrey or Saladin fast and mourn on the Ninth of Av, the day the Temples were destroyed?

Is it not true that only the Jews have done so for nearly two thousand years? What other nation has wept over the destruction of its capital after even two hundred years? Did the United States do so for New York, Britain for London, or France for Paris?

The well-known Israeli author, Shmuel Yosef Agnon, wrote about the unique relationship between the Jewish people and the land of Israel. When he received the Nobel Prize for literature in 1966, the King of Sweden, Gustav VI asked him where he had been born. Agnon, a deeply religious Jew, answered: "Majesty, like all Jews I was born in Jerusalem, but then the Romans came and moved my cradle to Buczacz."[3]

This most powerful answer, which captures Jewish history within a few words, has without any doubt been the answer the Jews have given to any invader, king or emperor in the last two thousand years! What other nation has ever shown so much attachment to its land?

An Eight-Day-Old Zionist and the Interrupted Chuppah

When a Jewish boy is circumcised at the age of eight days, the Jewish community wishes him all the good things in the world. A prayer from the Sefardi tradition reads: "May he have the opportunity to ascend to the land of Israel and visit the Temple on the three festivals of Pesach, Shavuot and Sukkot."

In other words when the baby is only eight days old, the community makes him, without his knowledge, a genuine Zionist! As Jewish children grow up, what songs are they taught? For thousands of years, every Jewish child was taught the songs of David about the land of Israel and its Temple. What else was important?

As soon as that child grows up, is ready to marry and stands under the chuppah, a strange scene takes place that should raise some eyebrows among the uninitiated. While the rabbi reads the blessings, the ceremony is interrupted. If you were to ask the rabbi performing the wedding to explain this strange behavior, he would tell you that the Temple has been destroyed, and who could ever forget this tragedy? He then places a glass on the floor and asks the bridegroom to break it under his foot as a sign of mourning. The young man then informs the community that he will not forget Jerusalem and its Temple as one would not forget one's own right hand. Only after this does the rabbi continue the marriage ceremony.

---

[3] See *A People That Dwells Alone: Speeches and Writings of Yaacov Herzog.* London: Weidenfeld and Nicolson, 1975, 65. This outstanding work should be studied by anyone who wishes to defend Israel's right to exist.

On reflection, this custom appears bizarre. Why insert this moment of mourning in the middle of such a happy occasion? Why not wait until after the couple is married? The answer is that even at the highlight of one's life, at the moment of one's marriage, one still cannot forget one's yearning for the Temple and its city. This has been the custom for nearly two thousand years.

How many millions of glasses have been broken throughout Jewish history?

When a Jewish bridegroom and bride enter their new home, they will make sure that it reflects the memory of the Temple. Above the door or some other part of the walls of their new home there will be a space that will not be plastered or covered with wallpaper, but will show raw stones as a sign of mourning. After all, how can one live in a home that is fully decorated while the Temple lies in ruins?

When the Jew celebrates a special occasion and holds a feast, the table will be lavishly decorated with beautiful cutlery and china and candlelight, but one candle will not be lit as a reminder of the loss of the Temple.

All Jews Are Buried in Israel

Perhaps the most impressive statement that Jews make about their connection to the land of Israel is when they have died and their bodies are being prepared for burial. Where will their bones rest and their tombstones stand? Throughout all the thousands of years Jews said: Only in the land of Israel. No Jew will ever be buried outside the Holy Land. Some might point out that there are Jewish cemeteries around the world, far away from the land of Israel. Yet even if that this is factually true, the Jew will maintain that Jews were never buried anywhere else but in the land of Israel.

How so?

Jewish tradition demands that even when Jews are not able to bring the dead to Israel, they must bring Israel to the dead. Just before the coffin is closed, the burial society sprinkles earth from the land of Israel over the deceased's shrouds, so that the deceased will be buried with this earth.

Wherever Jews live, the Jewish community will always make sure that it possesses some earth from the land of Israel so that Jews may be buried in this holy earth when the time comes. While their tombstones may stand outside Israel, their bodies are buried in the land of Israel.

Even that is not the end of the story. As if Judaism knows of no limit when speaking of the land, it requires that those who visit the house of mourning not depart without making mention of the Holy Land. On leaving the mourner, they say: "May you be comforted with all those who mourn for Zion and Jerusalem."

Jewish Robbers and Jean Paul Sartre

Rashi, the well-known eleventh-century biblical scholar, makes a strange statement in his commentary on the first verse in the Torah. Quoting the verse, "In the beginning, God created heaven and earth," Rashi asks why the Torah does not start much later in human history. What is the purpose in telling us that God created heaven and earth? He answers: "If the nations of the world were to say to the people of Israel: You are robbers! You have stolen the land! – Then the Jew would be able to reply, 'In the beginning, God created heaven and earth. All the earth is the Lord's and He gave this land to the people of Israel.'"

It is difficult to see how this approach would be of any help. Did Rashi really believe that if an international body such as the United Nations were to discuss the question of who should own the Land of Israel, the Israeli delegate could actually argue that the land of Israel belongs to the Jewish people on the basis of a biblical inference? Rashi's statement is a conundrum.

It is only after reading a statement by the famous atheist French philosopher, Jean Paul Sartre (1905–1980), that we are able to appreciate Rashi's comment. Asked to comment on the Israeli-Arab conflict, Sartre answered, "I cannot judge the Jewish people by the accepted rules of history. The Jewish people is something beyond time and we cannot pass judgment on the Israeli-Arab conflict without taking this into account."[4]

Sartre's point is clear. The Jewish people is an exceptional nation. Jews have done the impossible, as if time and space had no effect on them. Jews have survived against all odds, violated all rules of history, contributed to

---

[4] Ibid., 51.

humanity out of all proportion, and they continue to baffle the world in every way possible. Such a nation cannot be judged according to the same rules by which other nations are judged. There appears to be another set of rules at work here that sets the Jews completely apart. This is the deeper meaning of Rashi's comment.

Israel Doesn't Even Have One Real Good Golf Course

In 1989, Mike Royko, a famous journalist in the USA, published an article entitled, "Come on, Arabs, Israel's a Runt" in a Chicago newspaper. In this remarkable article, he asked some penetrating questions concerning Israel and responded with even more unusual but candid answers. He wrote:

> When I look at the world map, I sometimes wonder what the insane fuss in the Middle East is all about.... If I look closely and squint my eyes, I can find a country that has about 800 square miles. That's Israel! To give you an idea how small that is, you could take 40 Israels and put them together, and the whole thing would still be smaller than Texas. There may be counties, even ranches in Texas that are bigger. Little New Hampshire, where just about everybody gets a handshake from a politician during presidential primaries, is bigger than Israel. So is Vermont. In fact, we have only four states that are smaller.... So we are talking about a mere speck on the map.... In acreage, Israel isn't as big as Belize, Burundi, Djibouti, and is only slightly larger than Fiji, but a little smaller than Haiti.... So when it comes to land size and population, we're really talking dinky. Why, during any really cold winter you can find more Jews in southern Florida (seven times as big)! But, if you want to talk big, just unsquint your eyes and look at some of the countries near Israel – those that have been trying to squash their tiny neighbor for the last 41 years. Syria, nine times as big with three times as many people, Iraq, 20 times as big with 17 million people, Iran, 80 times bigger, with almost 50 million people. Put that part of the world together and there are millions odd square miles with a population bigger than that of the United States.

And most of them, in one way or another, with guns, tanks, terrorists or oil money, have tried to squash a country that isn't as big as Vermont.... A tiny sliver of real estate.... Instead we have these vast, and in some cases, wealthy countries now entering their fifth decade of trying to take over a place you can barely find on the map. It makes no sense, I mean, Israel doesn't even have one real good golf course.

These words speak for themselves. Whatever our political views concerning the Middle East conflict may be, we should never forget that the Middle East is one of the largest areas in the world and that the State of Israel is a very tiny country. Much of the Middle East is uninhabited and can easily make room for many more nations without compromising Israel in the least.

One Hour at the Western Wall Did More Than…

Last but not least, we would be wise to remember the words of Yaacov Herzog, rabbi, statesman and Israel's ambassador to Canada: "Zionist propaganda and the Jewish Agency with all its power and influence, the State of Israel with all its ambassadors, institutions and supreme effort, encompassing the whole of Jewry in all its economic resources have achieved ten per cent of what one hour at the Western Wall did for the Jewish people."[5]

Indeed, we should never forget that it was not Zionism, Jewish nationalism or any other Jewish "isms," but rather traditional Judaism that kept the Jewish people alive. This simple fact holds a strong message to all those who are concerned about the future of the State of Israel. All efforts to make Israel into a purely secular state will ultimately lead to its destruction. In no way do we advocate an Israeli theocracy, but without a deep commitment to Judaism, the State of Israel will not be able to survive. Once Israel has made up its mind and embraces its goal of being a Jewish state rather than a state of Jews, it will become a great blessing to Jews and gentiles alike. It will become a peaceful place in the Middle East and will

---

[5] Ibid., 59.

witness tranquility among its citizens and neighbors. Yet until that day comes, we will continue to repeat what all Jews say when they reach the end of their discourses:

May the Redeemer soon come to Zion and Jerusalem.

Rabbi Dr. Nathan Lopes Cardozo is a world-renowned thinker, lecturer and ambassador for Judaism and the Jewish people. He is known for his original insights into how Judaism can rejuvenate itself, showing new ways to authentic religiosity. Rabbi Lopes Cardozo's writings are read by laymen, members of the clergy and academicians throughout the Jewish and non-Jewish world. He is a sought-after lecturer on Judaism and Israel at numerous institutions of higher academic learning, including Jewish study programs at leading universities, religious academies and rabbinical colleges. He is also the founder and Dean of the David Cardozo Academy, the Aron and Betsy Spijer Institute (also called the Beth Midrash of Avraham Avinu), which is dedicated to recapturing the ideological foundations of Judaism. The Institute is a think tank where rabbis, educators and professors under Rabbi Cardozo's guidance try to lay the foundations of a new approach to Judaism based on the classical sources. It is also dedicated to educating a new generation of rabbis, teachers and Jewish thinkers based on this philosophy.

The author of many books on Judaism, Rabbi Lopes Cardozo writes a weekly column, "Thoughts to Ponder," on his website (www.cardozoschool.org). Educated in Amsterdam, he received his rabbinical degree from Gateshead Talmudical College, studied at Yeshivat Mir in Jerusalem, and holds a doctorate in philosophy. Rabbi Cardozo is a distinguished member of the Portuguese and Spanish Jewish community and lives with his wife, children and grandchildren in Jerusalem.

Books by Rabbi Dr. Nathan Lopes Cardozo:
The Torah as God's Mind: A Kabbalistic Look into the Pentateuch (BepRon Publications, 1988), *The Infinite Chain: Torah, Mesorah and Man* (Targum/Feldheim, 1989), *Between Silence and Speech: Essays on Jewish Thought* (Jason Aronson, 1995), *The Written and Oral Torah: A Comprehensive Introduction* (Jason Aronson, 1997), *Judaism on Trial: An Unconventional Discussion about Jews, Judaism and the State of Israel* (Urim Publications, 2000), *Thoughts to Ponder: Daring Observations about the Jewish Tradition* (Urim Publications, 2002), *For God's Sake: Whose Land Are We Occupying?* (The David Cardozo Academy, 2000), *Explaining the Jewish Claim to the Land of Israel* (The David Cardozo Academy, 2002), *Two Lectures: Halacha as a Symphony and Tolerance and the Jewish Tradition* (The David Cardozo Academy, 2003), *Crisis, Covenant and Creativity: Jewish Thoughts for a Complex World* (Urim Publications, 2005), *Thoughts to Ponder No. 2: Daring Observations about the Jewish Tradition* (Urim Publications, 2006), *For the Love of Israel and the Jewish People* (Urim Publications, 2008)